SUSTAINABILITY

21ST CENTURY ESSAYS

David Lazar and Patrick Madden, Series Editors

Sustainability

A Love Story

Nicole Walker

MAD CREEK BOOKS, AN IMPRINT OF
THE OHIO STATE UNIVERSITY PRESS
COLUMBUS

Mad Creek Books, an imprint of The Ohio State University Press.

Library of Congress Cataloging-in-Publication Data
Names: Walker, Nicole, author.
Title: Sustainability : a love story / Nicole Walker.
Other titles: 21st century essays.
Description: Columbus : Mad Creek Books, an imprint of The Ohio State University Press, [2018] | Series: 21st century essays | Includes bibliographical references.
Identifiers: LCCN 2018010746 | ISBN 9780814254851 (pbk. ; alk. paper) | ISBN 0814254853 (pbk. ; alk. paper)
Subjects: LCSH: Sustainable living—Anecdotes. | Sustainability. | Human ecology.
Classification: LCC GE196 .W35 2018 | DDC 304.2—dc23
LC record available at https://lccn.loc.gov/2018010746

Cover design by Christian Fuenfhausen
Text design by Deb Jul
Type set in Adobe Sabon LT Std

∞ The paper used in this publication meets the minimum requirements of the American National Standard for Information Sciences—Permanence of Paper for Printed Library Materials. ANSI Z39.48-1992.

Contents

Acknowledgments

USUALLY, I THANK Erik last, but since this story is as much his as mine, I want to thank him first for bearing the burden of being married to a writer like me. I thank my kids too, who don't mind it when I write about them but also feel like they have final say on the last word. Which I generally let them. I thank Misty Cummings for inspiring me to think about hypocrisy and sustainability and for teaching me to crawl up the rocks of Eagle Creek, which is currently on fire outside of Portland this week. If anyone understands the Oregon/Arizona divide, it is she. I thank Erin Stalcup and Justin Bigos for publishing the first piece ever published from this book in Waxwing. Thanks to Ann Cummins for talking through these essays with me as we both worked on writing about the southwest. Thanks to Patrick Madden and David Lazar for creating this incredible series and for making this book one of the first in what I think is going to be an important imprint for the essay. Thank you, Steve Fellner, for being the one who pushed me and told me I'd be OK because at least I had a subject and something to say about it. And also for telling me that suffering looks good on me.

Thank you, Karen Renner and Monica Brown, for the writing days that made this book possible and to Angie Hansen for being such a great supporter of my work. Thank you, Ander and Megan, for living in Arizona with me since 2008 and making it possible for me to understand the Tucson part of the state. Thank you, Mary Cappello, for your words about this book and your from-the-beginning love and support. Thank you, Peter Covino, for publishing my first book and for keeping me in the writing world ever since and Julie Paegle who keeps me believing in words. Thank you, Kristen Elias Rowley, for your work to bring this book into fruition. Thanks to Katharine Coles, Melanie Rae Thon, and David Shields for supporting this project with their letters and their faith. Thanks to Robin Hemley and David Carlin for bringing me into the NonfictioNOW fold, where I found a great nonfiction home. Thanks to Paige Walker Ehler who works out the science with me and who tries to find some hope in this messy world and to Valerie Walker Koonce to remind me about the "human" part of humanity. And thanks, Mom, for teaching me to love books and making me believe I could write them.

Dear Rain

DEAR RAIN,

It has been a year of waiting for the fire. You scrape the pine needles from the floor of our yard. You capture the rain in barrels, water the yarrow from the bowels of the gutter-catch. Our son, Max, stands on the cedar play set. His hands move as if he's chiming in the percussion instruments, cuing the strings. He conducts the clouds. You can't hear from where you perch, summoning droplets from the spigot, that I ask Max, "Did you make it rain?"

"No. Not yet. I can't make it rain. I can only make the clouds move."

"Maybe tomorrow?" I say.

"Maybe tomorrow."

I sit on the porch, sip my wine, watch you take a bucketful of last month's collected rain to water the flax. I try to visualize rain. I sort of remember what it looks like. I get distracted by my iPhone. There's an update on the wild fire. I stare at the sky. Mind of matter. Try to summon clouds. Like Max, I fail to orchestrate the rain. Our daughter, Zoë, asks me, "Did you see that?"

"What?"

"The hummingbird. It tried to drink out of my ear."

I missed it. I was thinking about fire.

I should pay attention but the air zaps around me. The static distracts me like an iPhone. I miss my kids saying what they're saying. I miss the way you rake. By wanting something more, I am missing something all the time. The lack of rain makes me think I'm doing everything wrong.

Just June ago, I looked at the sky and said, "come." The sky didn't listen and I knew the words of my prayers were wrong.

I cannot order the clouds any more than I can order the gods I believe in to have mercy on my soul.

The bossiness of prayer does not become me.

Begging repulses rain.

Rain makes me think about loss and the loss of rain. I can't always remember Portland. I moved to Flagstaff for a reason. It is beautiful here. Within reach of nine national parks, including the Grand Canyon. The top tier of nine descending life zones. Close to Salt Lake where my mother lives. It is not Oregon and Oregon's perpetual sustainability but I chose this place. It is dry here but, so far, there is plenty of water to drink.

Rain should make me think about weight. Heavy land. Soaked clothes. Do you remember the time we went running in the rain? That was Utah and right after you made me believe we would return to Portland. We didn't. Instead we ate Portland at the lunch truck like Pok Pok, but not, sesame beef in a taco and then we drove farther south. The dirt turned sandy and you said, "You can see the whole world in a grain of sand," so I rubbed it into my eye. The doctor said the cornea scratched but that was just a record on a record player we played only twice. Talking Heads. Dire Straits. Johnny Cash. Now you, me, and sand. Nothing between us.

As one. Pure metaphor but I can feel the sand in my hair, and the sand in you. Together. Forever?

It was only two Junes ago that we faked a Portland and went to the coast but without tacos from the food trucks. We knew we were only posers. Water tourists. It rained but I was mad as a crow. How could it rain in June? I remember Portland in June and a flat creek outside of town, Crow Creek or Eagle Creek, and we (not you we, another we, a we that's mostly the same as us although she was thinner than me, thin as you) lay on our stomachs and crawled up the river, holding rock by rock as if the river were strong enough to push us down to the Willamette, out to the Columbia, and off to sea. We'd turn over and sit on our butts and eat blackberries that grew right over the stream. It was hot in June and sunny and Portland was best not because it didn't rain, the rain is great, but Portland is particularly great when it doesn't rain in June.

When we visited Portland for the first time since Zoë was born, it rained in June.

But it does not rain in June in Salt Lake City, Utah, and certainly not here in Flagstaff, Arizona. The clouds congregate. They congress. They parliament like owls. But for all that swooping and hoo hooing and mak mak making they sit in the sky like asphalt. They give nothing. Don't even bother asking.

The Ogallala Aquifer, one of the largest in the world, runs through eight of the United States—Colorado, Kansas, Nebraska, New Mexico, Oklahoma, South Dakota, Texas, and Wyoming, and it is shrinking. It is being depleted at record rates. We are the fastest on the planet, faster than cheetahs, fast to prayer, fast to begging, faster than a fast-ing monk thanks to MSN.com, which brings us the news faster but rarely news of climate change because why brook that controversy. Brook trout instead! But the water, finite, is going fast. Dinosaur pee. Drink it while it lasts. Going out of business sale! In 1960 the Ogallala aquifer had been depleted by 3%. By 2010, 30%. Mainly drawn upon to irrigate agricultural fields where they usually grow corn to feed either cows or cars or occasionally crows, by 2060, 69% of the aquifer will be depleted of water if used at current rates. That's too bad, they say. They say, no wait. It's not so bad. There is a man on the field who is receptive to new agricultural practices. His name is Charlie and he is interested in the future. His great-grandfather inhaled the dust storm. Charlie wants to be the one that blows that dust out of his nose, back into the field, nutrition, not nitrogen oxide, which is toxic to everything in Lake Erie except the algae, which it instead makes bloom.

There are new technologies for crops. "Things are getting better," Charlie says. "Water use efficiencies have increased by about 2% a year in Kansas, which means that every year we're growing about 2% more crop for each unit of water." But this is bad too. Less water means more salt left on the fields, fields soon to be better known as sand, salted sand, of which each grain holds whole worlds. Think how much water each grain needs. Most people say, "Drink up while it's here. Drink a whole unit." We are only a blink of the eye in the history of the earth. It is hard to conceive beyond my children's birth, let alone their death. I am thirsty now. I probably shouldn't have eaten that pretzel. Everything has a consequence, which makes the world, and the rain, seem so heavy.

The earth doesn't mind the way we redistribute her salt or her water but Charlie has a few more years to reorganize his dirt. He would like to leave his dirt to his children. To his great-grandchildren. He would like the dirt to be good and useful. We keep having children because we believe that dirt can be made good. I had my children because I keep believing, contrary to my iPhone research, that the world is getting better. Perhaps we will find an antidote to salt. A recent report suggests that too little culinary salt is as dangerous in your diet as too much. So many reports. I hand the man on the field some of my Benicar for my altitude-induced high blood pressure. When I tell people about my high blood pressure, because I'm a confessor and a deflector of blame, I always say "altitude-induced" to remind the people who look concerned at me that it's not my fault I have high blood pressure. To let them know I'm not that old. That I'm only dying because I got a job in a high-altitude town, not because I ate too much steak with salt on it. All confessions require some self-deception. Conduct your myth. Organize your clouds. Pretend Portland goes on forever.

Charlie is saving whole units of water. If only a unit of water was all we needed. Look at those clouds. They won't even give up a single one. My neighbor is in the front yard watering what appears to be his ladder. I do not think this bodes well for our aquifer, Ogallala or not.

> Random House Kemmerman Webster's Dictionary has my favorite definition of *aquifer*: aq•ui•fer ('æk wə fər) *n.* a geological formation of permeable rock, gravel, or sand containing or conducting groundwater, esp. one that supplies the water for wells, springs, etc.
> [1900–05; probably < French *aquifère* (adj.); see aqui-, -fer]

At least this is French I can speak. Conduct as Max conducts the clouds. You can conduct water. You don't have to contain it, dear clouds. Let it be free. Let it be French. The abundance of etc. What else is there? Wells. Springs. The under burbles up. You can try to keep the water in the ground but it will find its way out of the center of the earth, into your bathtub. It will find its way to the ocean where like Charlie's fields, it will become salty too. Clouds are only saviors, desalinators, separators. Knowers of the heaviness of sodium and chloride. Knowers of the lightness of hydrogen and oxygen.

You tell me about a sinkhole half a mile from our house. It's one of the deepest and largest in the world. Geologists say the stream disappears into a limestone cavern and is not known to appear again. To you, this is wondrous. Where does all that water go? How deep can it be? You like to measure. To me, this is practical news. If we can get in there, we can get all that water out. Flagstaff and, therefore, our children will not die of thirst.

Hydrologist Don Bills notes in a PowerPoint presentation that up until 1930, the sinkhole was a tourist attraction. In 1991, four boys explore, two become stuck. Fire Department Rescue, along with the City of Flagstaff, attempt to fill with concrete and debris (source: the *Arizona Daily Sun* and oral communication, Lorri Hull, mother of one of the boys) but the fill just keeps disappearing. Later, cavers explore to depths of 1,000 feet and horizontally for about a mile, never finding the bottom. The sinkhole appears to be gradually expanding.

Geologists still wonder, where does the water go? Zoë has a baseball game tonight. The sinkhole is not fifty yards from her field. I want to look into all that possibility but when I get there, it seems to have been filled in, which they said was impossible, which makes me want for something yet again I do not have—infinity and accurate news reporting. I want both an abyss and I want a water source.

We named our son Max before we knew the name had anything to do with water. Maxwell, get it? Of course you do. I did not. A very large well of a son. Now he comes to us in his Batman shirt, asking us, "Isn't it great? I have to tuck it in because it's cute. Isn't it cute?"

You and I, we both fall into the cavern of adorability. The questions of a three-year-old are their own sinkholes. I could live inside them and never have to think about sand or rain or crows who look at me greedily, patiently. You will go, too, eventually, the crow caws at me.

At night Max says, "I love you, taco." At night he staves off birds with his Batman shirt and his great skills at tucking.

"I love you, burrito," I say back.

You, my love, who I love more now that I found that French aquifers apply to you. You who love sinkholes and aquifers. You who tell me that on this peak above that abyss of Kaibab and Sandstone sits the world's largest aquifer, underneath 300 feet of volcanic rock. Impenetrable as you must sometimes think of me. Who can get to this water? No one no one no one but at least you know the water is there just like I know Portland is there. It doesn't wait for me any more than the aquifer waits for you. At least you have your belief in sinkholes. Infinities.

I'm still the one standing on the front porch trying to talk to the rain. Aquifer. Sinkhole. Spring. Well. I quiver.

There is a place that is as stubborn as those clouds of Flagstaffian June, the ones parked on the peaks, the ones you could drive your car upon they're so black-asphalt and so unforgiving. This place sends me notes every time it rejects me, which is every time and every time it's the same note:

> Dear Nicole,
>
> Thank you for your unwavering patience in receiving a response from *The Believer*. Unfortunately, we won't be able to take "Fiction is just nonfiction that hasn't happened yet" for the magazine; however, we wish you luck placing it with another publication. Thank you for thinking of us!
>
> Best regards,
> *The Believer*

I think, what do they know about my patience? Maybe it's been wavering all along. Perhaps though they mean it in the long sense—like, we will always send you this note forever and forever. It is something to rely on, even if it's as comforting as a sinkhole. I hope they know I believe.

Now listen to me. This is a love letter. This is a combination of lyric essay and research about sustainability and abundance and scarcity. This is writing whose wage no one wants to pay. I get that. You don't have to read it. But listen. Even though you didn't take me to Portland, it did start to rain.

At first it rained like this:

I love tacos. Let's have turkey tacos and save all those calories that would be in the beef. Turkey tacos, never mind the crows.

And then it rained.

A taco is a taco, we may as well eat the shell. Who can afford the tortillas? I can I can I can, say the crows.

And then it rained like this every day.

Taco taco taco with sour cream and cheese. Taco with salsa. Taco with guac. Taco with pork belly. Taco with fried pickles. Taco with fried chicken and fried fish. Taco two ways. Taco three ways. Tacos up the yin yang, tacos up the butt. I knew you found me attractive, still.

And then Portland came to me, food truck and all. It came in colors that washed away the red. It came in curtains pulling Tennessee Williams. It came in locomotive trains, five engines deep. It came in Council Crest and West Hills. It came in La Cruda and Dots. It came in Hawthorne and Front Avenue. It came in Alber's Mill and Pearl District and La Brasserie. It came in Forest Park and Mt. Tabor Park. It came in Chanterelle and it came in Bolete. It came in St. John's Bridge and We'll Have a Very Nice Time on the

Ross Island Bridge. It came in twenties and reeds. It came in Mistied and Racheled. It came in Oaks Park and possum and one time otter in another river almost as shallow as Eagle Creek where someone left a diaper on the farther shore. What are otters supposed to do with a used human diaper? Oh how we give and give. Only the crows say thanks but that's the kind of abundance maybe we are looking for. Maybe with rain and otters come diapers and plastic. Perhaps that's what we can do with the sinkhole. You say they poured green dye into it and the green-dyed water never came back out. A wormhole is a sinkhole into which our excesses may slide.

I cried excessively when you left me.

I cried even though you came back.

I think sometimes you blame me for all this rain. I think sometimes I blame you for its lack.

I met another man once, no, not in that way, just a guy, who could observe the pattern of bird hop from stone to stone. It's only by looking at the bird tracks from every angle that we will begin to understand stones. He noted the bird's envy. He noted the stone's. I see the envy. The clouds envy the sky for all its absence. It's a burden to carry everyone's blessing around. The clouds do it heavily. They do it stingily. They do it meteorologically. They do it bumper-stickingly. They do it sexily. They do it heartily. They do it sinkholely. They do it like a taco and they do it like a crow. They do it fancifully. They do it aquiferily. They do it in eight states and my state and the state that I have turned into an emblem of you—even though you won't take me there. We can be stone. We can be bird. It's hard to be both but it's good to try to be one and then the other. Like the song I just taught Zoë, who is eight so will still sing with me, to sing, Baby you can't love one. Baby you can't love one. You can't love one and have any fun oh baby, you can't love one. Baby you can't love two. Baby you can't love two. You can't love two and still be true, oh baby you can't love two. And so on. Baby we can't live in Flagstaff and live in Portland and still be we.

Maybe it's just a matter of name. I'll call the bird, stone. You call the stone, bird, and in so doing, it will start to rain.

I am grateful for this Flagstaff you have turned into Portland. Nouns are often interchangeable. Even better, this Portland comes with lightning. This Portland comes with thunder. This Portland comes with tacos made in Mexico. This Portland comes with calories. This Portland comes with ravens instead of crows and built-in water efficiencies. I will miss this Portland when it's gone but all Portlands must go sometime. Portland falls apart just like a storm in the desert. It falls apart like love and Batman and *The Believer* and otters and bird's nests. It falls apart like prayer and god. Portland dries up just like everything, particularly in June when it rains even though it is not supposed to rain.

Are we going to make it? Is anything sustainable? Is love? Does love always come back? I am trying to see things your way but my own eyes get in the way.

I know I wrote this wrong but it was the only way I could write it when I heard the thunder.

Sustainability

A LOVE STORY

WE KEEP GOING. Keep living in Flagstaff. Keep looking for rain. Gathering water in our barrels. We keep on keeping on. It is a sustainable existence, in that here we are, doing what we do. Still.

Sustainability is easy enough to define. Keeping going what is already going seems like a good idea. Is *is* good. It denotes being. Aliveness. Fact. Tucked inside the word are other good words: *sustenance, maintain, able*—something we are doing and can keep doing. Present tense. Simple. We sustain. We are sustaining. We will keep life as we've come to know it, keep on keeping on. The word *sustainable* attaches to environmentalism, but sustainable is a reasonable, not-preachy kind of environmentalism. We resist the word *environmentalism.* It suggests not *is* but *no.* Stop driving. Stop heating this house. Stop powering this computer with ill-gotten electricity. But if humans are bad at one thing fundamentally, it is stopping. Animals. Animate. Going. Going is something humans do well. When I think of sustainability, I think of the possibility of cars. High-gas mileage. Electric-powered. Even solar-powered. But the solar-powered car. It only seats one. It goes slow. It's hard to drive on rainy days. I don't want no. I want forward. I want fast.

Sustainability has a ring of *lifestyle to which we've become accustomed* about it. Let's sustain what we have now. No one wants to make that many changes. And, to truly sustain the planet, not our lifestyles, we would have to give up a great deal of our lifestyle that we have been trying so hard, lo this industrial revolution, to sustain. I see my neighbor vacuuming his garden rocks. The clerk at Fry's wraps one item per plastic bag. I sit here, two computers whirring, fridge humming, dishwasher running, washing machine spinning. I'm eating an orange trucked in from California. What does sustainability really look like: Washing my clothes and dishes by hand? Or is it more extreme? Does it look like washing my clothes and dishes with sand? Despite the fact that I read all of Michael Pollan's *The Omnivore's Dilemma,* I still buy red meat from Safeway. I try not to think about the cows I've met and their bland, sorrowful eyes. I try not to think about Styrofoam. About plastic wrap.

Sustainable to humans most likely means I can still have my internet and eat bacon. I can take a plane to visit my sister in Baltimore. I can take my RV, hitch my ATVs to the back, tow an SUV behind that, just in case. I can go anywhere I want to as far as I want to with all the gas I want to use. I can drive to the grocery store, forget my wallet, drive back home, pick up my wallet, go back to the store, realize I forgot my canvas shopping bags, shrug my shoulders when the checker asks paper or plastic. Sure, I make certain to store my plastic bag in a plastic-bag-keeper until the plastic-bag-keeper explodes plastic bags all over my kitchen floor and I get mad and scoop them all up and throw them away.

What's sustainable to the human is not the same as what is sustainable to the otter. The otter prefers a cool planet. He visits his sister in the stream adjacent. His black, oily legs power him over to her den. Inside, she offers him crawdads. It is a good thing otters like their crawdads raw—it is hard to get a good boil going when it's twenty degrees outside. The water temperature, though, to the otter, is just fine.

What is sustainable to the crawdad is not the same as what is sustainable to the otter. The crawdad likes her water warm. Not so warm as to boil her, just warm enough that she can use the power of her plastic claws to fight back against the otter. Warm enough to lubricate her legs to kick herself a good hiding hole.

A hole finds the whole world sustainable. A hole is very Zen. It believes where one hole is filled, another will be dug. It has friends in crawdads, gophers, golf course designers, earthquake faults, geysers, meteors. What is unsustainable to the rest of us will be intoxicating to the hole.

I recycle glass from my wine and beer bottles but then, some people don't drink. Those people are probably the most sustainable of all. They'll live forever, healthy and righteous.

While holes are seemingly always sustainable, wind may well not be. Wind farms, at some point, may functionally stop the wind. Turbines absorb the wind, turn the wind into electricity. The flapping you hear against your house at night is not a breeze. It's the sound of pollen hanging desperately off the trees, crying, "We want to go there." Where? "Anywhere." Power lines have been routed away from trees. Without pollen, nobody is going anywhere.

•

What is sustainable to me is probably not sustainable to you. I won't let my kids eat a Lunchable but those parents who do insure their children, or at least their lunches, are preserved forever with BHT. The memory of their youth lingers on in the divided sections of plastic, disposable trays. My neighbors, three kids, then two sets of triplets, put two garbage cans out to the curb each Thursday night but on Monday night, no recycling bin graces the space where sidewalk and driveway meet. Still, if sustainability is in sustaining your DNA, these people have me beat by a multiple of four. My DNA is going nowhere fast, compared to my procreative neighbors. Diaper after diaper goes into the garbage can. There is no recycling of Pamper's. But my favorite part of Franzen's *The Corrections* was the fantasy of silicon becoming a precious resource in the future. Our garbage dumps will be our goldmines. I love speculative nonfiction.

Solar power seems highly sustainable. The sun won't burn out for another million or so years. But where is the comfort in that? The idea that my children's (insert exponential children here) will be freaking out when the sun expires in five billion years? Here's something that might make you wish Earth would explode right off the bat: when you Google "the sun will die when" some website says in 200 years instead of the more plausible five billion years. Because what's the diff, really, between 200 and five billion? Because the internet is full of accurate information only about once every ninety-seven (make it 200, it's an easier number) years. About five billion years old, the sun is about halfway through its lifespan. It does not have enough mass to go supernova; instead, it will become a red giant—overheating like a Chevy Nova (at least some things are nova). Things don't look good for Earth, five billion years from now. Even if Earth survives the initial explosion, all the water will be boiled off. If you don't frack it all to hell first.

Fracking uses a lot of water. I just went down the Google hole and emerged with, surprise, conflicting information. Some say fracking uses less water than burning coal or watering golf courses. Others say that the level of contamination in that fracking water is so severe we'll never repair it. Someone else went on to try to convince me that somehow the use of methane while fracking creates brand-new water, which led me to think I should stop reading that thread since last I heard, we are all drinking dinosaur pee and that is that for water, on this planet at least. Suffice it to say, when the sun turns from red dwarf to red giant, the water/dinosaur pee will be boiled off, the atmosphere will disappear, and all that precious water, potable or not, will disappear into space. Or maybe disappear into Google where from, as you know, nothing really ever returns. I'm still there now, trying to find out about this water vapor created by burning methane. If you ever get thirsty and you happen to have a farting cow and a match, so says the internet, you will be sustenance yourself.

The biggest threat to sustainability is the I/You conundrum. I love Italo Calvino's *On a Winter's Night a Traveler.* I hear his voice (in my memory, from my copy of the book that is still on the back of a toilet in a house I once owned in Portland, Oregon—that copy. That house. That toilet. Together they are sustainable), "You walk down a cobblestone street. Your head turns to the left. You see a man with a mustache. His eyes lift and fall on your white head." Some readers don't like this "you" business. "You can't tell me what to do. I will turn my head when and in what direction I want" they tell me in writers workshop. Some readers love this. They love that both the author and the reader are together in this. The "you" point of view is unsustainable. But the "you" point of view can lead you down a path of goodness, unsustainable goodness but goodness nonetheless. To see a mother bear cling to her baby bear on an ice-floe that is melting in the middle of the arctic sea will remind you of the daughter that is coughing in her bed, and while the polar bear's apocalypse is real and your apocalypse is, in the twenty-first century, full of nebulizers, inhalers, and portable oxygen, pretend, you can fall in love with that mama bear. You can approximate, metaphorize, resemble her. That polar bear loves her baby as much as you love yours (even though mine has been coughing on me and keeping me up all night with worry. The mama polar bear. Does she worry like you?) You will save that polar bear like you will save your daughter. You insert one more vial into the nebulizer. You donate fifteen dollars to Greenpeace. You can sustain your conscience one more day.

But the metaphor falls apart as it does in any second-person narrative. At some point, the "you" is just too insistent. Too preachy. Too full of itself. You want your "I" back. You are tired of polar bears. Come on down to the lower 48. Adjust. Adapt, you tell the polar bears. Shift your perspective. You think Greenpeace should have enough cash by now to let the bears catch a ride on their big boats, giving the bears a break from swimming from ice floe to melting ice floe. Or you imagine Greenpeace throwing seals off the bow of the boat (You can swim! You have flippers. Lazy seals.), trawling flotation devices behind for the hungry bears. Then you start to feel bad for the seals. You can't take this anymore. You jump off the boat. Join the seals and the polar bears. This *you* has gone on too long. Jump!

As Jacques Derrida and Jim Morrison assure us, no one here gets out alive. There is no jumping off the boat. You are the boat. I've been stuck in my own boaty head for years now and the only way I get anywhere near off of it or out of it is watching the ground squirrel figure out how to carry four acorns at once or the raccoon open the latch on the garbage cans. If the only animals that are going to survive are rats, deer, squirrels, roaches, and raccoons then I should learn the ways of the roach. Skitter. Congregate. Learn how to fly. These animals have one thing in common. They have adapted toward humans, the roaches best of all. The small adapts much more quickly. A bug moves quickly away from a falling stick not because he himself is small but because he pays attention to the small vibrations in the earth. And that by paying attention to the small, we can make our big selves adapt. I smell lilacs. It is spring. I should prepare for drought by sucking milkweed. The monarchs. They live. I learn to love the sour taste. I'll fight the cockroach to quench my thirst.

Maybe humans are too multi-tentacled to adapt. We make too many associations, too many mental leaps. Nothing is just one thing. Information is not cold numbers and hard facts like it is to a squirrel. We weigh facts. We caress facts. We warm ourselves by the dream of a technology that will save us. Solar power. Solar power. We chant to the sometimes-still-moving wind. We form emotional attachments to facts, which turn them from facts into feelings, numbers into hope. I love the number three. I loved being three. When I was ten, I pretended I had a three-year-old daughter and when my daughter was three I loved her most and I love my son most at three too so if you tell me that in order to stop global warming, I'm going to have to give up the number three, that three is the number of carbon dioxide and forcing sad swimming polar bears then I will tell you that the globe will then have to be hot. I love the number three. I think we can save three polar bears. That is how much I love three.

It may be metaphor that kills us. Grazed by bullets. The bullets are not deer, eating gently at our cheeks. The language itself is too soft to save us. Drowning in information makes us forget there is no water around. Angel hair pasta has neither angels nor hair in it. These are the salad days is only a good thing when you weren't required, for your heart, for your cholesterol, to eat a salad every day. We take grazing and drowning and angels too lightly. Figurative language is the reason people need pictures of four-year-olds with holes in their face.

But that is horrible and the horrible won't save us. Maybe I'm wrong. Maybe metaphor will save us. I would die without you—as long as the "I" and "you" simultaneously means caterpillar and squirrel. Frog and leopard. Jelly fish and termite. Ahi and ostrich. Panda and koala (all the yous of the nonbear bear family). Dust mite and dust mote. Hawks and ravens (even if the ravens seem to bully the hawks). Goldfish and monarchs. Jim Morrison and Jacques Derrida. Lactobacillus acidophilus and yeast. Elephants and elephantitis. Rattlesnake and bumblebee. Daughters and rock-vacuumers. Crawdads and otters. Solar power and holes. Roaches and Google. Triplets and Pampers. Raccoons and Michael Pollan. The bagger at Fry's and the RV driver. Italo Calvino and the polar bear. You and even maybe me too.

Cautionary Tales

IT'S HARD TO change the mind of the farmer in West, Texas, that this isn't just another drought. His dad suffered droughts. His grandfather. His great-grandfather. And even though he might admit this feels a little different, a little longer, a little drier, he doesn't think that it's the way he waters the feed he grows for his cows that might have something to do with the lack of water in the Ogallala aquifer. The Texan is a believer. The water will come or it won't and it will be God's will. St. Teresa of Avila, *The Life of St. Teresa of Avila,* ecstatic poet, saint, woman of the body wrote, "We must be always looking out for one water when another fails. The heavenly rain very often comes down when the gardener least expects it." There is hope even in a blue sky. St. Teresa of Avila can be read literally. The water will come. Because there is nothing else but hope. It wasn't until recently that I understood the full meaning behind "hope" being the one fury left locked inside Pandora's box. I always thought it was extremely unkind of the gods to keep hope away from the humans. But hope can be, when your crops fail, the most desperate.

The farmer hopes for rain. The owner of the house at the bottom of a landslide dreads it. You illustrate the dryness of the ground for the farmer. You make it hit home. It is like the cracked skin of your forehead. You show him your forehead. It is like the blazing heat of the forest. You light a match. This drought is the dust bowl times two thousand. But he is an artist of his own. He sees a mote of dust and knows a mote signals an entire storm. He carries his dust mote, the end-of-the-drought therein, and walks away, leaving me in the fields, thirsty. It is only when the farmer forgets his hat, it begins to rain. The drops make big holes in the ground. Each grain of sand greedy.

Perhaps it's because I'm a teacher. Maybe because I'm a mom. Maybe it's because my mom didn't have any compunction about telling a stranger-kid riding his bike down the street to put his helmet on. Maybe it's because I believe art can persuade. Maybe it's because I write about how small changes can make big impact but somewhere along the line, I became someone who thought it was my job to change people's minds. I try it in subtle ways, like, shouting really loudly to my kids when we're walking through the grocery store parking lot that "NO ONE NEEDS TO LET THEIR CAR IDLE IN THE PARKING LOT. GLOBAL WARMING." My Zoë learned early in life that subtlety isn't really one of my strong suits. She walks as many paces in front of me as she is old. One day, the gap will be big enough that she and her fellow shoppers will shake their heads at me in pity.

It's hard to make an impact. No one wants to listen to a short, blond woman who is mostly a hypocrite anyway, who eats cows, drives a gasoline-powered car, who owns no solar panels, tsk tsking them. Do you know on whom you can make an impact? Your little children. If you trap them in the bath, they have to listen to you. And you're not so short to them and your blond hair is not yet the blond of the jokes that will come.

How do you train the children about danger without turning them into anxiety-ridden doomsday-sayers? In our living room, we have a gas fireplace. It's the not-that-easy kind. The kind you have to turn the gas on and then use a match. I can never find the matches—not so much because we have kids and Erik and I would like them not to burn the house down but because we have a wood-burning stove in the other room that requires the one book of matches we do have. The kids are likely to know where they are. We ask them, "Have you seen the matches?" They answer "yes," meaning we should have hidden them, or "no," meaning they have found them and hidden them and will find them again sometime when we are not looking and they practice seeing what this red thing does when applied to this black thing. The fire forecast for our house, thanks to our inability to keep track of our matches, is about as bad as it is for the forest where it has not rained for over three months. We are mostly doomed.

Zoë brings the matches to me. The gas has been streaking out of the fireplace for a full minute now. I'm going to lose some eyebrows.

"Can I light the fire?"

"No. You'll lose your eyebrows. But you can strike the match." I think it's better to teach kids how to do things carefully rather than to not do them at all. Unless I think the opposite an hour later and tell her never, ever touch matches. In this case, I tell her to pull out a match. I show her how to fold the cover over match. "Pull it fast." It lights. She drops it. On the wooden floor. I stand up. Step on it. I turn off the gas. Maybe no fire tonight. This is as much danger-lesson as I can take.

In the bath, Max, dumping the contents of his purple cup that reads *Zoë* since she had two cups, this purple and another pink one, when he was born and why buy more plastic? over his head, cries. He needs a washcloth. I bring him a green washcloth but he wants the gray one. Zoë dumps her pink Zoë cup over her hair. She blinks the water out of her eyes. She doesn't cry. She's eight and not Max, but I hand her a washcloth anyway. Hair wet and bodies naked, their eyes look even bigger than usual. Disney's movies may be influencing our DNA. The kids are all audience and water. Worried about the matches and the fireplace, I have them trapped to hear a cautionary tale. I tell them about the Schultz fire.

"Where did they live?"

"By the fire."

"What were their names?"

"I can't remember. Do you want to hear the story? Two little kids just took some matches from their mom's house. They pulled them right out of the drawer. Didn't even ask. They wanted to pretend they were camping. They left out the backdoor and walked up the hillside. You know how Flagstaff is. One big forest. They found some wood, put it in a pile. Then, they pulled out the matchbook. It's so dry here. It only took one strike before the fire was lit. They pretended to roast marshmallows. That got boring. They started goofing off. Playing swords with their roasting sticks. When a wind came up, they didn't notice. The one kid broke the other kid's stick. The broken-stick-one chased the one-who-broke the-stick. They ran out of sight of the fire. The wind carried a spark to a small pile of ponderosa pine needles. Dried by sun and lack of rain, the pine needles didn't need much help to burst into flame. The flame wouldn't have been so bad if it hadn't been so close to a tree that had been attacked by bark beetles. It was defenseless."

"What's a bark beetle?"

"It's a beetle who ate bark," Max says to his older sister.

"Right. And bark beetles eat trees that are already susceptible to disease."

"What does *susceptible* mean?"

"Likely to get it," Zoë tells her younger brother. He knows more about bugs. She about contagion. They both take a break from the story to give me their zombie faces.

"We will eat your brains."

"Ok. That's it. Out of the bath. You know I can't sleep with zombies on the brain."

"No finish. Finish."

"It's not a happy story. The tree is on fire. The branches from that tree touch another tree and then another and soon the boys are running and an acre is on fire and then ten acres and then a hundred acres. Fires grow exponentially."

"What does *exponentially* mean?"

"To a greater power," I say.

"Like Jesus," Max clarifies. Max goes to a Lutheran preschool.

"Kind of." Definitions are exhausting.

"The fire people try to put the fire out but it's too big."

"The firemen?" Max is also very into gendered definitions. I blame the preschool.

"Not just men. People. Your Aunt Joy was a Hot Shot for the forest service."

"What's a Hot Shot?" Max asks. Zoë laughs to think of her aunt as a show-off, which she is anything but.

"It's a forest fire person."

"Fireman."

"No. Max. Stop it or no more story."

"OK." He does it because it bugs me. He laughs himself crazy, how easy it is to get me lecturing. His grin cracks wide. I can't help but like him even if he interrupts.

"It's not a happy story. The firefighters can't put the fire out. There are houses right below the fire. Everyone has to evacuate. Get out of their house. They can only take their most precious stuff. And where do they go? To their mom's? A hotel? A church? Drive up to Salt Lake and pretend they're on vacation? Down to Phoenix even though it's 117 degrees? Might as well stay by the fire. It burns and burns. The firefighters make a fire line, try to stop the fire from coming close to the houses. They set other fires away from the houses, and the city, for that matter, to make the fire go in the other direction. The fire burns. A guy from the news in Phoenix calls your dad to go take a picture of the fire."

"Why'd they call Dad?"

"Because he used to work for the news."

"Where does he work now?"

"Focus on this story. Dad goes and takes a picture. He can only get as close as the gas station. From there, he took a picture of the whole mountain swirling up into clouds of smoke. This is the worst part. Eventually, they put the fire out, but if you look at the mountain, there are no trees. Do you remember when we were driving back from Salt Lake and we got stopped for an hour?"

"I do! I do!" They both say, raising their hands, but Max was only one so I doubt he remembers. I remember having to take Zoë to pee behind a tree on the side of the road while the trail of cars in front of us stretched for miles. At least there was one left standing after the fire to pee behind.

"But I'm not kidding. Listen. It's sad. It had been raining while we were gone. The trees that used to hold back the water and the dirt were gone. A river popped up right below the houses and a little girl went to look. The bank fell away and the girl drowned. They stopped traffic that day because they were looking for her."

"Wait. What? Someone died? How? How did the river just come? Why does the bank fall away?" Zoë asked.

"The rain came down. It pooled in certain spots, drained in one direction. The girl didn't know there would be more water. She was looking at this new stream in her backyard and then the stream turned into a river and she fell in."

Which is, I guess, two cautionary tales. Don't play with matches and don't stand too close to the edge of the river, especially when where there was no river yesterday is a river today.

This bath is full of fully treated water. Potable and pure, the kids can drink it out of their "Zoë" cups. I try not to think about the soap and dead skin cells they're gulping. Because we have so little water in Flagstaff, Flagstaff waters golf courses and parking medians green their lawns with gray water. Unlike the water we drink, which is pulled from reservoirs and wells, and then treated, gray water is water that has been flushed or has run off into storm drains, is treated with microorganisms aerobically and anaerobically, and then is sent to those golf courses and medians. The water my kids are drinking was cleaner—at least until they shed their alleles into it—processed by humans and then by nature and then by humans again. Recently, the pumps at the water treatment facility that processes the gray water had broken down. As I drove past the golf course, I watched them water the grass with perfectly potable water. I wanted to know what the difference between treated as "gray" water and "rigorously" for potable was. My sister teaches biology and chemistry to high school students, sometimes middle school. She would know, so I called her.

She answered, "Who died?"

We don't talk on the phone that much.

"No one," I said. "You're the one who calls when people die. I'm calling you about the microorganisms they use to clean the water."

Paige had to call me when my dad died and she called me when my grandma died. She called when her ex-boyfriend Gabe died and she called when our Aunt Mary died. There was no reason for her to be suspicious of *my* calls. I should worry when *she* calls me. Except it goes to show that I don't call her enough. I'm distant when I'm distant. I don't do a good job bridging the spatial gap. Five hundred miles apart is far, mentally and physically. But I call a lot when I need help to understand genetics and microorganisms or to ask why all the bald eagles are dying in Utah. They think it's possibly bird flu. Or Monsanto. Neither sounded good.

"I don't know the exact name of the organisms they use at water treatment plants. I'll look it up when I get to school," she tells me. Paige teaches at an alternative school for pregnant teenagers. After they give birth, they can bring the baby to the school day care. If the babies need to eat, the moms are called to pick them up. They can bring them to class when they're really tiny. I thought it was the perfect job for my sister who had just had a baby.

"You can bring Blake to school! He'll be right down the hall from you."

"Nope. They won't let staff or faculty use the day care."

Instead, she took her six-week-old new son to my friend's in-home day care. For Utah being such a family-friendly state, the state isn't so friendly to families, especially the families where the mom has to work.

"How do they know which is the gray water and which is the regular water?" she asked me.

"There are signs all over town. On the toilets at the university. On sticks on the golf courses," I told her.

"But do they have different pipes, going to different places? Gray water pipes to toilets, regular, fully treated water to sink faucets?"

I told her that I would have to get back to her on that. I was almost at Zoë's school. I didn't have time to tell her about the Hopi injunction to stop the ski resort from using gray water to make snow on what they consider to be the holy Kachina Mountains. We'd get back to each other, we said, but maybe this is why we don't call so much. Teachers both, we are always giving each other homework.

That night, in the bath, after the forest fire cautionary tale, Zoë begged for another cautionary tale. I felt conflicted. How to tell this as a morality play without making it sound like I judged Janie? Unlike my dad, it wasn't Janie's fault she fell. Paige said she'd been diagnosed a few weeks earlier with breast cancer. She had just quit smoking. She was going to come to my reading at the King's English Bookstore in Salt Lake but the quitting smoking was driving her crazy and she just wanted to sleep in bed. After the diagnosis, she started smoking again. Maybe her body couldn't take the stimulus. Most likely, it was just bad luck after bad luck. If anyone deserved some good luck, it was Janie. Her bad luck was Mormonism. Was conservatism. Was expectation. It wasn't fair, using Janie's story as a cautionary tale, but I had been thinking about her and what her life was like and how as she lay in the hospital her grown children, ages twenty-four, twenty-two, and eighteen, must have felt as little as my kids, ages eight and four were, here in the bath. Janie was only a few years older than me. I wanted to go and collect her kids. I wanted to go back in time when I put her oldest on my lap and we watched the fireworks in the park at Lindsay Gardens and her wonder at the lights in the sky made me realize I wanted to have kids, even if bringing them into the sometimes grim world was selfish on my part. I wrapped my arms around Janie's daughter and watched the grimness fall away. In her eyes, through her eyes, was only red spark and expectant smoke. The kind of smoke that could take you somewhere.

"OK. Listen. This is why you shouldn't have sex too young. My friend Janie. When she was sixteen, she got pregnant."

I had told both of them the short and clinical version of penis-vagina sex. Max had no idea what I was talking about. Zoë said, "Weird." But they knew the fundamentals of sex having.

"Now listen. I had sex too young too. Don't do it. But if you do. Use condoms. Janie got pregnant. And in her family, if you got pregnant, you had the baby. Her parents and the guy's parents made them get married. Or maybe they wanted to get married. At sixteen, getting married seems like a lot of fun and not a lot like living at home with your parents. So they got married. But he joined the army because they had no money and hadn't graduated from high school. What else were they going to do? So they moved to Anchorage, Alaska, thousands of miles from home. And it is a lot like living at home with your parents except you have to pay all the bills. It's another reason not to have sex early. If you get pregnant, young, you probably don't have a lot of money. There's never enough to go around. Janie didn't have her mom to help her or her many sisters. She was from a Mormon family and sisters and moms help with the babies but not if you live in Anchorage. She had her first daughter. She had a second. Her husband, though, was not very nice to her. He hit her sometimes."

"He HIT her?"

"Yes. It was very bad." I wonder to myself, what is the cautionary tale here? Husbands? Pregnancy? Anchorage? Scarcity? Abundance? No. It's condoms. Even though I loved that daughter of Janie's as much as I've loved any kid not my own.

"So finally, she left him. It was hard because she didn't have any money and still hadn't finished high school. But she came back to Utah. She got married again, had a son, but this husband was a jerk too. She left him. She found a job at Ex-Wives Place, the bar where your Aunt Valerie and Doug met. They were all friends, which made me happy, even though I lived far away in Portland." The bar part of the story was an unnecessary detail but mentioning Zoë's Aunt Val made Janie seem all the more real.

"Janie quit working at the bar. Became a mortgage underwriter, which she didn't love because she loved to be around people and dogs and smoke cigarettes and drink beer, like we all do. But she had to work and her kids were in school all the time. In a lot of ways, she did pretty well. Her kids are amazing—smart and funny. But she was only forty years old."

I've lost the thrust of my argument. The bathwater is cold. Now, I'm just feeling sad about my friend who is in the hospital. It's really more a story of injustice rather than caution. Maybe the caution is, don't have an aneurysm or your friends will be sad, even friends you haven't seen in over ten years.

"My point is. Don't have sex too young. And always use condoms."

"Tell us one more."

"Prurient interest," I remind her. But who besides my children wants to hear my morality plays? "Get out of the tub. I'll tell you one more."

I dry off Max's tiny butt. I try to commit these butts to memory. Is all fear of the future merely the fear that you will never again hold hands this tiny, this healthy, this clean? I dry his feet while Zoë twists her towel into a Breck commercial on the top of her head. How did she get so big? Her breasts are still flat. Her hips still narrow but her body is on the verge. She's like ground under which you can hear the mycelium prepare to mushroom. I'm on the floor with Max so I am eye-level with her vagina. Is this the last day it's appropriate for me to be this close to her? Tomorrow? Her body, sensual, is so non-sexual. In the parking lot by the swimming pool, twelve trees bloomed. The scent was both overwhelming and fleeting. I could not quite hold it. When I held a branch directly to my nose, I could smell nothing. It was only by smelling the flowers as they dissipated on the wind that I got any sense of spring at all.

These bodies. I cannot keep them here. I can't even keep them perfectly safe. Maybe I can keep them imperfectly safe.

As I rubbed lotion first into Zoë's legs, then Max's: "Scott had never seen a gun. His parents didn't have them. They didn't even let him have toy guns. So when he went to his friend Tony's house, he didn't hesitate when Tony asked him if he wanted to see his dad's gun. Guns, really. There were lots of them, all kinds. Long ones and short ones. Some black, some silver. Scott asked if he could touch one. Tony said sure. He did it all the time. Scott asked if they were loaded. "No way," Tony said. His dad was really careful. So they each took a gun out of the cabinet and started fooling around, pretending they were in a shoot out. Tony hid behind the couch. Scott around the corner. One would pop up, the other would hide. The guns went click click. Empty sounding. Click click. Tony stood up and shot at Scott. Click click. Scott shot back at Tony. They clicked. They got bored. They decided it would be more fun to be snipers. They got different guns. From the upstairs loft, Tony put Scott in his sights. Click click. Scott put Tony in his sights. This time, the gun made a new sound. Not empty."

I didn't want to finish the story. It felt creepy. Who tells stories that are remembered poorly, dramatized so that the three-dimensional humans are turned into two-dimensional characters. Isn't that the problem with telling stories? The words become the humans and words are as flat as paper dolls. Plus, I tell a story that ends up brains splattered on the wall? I should have just let them watch *The Walking Dead*. Zombies are at least three dimensional-seeming.

I skipped over the brains. "Scott had to find Tony's parents. Can you imagine? Telling someone you shot their kid?"

"Why did he shoot him?"

"He was just playing around. He didn't know there was a bullet in that gun."

"Did he die?"

"He died."

"What happened?"

"To Scott. Nothing. He had to live with the fact that he shot his friend dead."

How old do you have to be to know what dead is? How close do you have to come? Do you have to touch it? The slow death the poets know—it's always coming. If I write myself dead, says Mark Doty, I grow into my death, if I see myself already dead in my own coffin, dissociating,

Now I lie in the box
of my making while the weather
builds and the mourners shake their heads as if
to write or to die. I did not have to do either.
perhaps death won't be such a shock. Perhaps death will
pass me by altogether.

Kids don't know what dead means. Nobody does. Everything else comes back—ants in the bathroom, grandmothers who live out of state, tulips in the spring, snow in the winter. Why should any of us believe the end of the body is the end of the body? It seems so unlikely. Entropy is all around us. But I show my kids my wrinkles. My forehead did not always have this big crease in it. Now, no matter how much I stretch my skin wide, you can see the trenches. "Now don't make my wrinkles any deeper," I warn my kids. "Don't touch guns. If you see a gun at a friend's house, leave. Do not stay in that house. Run straight home like their house is on fire because it is."

Max and Zoë look tired. "Can you tell us one more?" I'm afraid I have sounded too much like TV. Like I turned the real life into story, compelling narrative, escapist fantasy, instead of a gut-hitting, practical lesson on how to save themselves from the future. Art aestheticizes. I wanted ugly. I tell them all the time not to leave the front door open. "All the heat goes right out the door. Then the heater kicks back on. The gas spews its carbon into the air, hottening up the planet. What do I care? It won't be all desert and zombie apocalypse while I'm alive. It's you guys that are going to have starving refugees knocking at your door."

Crush their hope like you should crush the farmer in West, Texas's hope. It is not going to rain. It is not going to rain ever again. I will scare sense into you with my stories.

Instead of rushing over to shut the door, the kids again make their zombie faces at me. I don't know where they learned these faces, but they make their eyes big and the mouths square. These zombie children abstract themselves from themselves—dissociated, I can barely recognize them as my children. They are already turning themselves into stories. I wonder if my cautionary tales should have warned them about art.

Fire Question

"WE SHOULD MOVE." I say this to my husband, Erik, after Brady Udall's visit.

Brady and I ate blueberries, sitting on my back porch, looking over the slight depression in the landscape where both Route 66 and the Burlington Northern train tracks run east and west, alongside rock-covered and cell-tower-topped Mount Elden where most of the vegetation burned in the 1977 human-caused Radio Fire.

Erik and I feel close to Brady Udall author of *The Lonely Polygamist* and *The Miracle Life of Edgar Mint*. We are from Utah. Erik's mom is related to Brady by marriage, through polygamy. The Udalls, an important political family in Arizona, married Erik's mom's great-grandma in St. John's, Arizona, after her first husband died. They had no children together, so Erik is not related-related. But I read his books, so I feel related-related to him.

Brady scans Mt. Elden. I follow his eyes as they climb the hill that leads to my house.

"My friend died last summer. She lived in a house like this. Her husband got out. So did she. But then, she went in to get her cat. She and the cat both died."

"Did they live in the forest?"

"Yes. Like this. On the top of a hill. The fires come up over the ridge so fast. You have three minutes, maybe, to get out of the house."

Brady's just trying to scare me, I know. I forgot to order the books for his reading. I deserve whatever he dishes out. Still, it works. I'm scared.

So I tell Erik we have to move. Global warming will hit Arizona first—even in Flagstaff. The fire is coming. The drought is already here.

"What are we going to do? Spend our lives chasing water? What will we do for jobs?"

I know. I know. But isn't staying some kind of suicide? I look at the line of vegetation on Mt. Elden, where it stops, just above Linda Vista, the street by our daughter's elementary school. There are lines of green surrounding all of Flagstaff and then lines of deep brown. Fire lines, firebreaks, fire zones, fuel breaks. Lines wrought by bulldozers and firefighters with shovels meant to stop the fire from moving over. A boundary between them, fire, and us, home. But, as Brady Udall pointed out, sometimes we are *they*. *They* are *us*.

The End of the Coffee Is the End of the World

I ASK MYSELF important questions in the morning. Which would be harder to go without: coffee or a hot shower? Coffee gets the grit off your teeth. The shower scours the sleep out of your eye. I answer, cynical: Could have to give up both. A coffee fungus, made much more deadly to coffee plants, because temperatures in coffee-growing climates have risen enough to let the fungus thrive, could destroy all coffee plantations. So no coffee. But I live in Flagstaff, arid Southwest, where the drought is predicted to only get worse. It usually snows 115 inches each winter. This year, in my backyard, it is May and has snowed only twelve. Perhaps there will be no water. The grit will stay on my teeth. The sleep will cover my eyes.

And then I think, either way, I'll be dead soon enough. I'll miss coffee. I'll miss showers.

I'm a lot of fun in the morning. My friend Chance, whenever I see him, says, "The minute we are born, we start dying." He's even more fun than I.

I didn't used to mind dying so much. Most of the time, it seemed like a fine idea. Life is hard. There are too many people on the planet. People struggle for liberty and justice their whole lives and die anyway. What makes me so special, me here, with my coffee and my shower and my computer that lets me think I'm talking to someone. Or myself. A call and response. A collaboration. Is that what it's all about? Asking yourself why go on when Monsanto is killing the milkweed and now there will be no more butterflies and the Supreme Court says that corporations get free speech and money is speech and affirmative action is dead and then my heart is broken and my kids are at school so they can't cheer me up and they're stuck with this planet anyway and it's never going to rain again and I answer, there is a good reason to go on: Coffee. And a shower. Samuel Beckett, who died of a respiratory infection, not suicide, whose obituary in the *New York Times* read, "In no way could he ever be considered an optimist," drove Andre the Giant, of *Princess Bride* fame, to school every day because Beckett had a truck big enough for Andre the Giant to fit in. Beckett was the one who wrote, "I must go on. I can't go on. I'll go on."

Somewhere in the grittiness of poverty where, as Cornell West calls the nihilism of poverty, the kid chooses the gun. Somewhere in the griminess of too-young-sex, which America calls the nihilism of the body, the kid chooses the gun. Somewhere, in the gaudiness of the internet, which the chat room calls the nihilism of anonymity, the kid chooses the gun. The kid chooses the gun. The parents choose the gun. The scientist chooses a gun to block out the sun. Everyone chooses the gun because the world is dying anyway. I would choose a gun.

But wait! The world may be dying but look. But look. Here is a crocus. But look, a 3,200-year-old tree. But look, there is my love driving into the garage, bringing me a six-pack of beer from Founders—the beer that was a primary reason he was tempted to stay in Michigan. I don't even drink beer, but I'll drink this. Because he brought it. Did you see the lilacs? I think they're going to make it this year. This life is unsustainable but the beer is cold and the lilacs remind me of my great-grandmother's house in Evanston, Wyoming. Everywhere the lilac grows, now I have been. Lilacs almost always come back.

Every year, Manuel Santana returns to his coffee plantation in Ahuachapan, El Salvador. He lives in Flagstaff half the year, selling his coffee. The other half of the year, he flies home to the farm his parents owned and now he owns. I wait for Manuel in the parking lot of Beaver Street Brewery where we are supposed to meet at 10:00. At 10:15, I call Manuel. He forgot. Can I drive out to his house? He gives me directions. I think it's about five minutes away. I only have an hour because I have to pick Zoë up from school and get her to piano by 2:00. As I start driving, I realize Manuel lives as far away as you can be from downtown and still call it Flagstaff. I drive illegally fast.

I am an artificial interviewer. I bring a notebook but I take no notes. Manuel wears a blue button-down. He's short and square, like me, but his daughter is tall and thin. She's on his computer, which he needs to borrow to show me pictures of his farm but first he'll make me an espresso. I know him from the farmer's market but I don't really know him at all. I stand too close to him. I make jokes about how he's running a regular Starbucks in here, three espresso machines, burlap sacks of coffee, dishes stacked in the sink. I smile too much and laugh too loud. He hands me my coffee, asks if I want cream. I hug him a little. I do want cream. He steps back. I've made him uncomfortable. I have this ability with strangers as well as my own husband. I'm too much "yes, please." I'm bubbling over. Sorry. Sorry. This is supposed to be an interview. He sets the cream down by my coffee. I have twenty-five minutes until I have to be back downtown. His daughter has opened the files on the computer she knows he wants to show me.

"Do you go down to El Salvador with your dad?" I ask her.

She doesn't look at me like I'm an idiot but she might have paused a little to give me time to figure it out myself. "No. I have school."

Manuel starts telling me the history of the Farabundo Marti National Liberation Front (FMLN) in El Salvador and the civil war and what happened to coffee prices. I pick up my notebook but I'm still looking at his daughter. He leaves her every year from November to March. What business would I do that for? Coffee? Lima? Magic?

"Isn't it hard to be away from your kids that long?"

Manuel does look at me like I am an idiot. Of course it is hard. I sip my coffee. I have thirteen minutes and 497 images to go.

As Manuel flips through images, I can see the coffee fungus decimating the plants. Maybe he should give up farming. Stay with his kids in this house full of wood and coffee on the edge of Flagstaff. His wife works at my school. Isn't that enough? But sometimes, the most obvious questions are the ones you can't ask. Instead, I ask him what is the going rate for coffee. I buy his "for $15/pound" because I know him, a little, enough to nearly spill my coffee onto his laptop and enough to forget to thank him for the coffee and the cream as I'm rushing out the door, to ask if it's safe to travel to El Salvador, if I can visit his farm in Ahuachapan. "Yes, yes," he says because he sees me wanting him to say yes. He waves as I drive away and I can't tell if we are new friends or if he's glad to see me go. I promise to come back. Does Manuel laugh or does he shake his head? I say, "It was so good to meet you." Even though I've already met him. Because redundancy is the beginning of how we begin to understand our story.

•

You don't have to understand your story to narrate it. My son Max narrates everything he does. "I'm going over to the couch now. I'm picking up the remote. I'm turning on the TV. How do you turn on the TV?" I walk over to the TV, press the button on the remote, show him how "select" can also mean "on." He pushes "select." I walk away. He wants me to come back, choose *Curious George* for him. He has already chosen the show. He wants me to see how he's done it. If we narrate it, we'll remember it. Every memory, a reincarnation. Max wants to be sure I'll come back. Stephen Burt, the poet and critic, when I met him at a conference and complained about how hard it was to leave my kids, said, "But that's the reason to go. To teach them that you do come back."

Hoc opus, hic labor est. That was the problem. This is the hard work—figuring out how to come back. We come back to the living room, we come back from the trip, we come back from the dead in our lovers' letters, even if we were our only true loves.

This writing is an echo chamber. I can hear me just fine. It reverberates. Humans like to hear themselves talk. It is our gift to the world, these languages, even if the dolphins and whales too can speak they speak only in the moment. Humans, with their voice recorders, their pens, their typing systems, their status updates, their narration, make our voices go on forever.

Humans are not so worried about other voices. Navy sonar practices force whales and dolphins deep under water where they suffer from the bends, just like humans. Many go deaf. A deaf whale is a dead whale. But then, sometimes, the humans surprise you. A sailor and his friends fishing from a boat spent three hours freeing a humpback whale trapped by an abandoned fishing net. First, the sailor dove into the water and carefully cut the netting from under the whale's belly. Dangerous work. The whale was scared and huge. One flap of his tail could break the diver's neck. As he cut, the people in the boat pulled the netting off the whale, cutting when they had a chance. One pectoral fin to go, the whale dove, threatening to pull the boaters into the water. But the net slipped off. The whale was free. The boaters pulled the net into the boat to prevent future snaring. The whale paid them back in kind with a whale thank you. He breeched the water, spun, rose and crashed and then spun again. Maybe he was just joyful to be free. But maybe he was grateful for their hard work. Either way, their accounts were settled.

Humans are accountants as much as they are artists. Tit for tat. Karma. Do unto others. Somehow, we think the balance sheets will equal zero in the end. If we die, something else may live. If humans die, the other species will make it. If another frog species dies out, well, a human may get to drink her coffee AND take her hot shower. Cost-benefit analysis. Perhaps I should compromise and drink my coffee cold.

Are We Going to Make It?

ANOTHER KIND OF SUSTAINABILITY

IT'S HARD TO worry about the distant disaster when everyday disasters are so immediate. On the one hand, our friends Ander and Megan were in town for the weekend. Erik and I should be on our best behavior. But marriage doesn't behave just because dinner guests have become breakfast guests. The day pokes its head in. Where night is social, only some visits can handle the diurnal. Our friends arrived on Friday afternoon—I'd cleaned the house, gone to the store, made dinner that night. In the morning, I made breakfast: hashbrowns with habaneros, spinach frittata. Erik, cleaning up, opened the Tupperware drawer and said, "My god. I can never find a lid. Someone has to go through this. It's a disaster."

I said, "No it's not. I go through it every day. Every lid matches."

An old anger bubbled up. Unappreciated. Unperceived. Unsung hero of the Tupperware organizational system. The air became as tense as plastic. BPA-ridden. Toxic. Ander and Megan tried to make conversation through the petroleum jelly of our marriage but even their words, "these were good eggs," couldn't penetrate the muck. Who wants to see the inside of a marriage? It's like watching an oil spill. You want to cup your hands to pick it up, cradle it, rock it back to sleep, but the oil slips through your fingers.

The friends left early the next day.

I'm not certain there's a correlation between our bickering and their leaving early but what if there is? What if they left because we argued about Tupperware? It's not the arguing, necessarily. It's the symbolism. I extrapolate. If you don't appreciate my skills with plastic, you don't appreciate the way I wipe down the counters, nor the way I pick up the kids, nor the fact that I fold your laundry, then you don't appreciate me at all. The Tupperware is a match. My brain is tinder.

The forest is burning down. It wasn't easy to set on fire but once we did, well, can we put it out? Once the trees are gone, stand in the burn. In the black, firefighters call it. It's the only safe space. From here, where everything has already burned, you can watch the flames take out every fertile thing. We're lucky we already had kids, he and I. Our fire line.

The next night, we bickered again about something stupid. "I read in the paper it rained twelve inches."

"No. They said thirteen."

"I just read it. Twelve."

Erik's a carpenter. He believes in precision. The back and forth. It's who we are. Stubborn believers in our own ability to read and retain facts. To organize Tupperware drawers. To think that somewhere in the world, someone is keeping score, that somewhere, someone knows who is right and who is wrong. What a great belief, a god of sorts, a refereeing god who will come out at the end of our marriage and say, all right, Erik 458 points, Nicole 459. You're the winner. Here's your prize. The prize is a bag of organized Tupperware and an inch of rain. I'm left holding it. Erik's moved on to someone who has a capacity to agree.

On the other hand, I am having a rough year. It should have been a great year but I failed a friend by promising her a job and then not delivering and then another would-be friend by delivering too much by writing about her, her mother, her friend's cancer, and I didn't mean it in a bad way but I betrayed her. I have a hard time knowing where my stories end and where other people's stories begin. I like to believe we all share stories but when I'm the one typing, I'm the noun, everyone else is the direct object. The book I'd just published about growing up in Salt Lake was hard on my mom but she invited her sisters to read it, her friends at work, her book club. She was proud even though it was hard and that's how I thought everyone should be. But I am not everyone's daughter. People asked hard questions and that was good because I am not shy about nouns or direct objects. Parts of the book are about having sex too young and led to two days of talking about that sex, calling it what it was, what it wasn't, telling Erik's cousin, Emily, all the details—the babysitter, the two years it went on, the lack of real coercion, the fact that I put myself in the situation—I once called him to see if I should come over. I explained how I saw myself as separate from myself, an actor in my life. It wasn't me so much as a character acting out a soap opera of her own. I could dissociate. Leave my doll-playing, stuffed animal-loving, feed-my-bicycle-grass-because-it-is-a-horse self at home and go to the neighbor's house where I was Laura from *General Hospital* or possibly Hope from *Days of Our Lives*. I told her about how my parents had books. So many books that I could read: Sidney Sheldon's *Shogun* and Aldous Huxley's *Door of Perception* and Alex Haley's *Roots*. I could read Judy Blume's *Tale of a Fourth Grade Nothing* and Judy Blume's *Forever* and Judy Blume's *Wifey*. The romantic life of a twelve-year-old. Almost twelve. I had big, romantic thoughts. I told Emily about my imaginary daughter, Debbie, who was three, and my other imaginary daughter, Amber, who was just a baby. I took Debbie skiing, stopped on the hill to make sure she caught up, told her we had to get home to check on the baby. Follow my skis, imaginary daughter. An imaginary husband wasn't too much of a stretch. It did not hurt. I had read the books. I knew how to make the right noises and the right tilt of my head. I could watch myself in the movie of my life. I was my own referee, letting an ugly fifteen-year-old play a bit part in a scene that I would never be allowed to forget. Emily asks me, "Do you talk to anyone about it? Take it out on anyone?" Erik, my real husband, who I know has this scene of me being squashed naked by an ugly rapist flipping through his head, sits next to me while I talk. He doesn't push my hand away. I realize I deflect by fighting about Tupperware. And, I find out later, Erik's right. There are more containers than lids.

How does someone love someone after all that previous squashing? How do you reintegrate a divided self? The self that can write the event and the self that had lived it? The self that can see herself as if in a soap opera and the real self that looks at a twelve-year-old and finds that her real stomach hurts? It takes a carpenter to build a bridge from self to self. It's hard on that carpenter. Sometimes, all he can do is make a bridge with his hand over the abyss that is the couch of questions.

In a ruined forest, burned, destroyed, the trees might come back. They don't come back with sweetness. They don't come back through kindness. Trees come back through hardness, a seed through the bumhole of a mammal whose digestives juices have rendered a hard-husked seed soft-husked and viable. When I teach my students to write traditional forms of poetry, I tell them that it's important to have something to work against, to fight with, some structure in your form. Writing in form makes my language tighter, less floppy. Facts work as structures too. It's memory you work against, offering form. It's research you work against, tightening your thoughts. It's the marriage between the idea and fact that forces the words into resonance. Erik is my sonnet form. I stuff my thoughts into him. In the stuffing, sometimes there is singing.

So we don't move. We stay put. The fires come closer every year. We have created defensive space around the house. We keep saying "we," as in, "perhaps *we* should organize the Tupperware better." It is he who rakes the pine needles, stuffs them into plastic bags, hauls them to the side of the road to be picked up and driven to a let's keep-the-fire-over-there destination. But we both keep our eyes out for smoke and, in doing so, sometimes spot a bald eagle flying over our house whom we also like to think of as "we."

Erik moved with me away from Salt Lake, away from his home for twenty-nine years, to Michigan so I could take a job. What kind of previously squashed person deserves that kind of love? Some people take marriage seriously. Erik is one of them. Even if the love dies, these people, these Eriks, believe love can be reborn, regenerated.

Regeneration

ALTHOUGH WE HAD lived separately in the northwest, we met and got married in the desert. Erik and I did try to move together toward water. It rains 38.27 inches per year in Grand Rapids. In Salt Lake City, 16.10. In Michigan, we could stave off the effects of climate change. We could stop looking at brown mountains, brown parks, brown grass.

Every house in the summer needed a fan. Every house in Michigan in the summer needed a fan and a screen door. The fan pretended to move the air around. The screen pretended to keep the mosquitoes out. Our house in Michigan had no fan, and yet when I looked up from the television as I sat in the hot living room, sweating and swatting at flies, something brown and fan-like gyred on the ceiling. There was a bat in my house. I fell to the floor, army-crawled my way out of there. I barely like fans. I cannot stand bats.

Erik, who is making a movie about bats, introduced me to Carol Chambers. Carol Chambers, professor of forestry at Northern Arizona University, loves bats. She tucks her hair behind her ear because she knows, as everyone knows, that's where bats like to get tangled up. I, who do not work with bats, forget my hair and twirl and twirl it between my fingers. Chambers probably thinks I'm one big bat lure. She wouldn't mind if one got stuck in my hair or her hair either, for that matter. She thinks bats are great.

She tells me, "I always wanted to work with bats. I like being out at night and I think they are really interesting creatures and we don't know a lot about them because they are harder to study. They are very fast. They are in the dark and humans aren't really adapted to being fast in the dark in general. And the truth is, bats do not get tangled up in your hair."

Bats are surprising. Bats don't do what you expect. Bats are the antithesis of human. Humans are not fast in the dark. Humans are slow and stumbling and prone to army-crawling their way out of tough spots slowly.

Although slow, humans are naturally optimistic. We think we can crawl our way out of all tight spots. This global warming thing? We'll figure it out, we tell ourselves. Technology has always saved us before. In London, during the industrial revolution, whole houses were coated in soot from coal fires burning in chimney after chimney. The advent of natural gas and of filters for coal-processing plants saved the London skyline from permanent darkness. Now that the skies are clear but the air is hot as a greenhouse, we look at greenhouse technology. We will find a way to air-condition this whole planet. Open the window, we say! Let the hot air out! A giant fan is all we need. Whitewash the windows. This greenhouse is going to be fine.

We like to look at the bright side of life.

The dark side. We'll leave that to the bats.

The most logical way to get a bat out of your house is to open the screen door and talk him out. "Go on, bat. Go." Bats hear in two ways: the same way humans do, and they echolocate. You repeat yourself in highly resonant tones—

"Go away bat go away bat go away bat go," you sing. The mosquitoes fly in. The bat flies around. The bat seems to fly outside. You close the screen door. You think he's gone. Why would a bat stick around? What use are you to him? You and your new mosquito friends ask each other. If he can hear you twice as well, why won't he listen?

•

Carol Chambers also likes bats because they are so useful. "Bats do a lot of things for the planet. They help control insects because some bats feed on insects. Other bats feed on nectar or pollen or fruits of plants so they can help pollinate or spread plants." Bats help keep mosquitoes in check. She is currently studying to what degree bats keep mosquitoes at bay. When you're camping and the sun goes down, the mosquitoes come out. The bats follow. More people are bitten by mosquitoes than bats. One would hope.

•

Humans have a biological belief in regeneration. We cut our toenails, and they grow back. Every four to six weeks, according to our hair stylist, we should make another appointment to have our hair trimmed. We sit and stare in the mirror and make conversation about wind and Flagstaff. You tell the hairdresser that you heard that within our lifetime, the ponderosa pines will have died out from drought, bark beetles, and fire. She shrugs her shoulders. She's from Phoenix. It's already all brown there. Dead as hair even though every year, the monsoon comes back.

My students in Michigan told me their parents kept tennis rackets around for bat outbreaks or infiltrations or bats that slip by the system we call indoor/outdoor barrier. A bat is a fragile thing. Softer than a tennis ball, it relents almost too easily. One tennis racket swing to the head and the bat falls dead. I didn't necessarily want the bats to die. I just wanted them to go and not come back. I had Critter Gitter come to the house. They got no critters but they did place loose nets on any hole greater than a quarter that led into the house. The bats then could leave but they couldn't get back in. You not supposed to kill bats. They're a protected species. But you can encourage them to leave your house and never return. The bats slide through the net but can't return through it. Gravity of lacy things.

Is it a human's great gift or her great curse that a parent's first thought-reaction to any sort of news or disaster asks, what about my children? Not all children, just *my* child. Before I had kids, I had all kinds of causes. Save the whales. Save the cougars. Lawn watering. Pulp factories. Stray cats. Now that I have kids, I have one volunteer project: to make sure my kids survive the day. Carrots. Seat belts. Helmets. Sunscreen. I am still an activist. The sun shivers at my ability to deploy an amount of sunscreen worthy of an eclipse.

In the night, I am awakened by a noise. I run down the stairs thinking that somehow Zoë, then two years old, has crawled out of bed and fallen down or someone has broken in to kidnap her. I run the stairs. I do not take my tennis racket. Something touches my shoulder. Burglar. Rapist. Killer. I drop to the floor and scream bloody murder. There is a bat trapped in my hair. That's it. I'm moving. I'm outta here. I am leaving Michigan.

Erik runs down the stairs. He would tackle the burglar, the rapist, the serial killer. But he is seriously freaking out to have to deal with the bat.

"Go upstairs and get a blanket. I will scare it to the other room. You have to block the room with the blanket so it doesn't fly back in." We're going to try to get the bat into the back room, meaning we have to urge it out of the living room, through the dining room, the kitchen, and then blanket it out the back door. "Hold it high."

Erik's instructions are similar to instructions he gave to remove mice that the cats brought in to the house in the Avenues. Erik sweeps the mouse into a corner. I am supposed to usher the mouse into an empty tissue box and take the mouse to the field outside. But I drop the box on the mouse. It runs away. Box the cat makes his low, mouse-killing noise. Erik sweeps the mouse to the front porch. I manage to open the front door. I hope Box doesn't bring it back before morning.

With the bat, I'm not tall enough to block the passageways even with my arms held high, holding the blanket over my head. The bat flies over me, back into kitchen.

"You take the broom." This is what happens when I fail my easy job. I get the worst job. I sweep the air for the bat like I'm exorcising the devil. I'm whirling dervishes, wailing at walls, purifying the room with my broom as censer. The bat must have sensed my missionary zeal, or at least my commitment, to getting him out of the room. He flew out the open door thanks to Erik's ability to accomplish two jobs, holding the blanket and opening the door at once.

After the bat leaves, it takes me twenty minutes to remember that the reason I got up was to check on Zoë. I forgot all about Zoë. There could be bats flying all over her room but I do not want to encounter any more bats. I put my ear to her door. I don't hear anything. I go back to bed. Maybe parents don't *only* think of their children. Put your oxygen mask on yourself first, then attend to your child.

I'm sitting in the corner of the bookstore where they sell coffee. I bring my laptop, which screams "dorky writer." Everyone is looking at me, waiting for me to spill coffee or wiggle my writerly eyes at them or straighten my writerly turtleneck. I put them at ease by opening Facebook. It's embarrassing, writing in public. I wish I could sit and chat and talk with someone but even though I practice my overfamiliarity with the barista, "Which is the tea that tastes like popcorn?" she shakes her head at me and offers me something gun-metal. I sit and stare at Facebook but I am listening. I flip between screens, Word to Facebook. No one is really looking at me anyway.

The coffee shop must be a regular place for the forest rangers to meet. On their agenda, the overused trails at Wupatki and Walnut Canyon. The loud ranger complains that the rest of his office voted against him. He keeps apologizing to the two quiet rangers. "I'm sorry, but you have to know this." The concern seems to be who will support a Master Gardeners class for loud ranger. The quiet rangers I cannot hear but I'm pretty sure they are going to vote on the up or down vote.

Maybe I am wrong about the small. That if you can make small changes, you can make big impacts. Maybe rangers only see the forest for the trees. Or the flowers that he wants to plant in front of the entrance to Walnut Canyon. He's drumming up support for petunias. Everything is political. Even the fact I can't hear a word the two rangers say.

A guy is sitting next to me with cornrows. "Being on this trip with you has opened my eyes," he says into his cell phone. "You know Keesha is black. It's harder on her." I think that he is leaving his black girlfriend for the woman on the other end of the phone. "We can just hang over at your house. I can bring over some flavored vodka." He definitely wants a new girlfriend. I wonder, how is one girlfriend different from another? Sure, maybe she listens to better music, tells better jokes, wears tighter Levis. But the problem with changing partners? You realize that you are still you. No matter how many petunias you put in front of the ranger station at Walnut Canyon, native juniper will dominate the vista. Learn to love juniper. Juniper is you.

There are three trees in blossom. What are those aggressively pink trees cracking against all this green and gray? Japanese maple? I will have to come back in the summer to decipher the leaves. I'd ask Loud Ranger/Would-be Master Gardener but he seems busy. Four ponderosa. One too many honey-locust in the parking lot.

The ponderosas might be a thing of the past. As the forests burn, they might not come back. This year, there was no snow. Maybe 12 inches. The year I moved here? 115 inches in my driveway over one two-week storm. I worry about the water I'm going to drink. But it just occurred to me that this is a snow-driven forest. Ten feet of snow to water the ponderosas slowly over the year. It sprinkled today. Not even the blossoms of the trees that are indigenous to neither Flagstaff nor to parking lots got wet.

The ponderosas may be a thing of the past. What will replace them? A short juniper forest. Junipers aren't as magnificent as ponderosas but they do make berries for gin. We can drink while the water evaporates. We can, like Nero, fiddle while Rome burns. At least we'll be singing.

There are bad things in the forest. Most of them are not bats. Most of them are human-borne. In an *Arizona Daily Sun* article about the 2002–2003 pinyon-juniper die off, Cyndy Cole spoke with Neil Cobb, director of NAU's Merriam-Powell Center for Environmental Research. "About 16% of the Southwest's forests have had 'massive' mortality in recent years—25 to 75% of the trees in a stand are dead," he said. "As it gets warmer and the likelihood of extreme events increases, yes, we definitely predict that these massive outbreaks and die-offs will continue."

How do you stop a forest fire? With water. Where do you find water in a drought? How do you stop inertia? Where is the metaphorical broom and blanket?

•

The evidence of global warming is overwhelming. The glaciers melt. The Antarctic ice sheet crumbles into the sea. The average temperature is between two degrees and seven degrees higher where you live. The coffee fungus thrives.

The coffee plants weaken. Forests burn. Seas rise. So many active verbs. So overwhelming that it whelms the brain. Overwhelmed, you look around. You make statements contrary to predictions. It's actually cooler this year. You give up verbs. Turn to nouns. The rain. It soaks the ground. The snow pack for the 2012–2013 winter season was deeper than it was in 1913. The human's capacity to argue anecdotally is the best way it can inoculate itself against its biggest fears.

My favorite is this idea: Global warming will be better, not worse. Maybe it won't be drier. It will be wetter. Arizona, soaked, will become tropical. Rivers will flow. Mosses will grow. It will be Oregon everywhere all over again. I will leave this Michigan warmer, this Arizona wetter, this Utah more lilac-ridden for my children.

Oh, our big, bold, hopeful brains.

The bat is back. We thought he was gone but twelve minutes later, the bat is spinning in circles. He is flapping like a bird, flying like a bird, and even though you know he's not a bird, he's a metaphor for a bird. But birds as metaphors usually signal life and light and hope. Bats signal vampires, bloody teeth, an open, screaming, biting mouth.

You open the door and find a broom. Maybe you can guide him out with more encouragement than song. For a while, you think, "He's gone." And then you look up at the columns protruding from a shelf near the ceiling. What are those columns hiding? One bat? For all you know, a cloud of bats is just waiting up there to rain sheer terror down upon you.

This is a truth that is not a metaphor: neither a bat nor a bird in the house is a good sign.

I try to peek around the columns from behind the kitchen door. I can't see anything. But now with so many mosquitoes in the house, why would he leave? Why would any bats leave the comfort of my mosquito-ridden home?

•

Carol Chambers does not think of vampires in her research. The idea of pointy fangs and wind screeching through night wings doesn't bother her in the least. "Bats are very diverse. You can find a species of bat that does about any service for us on the planet that you can imagine. With over 1,100 species in the world they are the second most diverse order that we have for mammals and they are found on almost every continent." You can see on her face the way she loves the numbers. She doesn't love that bat populations are being decimated in the eastern half of the United States. White-nose syndrome is a kind of fungus that is killing off huge numbers of bats. The fungus appears to make them lose their bearings. The bats forget what is night and what is day. She has heard of whole bat colonies dying in the east. Is the white-nose fungus coming this way? Yes, probably. Chambers and her research colleagues catch bats by the lake. They use Q-tips to swab bats' noses to check for fungus. They use Lady Remington Personal Razors to shave the fur from the skin into which they insert needles and transmitters and other signals to let the indicator bats indicate what they need to let us know. The bats lie there complacently as the scientist buzzes the clippers over him. He doesn't squirm. Fear or pleasure?

Not everything that goes comes back. A lizard's tail, yes. An amputated leg, no. A patch of crab grass, yes. A potted geranium, no. The skin on the roof of your mouth after you eat a too-hot bite of pizza, yes. The skin on the top of your finger you sliced off with your mandolin, no. Winter. Sometimes. Spring. Yes. Summer. Usually. Tulips. Often. Water evaporating off a pool in Phoenix comes back as rain upon Lake Superior. If Phoenix builds a pipeline from Superior to Arizona, Phoenix will just claim they're taking their water back, so yes and no. The boyfriend who borrowed

$4,000 and sang Donovan's *yellow is the color of my true love's hair*? No. The boyfriend who borrowed $4,000 and sang "An American Tune"? Yes. The father who died when you were twenty-six? Not so much unless you think on the grand scale that the inhabitant of which spent hours in the garage manipulating the sprinkler system so not even one patch of lawn turned brown comes back as grass when you scatter his ashes across the Salt Lake Valley. Well, then. Yes. Everything.

Unlike mine, Carol Chambers' grandpa was not bitten by a rabid bat. My grandfather, camping with his Silverstream, grilling burgers by the fire, minding his own business, not even keeping mosquitoes about him, sprayed a bucket of deet over his skin. Over the meat, he sweat his own cloud of poison.

Out of the green of the trees, something brown raced toward him. It seemed to like him particularly. Or want him. Or want to get rid of him. It was hard to tell in the spin and gyre. My grandpa raised his arm to fend off the thing that flew right at him out of the pine trees out of the darkness. He flailed and he flung but the bat still bit him right on the proverbial neck.

He had flailed enough that he knocked the bat dead. My grandmother got him in the truck, towing him and the Silverstream back to the city.

Both my grandmother and my grandfather, having grown up near rivers and lakes and forests, knew enough about rabies to bring the bat to the hospital with them.

I could never be sure if the house in Michigan had been fully rid of bats. Close one eye and look behind the columns holding up the ceiling in the living room. Duck before walking by the lamp in the living room. What was that flitter in the corner of your eye? Erik and I were getting ready for bed. Zoë was already asleep in her crib. I went to shut the door so she wouldn't wake up to the noise of us brushing our teeth. Right next to her door, in the corner of the linen closet, was a balled up furry thing. The bats were moving fully into the house. I poked Erik and pointed. He pointed back. This time, we'd have to catch it to get it out of the house. From the rack in the bathroom, we each armed ourselves with a towel. Erik stepped forward first. I pretended to follow behind him but I knew if he missed, it was up to me to catch it. He stepped closer. I leaned in.

"Get me a stick."

"What kind of stick? There are no sticks up here. Do you want me to go outside and get a stick?" I handed him the toilet bowl scrubber.

"Will this work?"

He held the stick out toward the ball of fur. We held our breath. He poked it.

The fur ball didn't move. I got braver. We both stepped forward. Erik pulled a very large lint ball into his hands. It bit no one's neck.

Carol Chambers doesn't mind handling bats. When Chambers holds the bat, she strokes its neck to calm it down. The wings are as thin as parchment. Her main challenge: to not break the wing. The bat, fluttering in her hand, makes the challenge hard. Sometimes, they bite at her. I wonder if humans, like dogs, can get preventative rabies shots. It seems, after I see a bat bite her in the thin web between her thumb and forefinger, rude to ask if she's worried about catching the disease. "The three outbreaks of animals that we captured with rabies were skunks, striped skunks, foxes, I think there was a ring tail, there was a domestic cat but most of the animals were skunks and foxes. What was unusual is there a lot of different strains of rabies. The virus that has been detected in these animals locally is the strain that comes from bats, from a specific bat called the big brown bat." The rabies outbreak seems to be taking a break. Fewer bats, therefore, fewer skunks, foxes, and cats have rabies.

I like that my cat doesn't have rabies but that doesn't assuage my fears completely.

Rabies is something that always comes back.

What I am actually afraid of isn't what I think I'm afraid of. I'm not afraid of actual bats or actual rabies. If Carol Chambers held a bat in her hand and asked me to pet it, I would pet it. I'm afraid of the idea of bats, their shadowy selves, the idea that even when you think the bats have moved on to hang under someone else's eaves, they come back. What I'm afraid of is sitting on my deck on the edge of the neighborhood they call the country club even though this neighborhood feels more forest than country club and, from the eaves above where I sit, the bat will fly down from his sky-camouflaging heights and land on my shoulder and bite my neck.

I am afraid of myth. I am afraid of unpredictability. I am afraid of the future. I am alone on this deck. I used to look out at trees. Now I can see clear to the lake where the bats dip and swirl between meals of mosquitoes. My deck is made out of dead wood. My view is now mostly dead wood. The fires are coming. It's just me and the bats now.

Perhaps I am afraid of intimacy.

It was a good move, the one from Michigan to Arizona, in many ways except this one: Next to Texas, Arizona hosts the most number of bats. "With over 1,100 species in the world they are the second most diverse order that we have for mammals and they are found on almost every continent. Here around Flagstaff we have bats that are mostly insectivorous—they eat bugs. But if you go into the tropics or other parts of the world you'll find bats that feed on other kinds of food whether its insects, nectar, fruits, and so on. These animals can help our lives by revegetating areas, by spreading seeds, by pollinating plants, or simply eating the bugs that are going to chew on us, like mosquitoes."

It is the number of bats and the number of species of bats that is promising. If one species falls victim to white-nose fungus, another species may resist it. If some of the populations suffer from rabies or fungus or tennis rackets, the sheer number of bats may allow their numbers to be sustained. Every bat has a potential to eat a million mosquitoes. To pollinate a million trees. The bats bring plenty when scarcity abounds.

The first thing I notice about the new house in Arizona is the guano around the perimeter of the house. On the upstairs deck, I look up. I see a hole bigger than a quarter. No netting to convince the bat to leave and not come back. We live in the "country club." You think we could deter the bats by the sheer number of tennis rackets. One rare thing about our neighborhood is the number of tiny, man-made lakes. Mainly, they serve as water traps for golfers, as water features for the houses surrounding the course, and as a water source to water the lawn. We'll get our green somehow in Arizona, even if it means turning whole tracts of brown land into golf courses. The water also serves as a haven for birds. And for bugs. And, therefore, for bats. Chambers says, "What I think we are seeing is the large number of maternity colonies of big brown bats that we are detecting over in that country club area mainly because of the water sources that are there. Because if you think about a bat that is pregnant and gives birth the bat is a mammal so they are nursing their young with milk and they need a lot of water. We're in a dry environment so that kind of water really provides a great resource for a mother bat." But I'm a mother too. What about my kids? They like to play outside when the sky turns pink and the shadows of their scooters loom large. They have enough to watch out for—cars speeding down the road, neighbor kids not inviting them to play. Do they have to watch out for rabies too?

If you take a ponderosa forest that once was green and lush, at least by Arizona standards, and you dry it out, burn it down, or eat it up, the brown will haunt you. It will hover in the shadows of what is now short stacks of fallen logs. Brown will tower over you, dripping regret onto you as your ponderosa once dripped sap. You will hear in the night a wild whirl. You used to be afraid of wind. Now you're afraid of a lack of it. Only the brown bat holds a green cure.

When my grandfather brought the dead bat to the hospital, the lab tested its flattened body for rabies. Rabies confirmed. I remember that for four years, once a month, my grandfather went to the doctor to have the two-inch, four-gauge needles injected into his stomach to prevent the rabies virus from swirling and fermenting and threatening to boil over. My grandfather had few friends. The nurse he saw every month became one. He invited her to his church where he could promise her the second coming.

•

Chambers doesn't like bats just because they are warm and cozy or because she has a strong ability to discern reality from fantasy. She likes them not only for their usefulness but for their godliness. If bats can revegetate whole areas destroyed by volcanoes, by earthquakes, by floods, maybe they can revegetate whole forests. Maybe bats—with their fur, their ears, their wings, their flight—are the anti-man. Maybe that's what scares us the most. It will take the brown bat to make the planet green again.

I imagine a big brown bat flying over the one-time ponderosa forest now covered scantily with juniper. The bat lands on a nearly fossilized ponderosa pinecone that still has a bit of pollen on it. Days later, the bat, rabid or not, lands on another pinecone. Together, this flying mammal brought male gametophyte to female pinecone ovule for pollination.

Matchmaker bat. The ground, with the help of enough bats, will turn green again. Marry dirt and water together.

•

Humans—browning, deadening force that they can be, aren't worse than other forces of nature. Think of them as big tornadoes or asteroids or volcanoes. Not much better than earthquake or fire at forethought, humans do have appetite and awareness of immediate danger going for them. We shouldn't hate them any more than we hate bats. Both can live in trees or houses. Both have hair that can be removed by the Lady Remington. Both can spread disease. Both can revegetate. Look at my greenhouse! Look at my forest! Both keep bugs at bay, some by eating them, some with deet. Both are alert to things coming at them in the dark.

The main difference? Humans are able to change their minds about what they like and what they don't. Bats don't like humans to catch them in nets. They don't like tennis rackets. They don't like the way humans heat up the earth or fire down all the forests. They may continue to experience the Lady Remington, but they won't change their minds about how they feel about it. Maybe the human's ability to change their minds means they can change their behavior, negotiate a different future, learn to like the night.

I take it as a job to change my mind. When I sit out on my porch at night, I look between the ponderosa pines. I force myself to stay outside and watch the bats. I still bend and duck when I see them diving at my neck, but I am learning to like them. I have to. I have to learn to like brown, if I want any green in the future.

Maybe Erik's hand on my lap, as I try to explain to Emily that sometimes a book is all the preparation you get, is a bat in our burned-out forest. And the bat is swooping in. He's dusting pollen from some still live forest on top of the burn. He's tucking some pine seed in the bend in his claw, dropping it in the burn. He's dust-bombing burnt pinecones with fertilizing guano onto those seeds that only sprout after fire.

Regeneration, does everything come back? I should look it up in a book but I want to sustain this hand in this lap for just a little longer.

Hegel's Dialectic

GIVE OR TAKE AN INCH

MY HUSBAND, ERIK, and I IM all day long. We wonder who will replace the retiring president of the university where we both work. I teach. Erik makes short films. He IMs me about his mannequin movie and I copy and paste rejection letters like this one: "Thanks for sending along the first pages of your novel. We've read them with interest and were impressed by the gripping drama and original storytelling. Unfortunately, we do not feel that we are the right representation for your work." And he sends a smiley emoticon and types, "yeah, gripping drama and original storytelling are so 1990."

I think I would die without Erik. Which I'm not sure is a compliment. Not necessarily because I would miss him so much or I need him so much but because he makes me see things in a perspective I don't naturally have. When I'm in some hand-wringing frenzy about the ravens picking on the hawks, he says something much more likely, obvious even. "The ravens are probably keeping the hawks away from the nests. It's hatching season." Perspective doesn't help the problems of what to do with dinner and dishes and the basic fact that we disagree on how many inches it rained last July but perhaps, if I had a little more, it would.

It usually rains six inches per monsoon season in Flagstaff. After a nearly snowless winter, this summer, it rained thirteen. I kept calling it the Pacific Northwest of Arizona. It made me think about Portland but the rain falls differently. In Portland, it rains all day from October to May with a brief dry spell in February. It may rain a little or a lot but the rain suffuses everything. It's a pervasive rain. In Portland, it practically rains indoors. In Flagstaff, during the monsoon, it rained not like a temperate rainforest but like a tropical one. Whole oceans of rain gathered in the southwest, spun around, turned over the peaks, the peaks popped the clouds like water balloons and then the clouds fall down onto ground that, unlike the northwest, distinguishes solidly between ground and water. There's only so much water the dirt will absorb. The ponderosas are used to a fifteen-minute-per-day dousing. When it rains oceans, even they resist by pummeling you with pinecones, catching you with sap. Sandbags come out. Sidewalks buckle. Streets turn into rivers. Water is so rare here—especially here—we don't even have any rivers—that the ground itself seems to shrug its shoulders and ask, what the hell is this?

In June, the monsoon hadn't started. The clouds circled and darkened and then broke apart. I would stand on the porch and lean toward them. I would almost beg them aloud to please let go. Please rain. It was all I wanted all of June. It is so much easier to love the rain when the ground isn't used to water. Supposedly, in Flagstaff, there's an aquifer 300 feet under organic rock that soaks up the usual snowmelt and rain. I'm going to be like that aquifer. I bought two rain barrels. I'm going to store up this rain. I'm going to Portland up this place and make it remember water. It's not a bad guy, the rain, unless your house is in the flood zone, I tell the ponderosas, I tell the dirt. It's good. Think of what we can grow.

Mushrooms and lettuce and woollybears and mosquitoes. It is a whole new world. We don't have to put up tomatoes this year. We can grow them all year long every day—this weird mixture of rain and sun will make it easy. Living will be easy. Like in Portland, where everything grows, even tomatoes, although they often never make it to red.

Sometimes we'd get two inches a day. Thunder that would make you check your ceiling for cracks. Lightning so close, you touched your hair. Pat down the static. Make sure you weren't on fire. You could sit, because it wasn't quite cold, on the porch for an hour and watch it rain and lightning and be the stranger you'd never met before, coming to town with a lot of money, a lot of horses, a lot of delicious cherries in his basket. You loved him because he was new and different and didn't make you worry about sunburn or drought.

My neighbor said it rained like this thirty years ago, when he first moved here. The monsoon season is almost over. It might not rain this hard again for thirty years. The clouds are swirling today and there is thunder in the distance but I can see ribbons of blue parting the clouds, reminding them who they are. Where they are. This is not the tropical rainforest. This is not even the temperate rainforest. This is Arizona and clouds should probably go back to where they came from.

It wasn't a regular summer. I couldn't take the kids swimming for fear of lightning. It was raining by 11 a.m. Our kids didn't like it. Max got tired of mud. Zoë got tired of clouds. But I do not think I will be missing a thing so much as I will miss this rain that is as big and loud and unbelievable as everything I've ever thought I wanted.

Erik says it was the second rainiest summer. I say it was a tie. We could look it up. We could but that would be like one of us, on a raft, in the ocean, pushing the other raft away with an oar. Facts are oars. We keep hoping our rafts will float toward each other and find a more romantic way to agree. We use the waves as guideposts even though we would both agree, probably, that nature is bad at leading the way. She's good at making up though, like any good relationship. Look at the way the seedlings stick their middle finger up at the forest fire that decimated parent trees. Look at the way the sand and silt and clouds filter that nitrate-filled stream. Marriage is the nature the human participants seek to destroy. Marriage is its own patient fixer. Give it time.

Between Me and You

THERE ARE THINGS that come between me and you, all kinds of prophylactics: condoms, Kevlar vests, words, expectations, history, our mothers, our children, sulfur dioxide.

Sulfur dioxide? Like a Kevlar vest, the sun sends bullets of rays down to Earth. The sulfur dioxide won't let them penetrate.

•

My mom never let me and my sisters play with toy guns. Our cowboys lost their pistols the minute they were peeled out of their boxes. If a friend gave us a plastic revolver for our birthday, my mom would hand it back to the parent, saying, "Guns are not toys." We couldn't even have water guns. Water balloons, yes. Water "launchers," possibly OK. But anything with a trigger? No and no. For some reason, our *Star Wars* dudes got to keep their phasers and we had plenty of light sabers around. My mom's dad hadn't been killed by a phaser or a light saber, was, I guess, the reason.

•

There is money in guns. According to *The Guardian*, there is no real way to know how many guns are sold each year in the U.S. because no one records that number. Between 1998 and 2012, 156,577,260 people applied for gun permits. That's half of the country not including those who buy guns illegally. Figuring everyone around you is armed, it seems kind of dumb not to have a gun yourself. But we've all seen every movie ever made. Two guns pointed at each other isn't necessarily a way toward a peaceful resolution. I feel very righteous walking around without a gun. It's a big trust, assuming people aren't going to shoot me for no reason. I'm white. I'm mostly safe. I should be nervous. Sometimes, I'm a jerk. I'm grateful for the gun-havers' restraint.

•

"Shoot out the sky" is a line from a poem whose author I can't find anywhere. F. Scott Fitzgerald wrote something along those lines, "When a new sky cut off the sun last spring, I didn't at first relate it to what had happened fifteen or twenty years ago," in his essay called "The Crack Up." There he writes about how skies eclipse suns and how you stay alive when it's probably the better idea to not do so. From this essay published in the 1935 issue of *Esquire* about depression and writerly success comes the well-known phrase, "Intelligence is being able to hold two opposing ideas in your head at the same time." Fitzgerald gives sage advice. Do not fall prey to niceties and etiquette. It's time, dear writer, to abandon whatever social roles have bound you and kept you from great art. Be free and shut the door in those time-stealers' face. But that idea seems inimical to his understanding of intelligence. If we're going to hold two ideas in our head at once, we're going to have to write letters of recommendations, go to dinner parties, read our students' manuscripts, and blurb other people's books as well as write our own as well as watch as the sea levels rise and the smell of smoke trumps the smell of water. Beware the two ideas collapsing into one. By the end of the essay, you stand alone.

•

Eclipses can mean two things at once: a complete blotting out of another entity and everything happening all at once, in a row. "Shoot out the sky" and "new sky cut off the sun" suggest holing up in your room with your typewriter. "Holding two ideas in your head at once" seems like a bear hug. Maybe a grizzly bear, but a hug nonetheless.

•

Whatever lyrical whimsy lies in the phrase "shoot out the sky," an actual plan exists to shoot, using military artillery, aerosoled sulfur into the sky to deflect the sun's rays, forestalling the sun's heat, thereby reducing the effects of climate change. There are some potentially negative side effects to disrupting the patterns of the sun: drought could occur more frequently in Asia. Sulfur dioxides might attack the ozone layer. The color of the sky itself could change. Solar energy systems would draw less energy from the sun. Coating an entire planet's troposphere with a substance presents technological challenges. Although sulfur is naturally occurring, distributing a layer of an aerosol, particulated small enough so that it doesn't just rain back down onto the planet, is tricky. One idea is to shoot it, using heavy artillery, from several locations throughout the planet. 10, 9, 8, 7 etc. The guns will launch, miles above the earth, the sulfur will explode. The molecules will combine and reach out toward each other. 156,577,260 particles stretching out across the planet like a lovely umbrella, protecting the humans from the aging effects of the sun. I can see us walking, safe now, along the Seine. No need for shade umbrellas. The sulfur umbrellas everyone. Renoir would be impressed.

•

Sulfur-slicked atmospheres come between Earth and sun. Guns come between people. They're like force fields. In the neighborhood where I go running, a Pathfinder's bumper sticker reads "What Criminals Want: An Unarmed Victim." If you have a gun and I have a gun, we each have our own force field. It's only in the Old West where two guns, fifteen paces, turn and shoot obviates the force field. Well, that and other places like with cops and robbers, gangster and gangster, late-night drinker and late-night drinker, Pathfinder-man and armed criminal, armed victim and rapist who knocks the gun out of her hand. The force field, like any mutually assured destruction game plan, only works if you're convinced the other person will shoot. Or won't shoot. You have to be of the same mind. The problem is, the gun itself is between you. You can never know a person's mind when the gun's force field is in effect. The gun eclipses you and the gun eclipses me. Only one idea per head when the guns erect their barriers.

•

When my grandfather stole the money from the cab driver, he did not use a gun. He used a pretend knife but even pretend weapons create a kind of force field. A weak force field, but a force field nonetheless. My grandfather didn't need a force field. He didn't even want one. He wanted a drink and the best way to get a drink is to get some money. The taxi driver was still a man. Maybe my grandfather apologized for being an asshole, taking the money. Maybe my grandfather's hand touched the hand of the taxi driver in a gesture of thanks as the driver slid him the money. If there'd been a gun, there'd have been no touch. If there'd been a gun, the man could not have heard the thoughts of my grandfather as he wrote to his mother that went something like this:

Dear Lady, I am sorry for the pain I have caused you. I vowed in prison that I would never drink again. But there's something hard about the outside world. When I went up to Wyoming to see Dee and the kids, Dee wouldn't look at me. She wouldn't touch me. How is that not its own prison? A world of untouch. Might as well have had a force field around me. I don't know why drinking makes me feel less alone. The warmth of bourbon swells inside me. I'm bigger. The bartender. His finger touched mine when he took the money I'd stolen from the taxi driver. I wish that finger had been enough. I wish the policeman at the door had taken my hand. My hand was not a gun. I lifted my hand, I reached out to them, to show them my hand was not a gun, I realized too late, the only criminal the police want is an armed criminal. Then the police and the criminals are even. Force field against force field. If they would have held my hand, they would have seen it was made out of skin and bone, not metal. If they would have reached out, even if to put handcuffs on me, they would have known that you, lady, never let me play with guns and then maybe I would have lived.

•

I was on an interview committee for a statewide student scholarship–awarding foundation. Education and poverty were constant subjects for the interview questions. "Why do you think some students don't graduate?" We asked the overachieving students about their peers. The students inspired me, even the ones who didn't make the cut. One spoke about teaching a kid with Down's syndrome. Another talked about tutoring several students who didn't pass the Common Core test. Another student noted how a particular teacher sat down with him in the third grade to see why he wasn't reading, diagnosed his dyslexia, and got him reading help. By the next year, he was reading two grade levels ahead. One-on-one. Individualized attention. One student spoke about robots and how they'll do all the menial work so humans can only do the meaningful work. We had long discussions with him about oppression and the definition of *meaningful* but we agreed: there is no technology that substitutes for the one-on-one interaction. But after the students left, we wondered about the one interviewee who didn't believe in global warming. About the one who couldn't imagine that clean water wasn't available equitably around the planet. About the optimism of each who answered their essay question, where will you be in 2044? No one said "dead" or "suffocating from sulfur dioxide poison" or "living in a refugee camp" or even a plain "not here." They believed the world would continue. That there would be clean water to drink. That there would be water and sun in equal proportion to grow food. That the world wouldn't be so hot that we'd all have to stay indoors in air-conditioning that made the outdoors even hotter. That "indoors" would be "slow-boil" and we would be the frogs.

One of my interviewing colleagues worked for the city council as a water-policy advisor. The other worked as a geology professor. I mentioned I was writing this book about sustainability and how one person's sustainability is another person's suicide. "Very interesting," he said. "I mean, I had meat on my sandwich." She said, "We each drove our separate cars here." "I run the air-conditioning all summer," they, both from Tucson, said. "And I run the heat all winter," I, from Flagstaff, said. "Our comfort trumps our knowledge." "And, we hold out hope. Technology will save us."

But we knew that the kind of technology that would save us would be more like the robots doing the menial work, a kind of morbid, uninspiring technology, than the stories about the individual teacher that saved the student from a lifetime of illiteracy. Technology is an external force. It requires its own sacrifices. We are bad at making sacrifices first. The roast beef with cheddar is so good. The sound system in my own car with the heat turned set to exactly my favorite degree is so perfect. The water in my plastic water bottle is so cold.

The technology will come.
We hope.

•

My friend posted a graphic on Facebook. School shootings since Sandy Hook.

DATE	CITY	STATE	SCHOOL NAME
1/8/2013	Fort Myers	FL	Apostolic Revival Center Christian School
1/10/2013	Taft	CA	Taft Union High School
1/15/2013	St. Louis	MO	Stevens Institute of Business & Arts
1/15/2013	Hazard	KY	Hazard Community and Technical College
1/16/2013	Chicago	IL	Chicago State University
1/22/2013	Houston	TX	Lone Star College North Harris Campus
1/31/2013	Atlanta	GA	Price Middle School
2/13/2013	San Leandro	CA	Hillside Elementary School
3/18/2013	Orlando	FL	University of Central Florida
3/21/2013	Southgate	MI	Davidson Middle School
4/19/2013	Cambridge	MA	Massachusetts Institute of Technology
4/29/2013	Cincinnati	OH	La Salle High School
6/7/2013	Santa Monica	CA	Santa Monica College
6/19/2013	West Palm Beach	FL	Alexander W. Dreyfoos School of the Arts
8/15/2013	Clarksville	TN	Northwest High School
8/23/2013	Memphis	TN	North Panola High School
8/30/2013	Winston-Salem	NC	Carver High School
9/28/2013	Gray	ME	New Gloucester High School
10/4/2013	Pine Hills	FL	Agape Christian Academy
10/15/2013	Austin	TX	Lanier High School
10/21/2013	Sparks	NV	Sparks Middle School

DATE	CITY	STATE	SCHOOL NAME
11/1/2013	Algona	IA	Algona High/Middle School
11/2/2013	Greensboro	NC	North Carolina A&T State University
11/3/2013	Stone Mountain	GA	Stephenson High School
11/21/2013	Rapid City	SD	South Dakota School of Mines & Technology
12/4/2013	Winter Garden	FL	West Orange High School
12/13/2013	Arapahoe County	CO	Arapahoe High School
1/9/2014	Jackson	TN	Liberty Technology Magnet High School
1/14/2014	Roswell	NM	Berrendo Middle School

The thread, even for my self-selected non-gun-bearing Facebook friends, still had someone arguing that guns are part of our culture, our rights, our heritage. She had grown up in Oklahoma. Everyone had guns. School vacations existed for hunting. She blamed a changed culture that contributed to wanton shootings, accidental shootings, obviously-only-black-people-in-this-situation-would-get-shot shootings. Where once was respect and at-table dinners, now was *Grand Theft Auto* and positive reinforcement. "I could go on and on about what it could possibly be, but perhaps some of it is the glamorization of the crime on TV or possibly the lack of parenting in our society. Perhaps it's the lack of consistent discipline/accountability in our country or how people don't seem to value other people and their lives as much (thanks in part to social media and the disconnect it has created—i.e., not seeing people as REAL people)."

Where are the real people? TV has made us. Everyone on TV also has a gun. Good guys, bad guys. Smart women. Responsible men. People who value other people. She's onto something. People who shoot people don't shoot real people. They shoot non-people, anger-making bags of blood and bones who deserve to die because they made them angry, and, as our Pathfinder friend notes, don't have a gun. Bags of bones and blood can't point a pistol. She goes on to argue that if we took away guns, only criminals would have guns. That people would instead go out of their way to build bombs to blow up schools. But if we are already such a violent people, if everyone is just a caricature of a human to each other, that perhaps we are all criminals already—schizophrenics who cannot tell ourselves apart from ourselves. You, bag of bones and blood, are not like me. You are just a bag. Let me show you. Kaboom. If we would choose the bomb as easily as the gun, well, then, maybe we should all arm ourselves. It's time for a shoot-out. Fifteen steps to the west and turn around. Or, even better, what if on TV only the good guys and bad guys started punching each other in the ribs, the sound of wooden sticks broken inside bags of flour, started noting that his bag of bones and her bag of bones and all these bags of bones hurt in all the same ways. There's something to be said for having to punch someone in the gut. Your hand hurts. It reminds you that their gut and your hand come from the same planet called Earth, not bags.

Guns are in between two people and no matter how shiny the metal, neither provides a mirror. It always makes a movie screen.

•

My mom has a letter from the policeman who shot her father. Does everyone regret their gun? He apologized. He thought he saw . . . Policy is . . . If he could do it over again . . . The policeman stood over my grandfather's body, his gun still hot in his hand, my grandfather's blood still warm on the floor. Everything smells like metal. Even the gun. Especially the blood. The policeman bends over. We've seen so many movies. Couldn't he be able to press "rewind"? Should he take his pulse? Should he check his breath with a mirror? Should he walk back out to his car, turn the ignition, and drive away in another metallic contraption that has the added bonus of being able to reverse time? To make a fake gun a real gun? To make a desperate man an armed man? The nice thing is, with a real gun, you can drop it to the ground.

As my grandfather's life circled into the bar's wooden floor, the bartender started to sweep up the glass that broke when my grandfather fell. There are fixable things. There are sweepable things but the blood on the floor still stains wood although that wood has been sanded and polished for fifty years and is now the floor of one of the breweries on a revitalized 25th Street.

•

The reason to pump sulfur into the atmosphere is so that something will come between us and the sun. We want that gulf. Or, we need it. If this drought continues. If the floods won't stop. If the ice is gone. Then, we'll invite that separation. The sun, which has modulated life on this planet by itself, with only a little help from the moon, will now be modulated by the humans. Like a visor, or sunscreen, we'll put a little layer between us. Maybe it will be fine. Sometimes, you have to choose between one idea and another. Maybe you can't have sun and water in equal proportion anymore.

But maybe, as when we lose vitamin D when we slather our skin with sunscreen, we'll lose something important with the direct contact with the sun. Maybe, like punching us in the gut, the way the sun beams at us reminds us that we are made out of skin, not bags.

21,000 Acres and Counting

WE ARE WATCHING Arizona's Oak Creek fire news from the relative safety of Helena, Montana. The fire started at twenty acres. Then twenty-five. It grew to 450 acres in a couple of hours. By night, the fire had grown to 4,500 acres. Oak Creek is the canyon that ties Flagstaff, the mountain ski town, to Sedona, the red rock/vortices tourist destination. The drive down Oak Creek Canyon is the only water you see rushing anywhere near Flagstaff. The West Fork hike is one you do in sandals so you can stomp back and forth across the creek as the trail winds through oak groves, juniper, and ponderosa pine. Flagstaff sits in the middle of the largest contiguous ponderosa pine forest in the United States. From the top of the hill heading in the opposite direction of Sedona, toward Payson, you can see waves of ponderosa forest stretching as long as the sea.

I wonder how many fires it will take to make the forest no longer contiguous. How many interruptions can the forest bear before the contiguity is ruptured? The forest, when it burns, does not come back so quickly.

There are two pictures on Max's wall. One is of the Columbia River before the dam. Three members from what might have been the Yakima, Umatilla, or Nez Perce tribe stand on the bank of the river. The river cascades over huge cliffs making a fat waterfall, excellent for the salmon to jump and for the water to swirl. Three beams, hewn from what must have been a 250-foot Douglas fir, jut into the river, signaling the future.

In the second picture, it is the future. Many men, fifty at least, stand on beams, posts, two-by-fours. They are making a dam out of the forest that surrounds the river. The dam will eventually provide hydroelectric power to a million people. It is not obvious that members from local tribes stand to watch.

In the very, very present, fully dammed river, there is no water falling. There are no cliffs, no rocks, no indication that the water is moving very fast, fast enough to power a city. The water is smooth. Smooth as a lake. Smooth as a forest with no trees.

In the spring and fall, we create defensible space around our house. Erik rakes 17 bags of pine needles. We keep the weeds pulled, layer gravel in the front yard. No tree limbs touch the roof of our house. We keep the hoses ready and we know which routes to take to get out of town.

Four years ago, we met our friends Rebecca and Todd to camp. We hadn't seen them in years, not since Zoë was born. She was now four, almost five. Max had been born in January. We left to find a spot to camp, near Payson, somewhere in the middle of the contiguous forest. But sometimes it's hard to find a spot in a contiguous forest. Why is one spot better than another? How will Bek and Todd find us without cell service in the middle of all these similar-looking trees? They have two sons, one two-and-a-half and one the same age as Max, just six months old. Who camps with two six-month-olds in the middle of a contiguous forest?

We don't, apparently. Every time we got out of the car to check for a spot, something was wrong with it. One was on the edge of a cliff where six-month-olds could crawl and fall to their deaths. Another seemed nice, until we noticed two guys with rifles coming toward us. Where was their car? The next place, we got out and were promptly bitten by fourteen thousand mosquitoes. Mosquitoes? In Flagstaff? Maybe we weren't in Flagstaff any more.

By the time we'd rejected this mosquito spot, it was getting late. Bek and Todd, driving in from LA, were still hours away. We bailed. Went home. Met them at our house where we had them sleep in our bed and we slept downstairs with Max and Zoë, where we almost always slept anyway.

The next day, we headed the other direction, toward Sedona. Off Forest Highway 535, we set up camp. The first night, I made trout with bacon and pine nuts. Good and easy but nothing too extreme. The next day, Rebecca, as always, organized an ambitious menu. For breakfast, spinach with ham cream. Whole whipping cream, sautéed with ham. Eggs were to be poached in ramekins with spinach but even Rebecca doesn't bring ramekins camping. She poached the eggs in the cream, topped the eggs with spinach until it wilted, served the ham-cream and eggs over fried hashed brown potatoes.

We stayed two nights. I can't remember what Rebecca made for dinner. Probably because I had been blinded by ham-cream. Campfires are disallowed in the forest in June, the time when it's most likely some spark flies from a pile of flames and finds a partner in forest revolution. We sat around a pile of rocks, drinking wine out of a box.

As we drove out of the forest, to the forest-town of Flagstaff, I turned my cell phone back on. There were fourteen messages. The recordings were intermittent. Service was bad. I'd start a message but couldn't make out who it was. And then, I pieced it together. It was Emily, our cat sitter, but I couldn't hear what she was saying. Then, in the next message, I heard something about "evacuation." I gave up trying to play through all the messages and called her back. The service was still spotty but I gathered this much: there was a fire near our house. A pre-evacuation warning had been issued. Emily had packed everything she thought we might want from our house.

How do you pack another person's life?

Emily did a great job. When we pulled into the driveway, she was still putting boxes of our stuff filled with Zoë's artwork that had been secured to the fridge. Our photo albums. Erik's guitars. Cat carriers ready to go with food and bottles of water. The quilt my mother-in-law made us. Rebecca's oil paintings. My computer and the journal beside my bed. Erik's grandfather's watch, my grandmother's coffee grinder, and my dad's matchbooks into her old Subaru.

She couldn't have known about the boxes full of mementos shoved into the attic. Tickets from concerts and letters from old boyfriends. Drafts of short stories that never got published. Zoë's turtle painting and the imprint of Max's feet from the hospital.

We helped Emily pull our boxes out of the car, piling them by the front door. We thanked her as she left but how do your properly thank someone for going through your life and finding what is meaningful?

Now, the Slide Fire is nearing Highway 535, where we had camped four years ago. Ash is falling on houses. Smoke is crawling up the canyon. The house may have defensible space but houses are still made of wood. How can a fire tell the difference between a forest and a house? Where is Emily when I need her? Where is Rebecca to distract me with hamcream? But mine is just one house. This scraping up of pine needles is a hollow gesture of self-preservation. Perhaps the self-part is what makes it particularly hollow. Did I consider how deep is Emily's defensible space? What is she drinking while she sits around the cold rocks without a campfire in the largest contiguous ponderosa forest in the world?

Revolution

A PLANET IS morally neutral. As Robert E. Laughlin, in *The American Scholar,* put it, Earth doesn't care if you drive a Prius.

> It doesn't notice when you turn down your thermostat and drive a hybrid car. These actions simply spread the pain over a few centuries, the bat of an eyelash as far as the earth is concerned, and leave the end result exactly the same: all the fossil fuel that used to be in the ground is now in the air, and none is left to burn. The earth plans to dissolve the bulk of this carbon dioxide into its oceans in about a millennium, leaving the concentration in the atmosphere slightly higher than today's. Over tens of millennia after that, or perhaps hundreds, it will then slowly transfer the excess carbon dioxide into its rocks, eventually returning levels in the sea and air to what they were before humans arrived on the scene. The process will take an eternity from the human perspective, but it will be only a brief instant of geologic time.

It's kind of worth dancing about, Earth's deep level of disinterest. Robert Laughlin argues that climate change comes and climate change goes and, speaking about eons, there's not much we can do about it. I am off the hook. Climate is not my problem, geologically speaking. Eonically speaking.

But I am living in the century. Global warming might become a problem for me and definitely will be for my kids. Laughlin writes, "Were the earth determined to freeze Canada again, for example, it's difficult to imagine doing anything except selling your real estate in Canada. If it decides to melt Greenland, it might be best to unload your property in Bangladesh." Um, what if no one wants to buy my land in Canada? How will I move? What if my kids can't get a boat to float themselves out of Bangladesh or New Delhi? What if we're stuck with the rocks we have already committed to? Is real estate our only concern?

Earth shrugs its shoulders. "Kill yourselves, or don't, like you do everything else" it points out, showing the way human encroachment annihilates species after species. I don't think Earth, big rock in space, cares about us or about the bats or the whales or the mushrooms. But perhaps Earth is more than a rock. Perhaps the "world" counts as the people and the other bugs on it. Perhaps Earth is saying something, offering an example in its hurricanes, volcanoes, and earthquakes. Perhaps these big eruptions are messages. Perhaps the world's riffs and geologies are a kind of speech and speech is a kind of caring: Earth, an advocate for evolution, believes, I think, in revolution.

The day the amount of carbon in the atmosphere reaches the 400 parts per million threshold that climate scientists say is the point of no return—that glaciers will melt, that the droughts will lengthen, that the weather will become unpredictable—I apologize to Zoë. We are driving with my mom and her boyfriend, Bart, down to Page Springs Winery, near Sedona, when I read the news on my phone. I should stop reading my phone and should instead appreciate the view. I should devote my entire attention to my daughter who is, at nine, almost as tall as me. Time is turning away from me and this phone isn't stopping it. But I do read and I do choke on the numbers, 400 ppm.

We take the long way. For each five hundred feet we drop in elevation, the scenery changes. At first, full-on ponderosa forest. Then a more sparsely drawn juniper landing—the soil between the trees in more yellow, harder looking than the reddish brown where the pines have donated their old selves to the color of the dirt. To the right, farther down, you can see the red dirt of Sedona. Iron ore revealing its rust in a closeted corner. Close your right eye and the red rocks are gone and all that remains is broken yellow sandstone to your left.

I'm looking at the back of my mom's head. She's let her hair go gray. I keep thinking she is fifty-eight but she's not. I have to keep reminding myself that she's ten years older than that. Eons.

The drive itself is geologic and, therefore, perspective making. When I am dead and gone, the red rocks will still be red. But I feel bad for Zoë. I don't want to leave her with this mess. And I don't mean to make the "parts per million" sound so dire but I have no restraint and my chest hurts, wondering what I've done, bringing kids into this future. Instead of dwelling on my heart problems, I go ahead and break hers.

"Why are you sorry?" she asks.

"For not doing enough, anything, really to stop it. This carbon. It lingers for hundreds and thousands of years."

"But why are you sorry to me?"

I should be a better mother. I shouldn't scare her. Or worse, subject her to my sensationalist imaginings. I'm a hypocrite. I'm always telling her, when she asks me, "What are you talking about?" when I'm whispering to my husband, Erik, about how I smelled alcohol on someone's breath at work, not to ask probing questions. But here I go, purposefully freaking her out, as we rocket down the Mogollon Rim toward Sedona on this regular Saturday as all chapters of Cormac McCarthy's *The Road* march through my mind. Some scenes of *Waterworld* interrupt to stave off complete dreariness with the promise of gills and dry land.

"I'm sorry we didn't stop the oil drilling and the coal mining in time. That here we are, burning old dinosaur bones, chucking their leftovers into the sky just to drive to get a glass of wine. It's just going to be bad. The weather will change. You won't know when to plant what. In the middle of summer, it could freeze. In the middle of January, a heat wave will dry out the ponderosas. They say there will be no more coniferous forests in the Southwest."

"What's coniferous?"

"With pinecones. The wild fires will be too many to control. There won't be enough water, or enough fire people, to put them out."

"Maybe Aunt George can put them out." Erik's sister, Joy, was once a Hot Shot firefighter. She is Zoë's hero. I should let Joy figure in to the wildfire story longer but now, I'm on a roll. Bad novelist who can't quit freaking out her nine-year-old.

"Maybe she can. But still, it's already been drier here than it used to be. This year was the third warmest on record. I want you to move to Oregon. But maybe that's a bad idea too. There, it will be so crowded. Everyone will go to get out of the sun, away from the drought and they'll bring diseases like cholera. It will be so wet and warm. And then malaria will make a comeback. The oceans will rise. You and Max on an island in the middle of the Pacific Northwest."

In my mind, I promise myself I will move them somewhere safe. Perhaps Reed's ski cabin on Mt. Hood. The oceans will rise but the sauna will work again. The ground, warm instead of covered in snow, will grow carrots for them. They will eat not enough but well. So many carrots.

So much vitamin A. They will be able to see. See what we did. See what we should have done. See when the masses are coming for their last carrots. Perhaps they will see ways to give everyone a carrot. Perhaps they will see things no one else has seen.

By the time we pass the exit for Sedona and are solidly in chaparral territory, these scrubby not-quite-trees gripping into the dirt as if dry soil was better than dry air. Zoë's face is cracked open like she's seen a zombie. She is staring at me, eyes wide.

"Oh, Zoë. I'm sorry. It's still true. But I'm still sorry. I shouldn't have said anything." Two stills at the same time. A good parent would pick an apology.

Now I feel doubly bad for having a car, heating my house, wrapping my half-cut onion in plastic, for doing my part to destroy the planet and then telling her about it. Sensationalistic.

We drive quietly for a minute. And she says, "Tell me again."

"No. Now I'm sorry for saying anything." I once had an agent who dropped me for being too depressing. Perhaps I should have taken the hint.

"No, Mom. I can take it."

I look for my own mother's eyes in the review mirror. "Jeez, Nik," she says to me. I can't tell if I've scared my mom too or if she thinks I'm just being too harsh for Zoë. I feel jealous of my mom. Most of her life, she could turn the heat up without worrying about climate change. But the car we are driving now is hers and it's a Prius. I know the planet doesn't care if she drives a Prius but I do. "Thanks for driving," I say. "Bart's the one driving," she corrects me. But that was not quite what I meant. And then I repeat myself. "400 parts per million. All that exhaust you can't see coming out of the cars. All of that smoke coming out of the refinery that you can." That carbon goes up into the air, makes a layer almost like glass. The sun comes in but the heat can't get out. That's why they call it greenhouse effect.

I am also a bad mother because the day before, my mom and I took Zoë and Max to see the third *Hunger Games* movie, *Mockingjay.* It is full of kids killing kids and Peeta, a main character, is being tortured. Katniss returns to District 12 after her rebellious threat to kill herself if President Snow doesn't let both her and Peeta win the hunger games. There she sees the skeletal remains of her friends, everyone from her hometown, sticking grayly out of the dust. The scene that scared Zoë most though was when Peeta tried to strangle Katniss. Individual people doing individual things. This is why no one cares about the end of the world. Everybody dies in a blanket of everyone's death. But no one wants Katniss, the individual, the hero, the main character, to die. No one wants Peeta to be the killer.

My friend Lynn and I were talking about how ordinary the violence seemed when thinking of American gun deaths or the recent massacre by Boko Haram in Nigeria and how just slightly exaggerated the divide between the Capital and District 13 was from our everyday, left/right politics.

I misunderstood, thinking that she could feel a swell of revolution coming. "That scene where they knock down the dam. Hayduke Lives! The revolution is at hand," I said.

She corrected me, "I meant, more like neither side is really more right than the other."

Then, I got what she was saying. The swell of revolution might just be the swell of an engorged media. "It's true. It's all marketing. I just yelled at the poor lady on the phone trying to raise money for the Democrats. I said, you just lost an election. You asked every three hours up until the election for money. Every six, I gave you some. And what did you do with it? You wasted it. What is your message? You cannot get your marketing people to get it together. Find a position. Stick with it." In *The Hunger Games,* and the democracy games, it is the cynical leading the cynical. The bad guys are in the eye of the beholder. The climate scientists say that 400 parts per million means the climate is irrevocably changed. Fox News says that climate change is a myth. The Nazis said Jews were to blame for the suffering of the German people. The Nazis had a good propaganda arm. Better even than Fox News.

But during the movie, when Jennifer Lawrence sings "The Hanging Tree" song, I don't feel the propaganda. The bad guys are truly the bad guys. Bad as Nazis. I can tell because Philip Seymour Hoffman is on the side of the good. I can tell because they march against the dam. I can tell because the song is paradoxical—we are winning by dying. They take down a prominent symbol of human power of nature. They lose some humans as they plant the bombs against the concrete. Concrete crumples faster when inspired by C-4.

There are lots of bombs. There are lots of guns. People keep reminding me how little value life has on this planet when they shoot the other for playing loud music. When Ted Nugent holds up the dead body of a two-hundred-pound mountain lion. The cougar's head hangs over Nugent's arm like a giant globe. Someone has given up all hope in man.

But in the night, when Max and Zoë wonder how does that hanging tree song go, I'll sing it even if someone gets hanged in the end. It's a song in a made-up world about a real person. Revolutions happen song by individual song.

If the planet does not care if I drive a Prius and if a good majority of the people do not care what happens to the planet, then perhaps it is better to go to the movies and sing songs and write bad novels about zombies in space. The planet isn't watching us. Once upon a time, when the carbon parts per million were four hundred plus, the planet bore the brunt of the dinosaurs. Heavy and toothy. The oceans, acidic, made acid-loving fish. The plants, carbon guzzlers, sucked big bolts of carbon into their carbon-sucking cells. There were no humans then. There will be no humans later.

Maybe the planet will look like the one in the movie *Wall-E,* all covered in garbage and wrapped in brown smog. Maybe it will look like the one from *Tank Girl*—all desert, only Kangaroo-hybrids live on the surface. Lori Petty defends what's left of the human race from drought and Malcolm McDowell. Maybe there will only be dinosaurs. Maybe my kids will like that. They like dinosaurs.

On the drive back to Flagstaff, up 3,500 feet, through Oak Creek, the landscape is less paleontological. The oak trees give way to ponderosa pines. Green to green is an easier transition than the obvious layers revealed by Highway 17. Driving up the switchbacks of Highway 89A, you can see the wide slit of the canyon cut into the earth. The slit looks menacing, cut by springs that erupt from Flagstaff's snowmelt. The springs gather together to make a river to cut through the lime and sandstone. From the highest switchback, you can see the tops of ponderosas, the dangers of rockslides, and the backs of ravens. Unlike looking over a bridge, you would not think, even in your most distressed state, of jumping. The fall does not seem cleansing, cathartic, clean, or easy. There are a lot of rocks. Some prickly pears at the bottom. Something called the pipeline trail, which is really just a ravine full of black-hearted boulders. Unlike a bridge, which might make you think, this life has been good enough, I can jump into that soft water, the cliffs in Sedona scare you with danger: these switchbacks, no shoulder, hard, prickly landing, make you want to cling to the road. Perhaps the difference is that jumping off a bridge is a sign of the contemporary—the random machine of the twentieth century—while these geologic-gravities reveal the significance of the unlikely evolutionary, time-bound existence of *you.*

The planet will not miss us although it may miss us missing it. It's not so much that because we notice it, the wilderness becomes significant, instead, because we notice *significance* itself. Things are changing. Isn't that the definition of semiotics—to note the difference between sign and signified? As the world changes, significance itself becomes more obvious. Things are getting wilder. Between wild and wilder, someone has to register the difference. Humans imagining the wild is reciprocated by nature. Wild imagined us.

I look out the window at a ponderosa in my ponderosa-filled neighborhood and swear I see a sloth hanging, in a swath of pine needles, in the crotch of a tree. I point it out to Zoë. She can't see it. "Sloths are very slow, you know. They look just like bark," I tell her. This sloth barely moves, just as most sloths barely move.

"I wonder why is there a sloth in Flagstaff, Arizona, when there are no known sloths in the area," I pretend to wonder aloud. Sloths are indigenous to Central and South America, not North America. Is everyone like the Jeffersons and just moving on up, thanks to climate change?

How the sloth came to like pine needles over fat, juicy, Costa Rican trees is a surprise to me, but maybe that's the surprise of nature. Adapters, some of those slower species.

"It's just a tree, Mom."

"How about over there? That could be a sloth, over there, in the armpit of Fredricka's tree. Maybe, maybe not. I'm just saying. Keep your eyes out."

If I squint hard enough, I can see anything I want to in trees. Sloths have existed for over sixty million years. Until ten thousand years ago, they lived in North America. My hallucination elides millennia. Sloths, even when they're not really sitting in the crotch of a ponderosa, signify all the possible surprise nature can offer. It teaches how imagination compacts the eon.

The 1966 *Oxford University Press Dictionary of Etymology* won't stay open long enough for me to type what I need to type. The spine is cracked but not in the right place. I take another book and a notebook, force the dictionary open, and slam the other books on top to keep it that way. I learned this technique from the rocks and the grass. Another metaphor for revolt? Book crashing into another book? The earth won't miss our books but it might miss our pressing. With one elbow pressuring the other books open, I can type this etymology out:

> Revolution: moving of a celestial body in an orbit, time in which this is down XIV (Grwer, Ch.); periodical recurrence XVI; complete change of affairs or reversal of conditions XV; overthrow of established government XVI. (O)F. *revolution corr. to Sp. revolucion,* It. *rivoluzione* or late L. *revolūtiō(n-).* Hence revolutionary. XVIII (1774; but in gen use only after F. *révolutionnaire* 1794).

There is much translation in the world, which is another kind of revolve: A. remove from one place to another B. Turn from one language to another.

If you need a metaphor for revolution, perhaps grass is the best bet. Grass will take down anything. That's why neighborhoods around the countryside rely on Roundup. One spray at that fledgling shaft, destined to upend your entire driveway unless you aim the trigger at it and shoot. I have a neighbor who wears a cowboy hat and pretends to draw on, with his real gun (we live in Arizona), the grass invading his concrete. Americans can find their enemies anywhere and although I am prone to finding my enemy in Monsanto, the company that makes the chemical that makes the Roundup that kills the plants, and, by extension, the bees, others find the grass itself to be his enemy. Driveways cost money. Still, regardless of our economics defense, eventually, the grass will win. Even if we Monsanto every plant, annihilate it like Katniss's District 12, the algae will crawl back from under the surface of the ocean to land upon one of our well-concreted dams. It will mildew itself up the cement surface. It will find a chip in the armor of your Army Corps project. It will find a hole in our façade. The algae will move in. It will spread itself or it will catch a seed from a Monsanto escapee. The algae will hook a tiny grass seed. It will provide enough friction to stick. It will make enough nitrogen for the grass seed to eat. The grass will grow up. Then it will take root. And then it will open the hole just a bit just a bit. The hole no one has tended because the plants are long gone. But here it comes again. Life as green and cracked as ever. It will crack that concrete. It will inch, then foot, then yard its way up and down that dam. Once there was a lake. Now it's a river. Hayduke lives. It's a kind of suicide, letting the grass grow up the dam. It's a kind of survival, believing that grass is in charge. The grass may just be the eons, crushing humans under their rocks like so many dinosaurs. Or the grass might be a solar-powered car or an antidote to carbon dioxide (we used to call it "tree").

Speeding up the Mogollon rim in the Prius, we emerge from Oak Creek canyon. We still have ten or so miles through flat ponderosa forest to go before we reach Flagstaff proper. Tree after tree. No coyotes. No squirrels. This is not old growth forest. A monoculture. No difference, that I can see.

Tree, tree, tree blurring through the windows except wait.

What is that? I have never seen that before. I've made this trip a hundred times and I don't remember any rocks there. I don't remember that algae covered limestone. Where once was flatness, nothing, red-brown dirt, surrounded by red-brown needles, candled with ponderosa tree trunks now stands a massive rock wall, cracked in half, like a tiny earthquake in the middle of this sea of trees. Nature cracks itself. It revolts. It is not necessary and perfect because it sits there, but because it moves.

Of course, so are kids, which is why, in spite of the horror we bestow upon them, they will inherit revolution too. And virus is revolution and drought is revolution and Oregon is revolution and the way Zoë practices her pirouettes in the kitchen is revolution. It's not quite sugarcoating it—turning is neither bad nor good, ask Fox News. Ask Monsanto. Ask any of us who like our thermostat set at 71 degrees. Our way of life is constant, we who hoover our garden rocks. We who use gas-powered leaf blowers. The same we who looks at the sun and think, my god that thing is bright. Almost as bright as my incandescent light bulb. A turning is what will happen, which is not to say the wall of constant burning, constant heating, constant driving, constant droning does not stand, but it is also to say there is a grass seed floating in the air. If the wall is made of carbon, planting a ponderosa might not tear the whole wall down. But it will make a difference.

Love in the Time of Global Warming

I DON'T THINK Erik and I had the "be as one" phrase in our marriage vows but there are days when it's true. It is usually in a car, driving. Johnny Cash sings, "If I were a carpenter and you were a lady would you marry me anyway? Would you have my baby?" June Carter sings "yes" and Erik sings along with her and I sing with Johnny. We are on our way to Home Depot. Erik is installing baseboards in the hallway. I told him the molding was fine but he's right, the old ones had been kicked and scuffed beyond repair. It will take him three weeks to paint the trim using his toxic, scuff-preventing paint. He does it freehand. He is perfect and precise. It's why he paints our daughter Zoë's fingernails instead of me.

But there are days not like that. Days at Sam's Club because we don't have a Costco in Flagstaff, Arizona, and the kids need thirty-six juice boxes to get them through two weeks of school and two mom-brings-the-snack events.

"I think we should cancel the membership. It's the same as Walmart."

"But we're sticking it to them by buying gas. The gas is actually a loss for them."

"But I hate Walmart so badly."

"I like the snacks," Zoë chimes in as she asks if she can have another sample of bacon.

Tillamook Cheese and $13 bottles of Joel Gott make it worth it to me. I won't buy the steaks there even though their meat is supposedly the freshest in town. If I'm going to eat meat, I'm only going to buy the kind from Flying M Ranch, grass-fed, local, which is $6.99/lb for hamburger. Three times what it is at Sam's. And I mean it. I won't buy it. Until I see the steaks and the hamburger on sale and I really want to make tacos. I put the Sam's Club meat in my cart. I hate being a hypocrite, which just makes me more of a hypocrite, which makes me grumpy and oversensitive and a FUN shopping partner!

But I'm still complaining as I continue to pile stuff into the cart. Erik puts his own addiction into the cart: a city of paper towels.

"No way. Not those. We do not need that many paper towels. Where will we put them?"

"I need them to finish painting the hallway." *Finish painting* words are usually golden words to convince me to go along with anything he says but not this time.

"They're not even recycled." Although I protest, we both keep walking toward the checkout.

"I have my own card." He puts them on the conveyer belt.

At first I let them sit there. Then, I shake my head. I'm snarking under my breath and then I get loud and say, "No way. We cannot get them."

I take them off the conveyer belt. Everyone is looking at us. I know I am embarrassing Erik, but this is beyond unreasonable.

"Everyone is looking," he whisper-yells as he puts the paper towels back on the belt.

"I don't care if they're looking. They're not recycled," I leave them alone on the conveyor belt but I keep yelling. "You don't even care. The planet's going to hell and you don't care if it's scorched and burned for your kids. Sorry, kids, get another planet."

"Oh, and your wine bottles are so recycled."

Oh great. Now it's not just drinking the wine that's bad. It's what the wine comes in too. There is no free drinking in this land.

"That's fine. Tell the kids to their faces that you don't care if they even have any trees left after we die." We leave. I'm still yelling. Paper towels purchased, in the cart.

We load the groceries into the car, handing paper towels and wine to each other, picking up one kid, putting him in the car, shutting the door for the other. We can shop with our eyes closed. We can argue with them closed too.

Erik gets in the driver's seat, "And you can go by yourself to Sprouts." He drives home. Climbs out of the car. Takes the kids and the paper towels, leaves me in the garage. I've ranted and raved and still we have nine hundred rolls of paper towels and fifty-dollars worth of non-grass-fed meat. Who wins by yelling about paper towels? Not me. Scorched-earth policies.

It's the worst thing he can do to me. Make me go to the store alone, on a Saturday, when we're supposed to be together.

•

When I lived in Portland, I worked at ORLO—an environmental arts organization. I was creative editor of the *Bear Essential Magazine*. I finagled having one of my poems published even though I was editor by submitting it under a pseudonym. I revealed that I had written the poem at the final publication meeting. Susan Whittier, the genre editor, was pissed but others thought that since it came up through the slush pile on its own merits, it was OK. I was an idiot but I was a desperate idiot. I so badly wanted that publication. I should have pulled it. Perhaps my whole writing career has been based on hypocrisy and subterfuge. Susan had just written a negative review of Terry Tempest William's latest book—not *Refuge*. In this book, Terry made love to the river, becoming one with the river. Susan kept making fun of the water flowing into her vagina, penetrating her. Susan did make the book sound ridiculous. In Portland, it's rare to find much complaining. There's so much to love there—all that water, those trees, those roses, Kornblatt's, Le Bistro Montage, DOTs, Wildwood, The Alibi, Alber's Mill, Powell's, all those books I wanted to be. It's harder in the desert. The lovables are farther and fewer between. Scarcity makes every living thing, even living dirt, lovable. Living dirt, the kind where the cryptobiotics knit the soil into the earth, does not turn to sandstorm. It does a loveable and good job of staying on the ground. But Terry Tempest Williams is from the desert. Water is other. Water is the opposite sex, or, at least, the attractive sex. Only someone from the bounty of Oregon wouldn't be desperate to fuck some plentitude. Susan didn't understand my desperation. She was from Oregon. I am from Utah where it's hard to find water and hard to publish poems.

•

Richard Primrack, a scientist at Boston University, and Charles C. Davis, a scientist at Harvard University, use Henry David Thoreau's journals to measure climate change. Blueberries flowered in mid-May during Thoreau's time. Now, they flower in April. The number and variety of plants in the Concord and Walden Pond area have gotten fewer since Thoreau. The purple trimmed orchid has been spotted only once in the past ten years. However, you can still find most of the birds. Our current day religion says, put out the recycling bin as you would put a sacred wafer into your mouth. We will detail our loss just as Thoreau detailed his pleasure.

Thoreau was a genius with detail, not so much with plot. Thoreau is writing scripture, not narrative. He becomes one with nature but fails, a bit, to become one with his reader. He tries to hum the bird sound, buzz the bee sound, "confuse the author's identity with gods," as Stanley Cavell writes of *Walden*'s religiosity. And as a prophet, Thoreau has been heard by the new religionists, our scientists who say, "It is getting hot. Look at the birds! I miss the orchids. I worry the birds will come and the blueberries will already be gone." But unlike Thoreau, the scientists murmur to themselves, narratively, "But a part of me likes these warmer winters."

In the wilderness, there is no comfort. It's an antinomian place from where all the apocalypses are witnessed. At home, in domestic sphere, we say to ourselves: Do not forget to put out the recycling on Tuesday. Cross yourself on Sunday. Count the berries on Monday. At home, we ritualize and withstand and fight about the little things because it's safe—just the right temperature—to do so.

There is something to be said for domestic sounds, the noise a household makes. Busying yourself with domesticity keeps you from confusing yourself with God. At home, the power is shared. No to paper towels. Yes to steak. Yes to driving to another grocery store to get the organic peaches they don't have at Sam's Club. No to glass bottles. Yes to wine in a box. In the indoors, it's safe to fight about nothing and to pretend that it is everything.

What I remember, later, after the paper towels:

Erik peeled nine artichokes. I had cooked them but hadn't trimmed the leaves. As he pulled each one away from the core, the hot, stabby leaves poked his fingers. While I chopped spinach, he rubbed out the out. Nine of hearts. A card game. A reason for butter and for mayonnaise. Our kids like artichokes as much as we do. Liable to poke you heartily and yet still delicious.

Carbon-Sucking Mushrooms Will Save Us but Whiskey Will Kill Us Anyway

IS THERE ANY kind of alcoholic beverage that is sustainable to drink? I mean, can you drink, sustainably, or, at some point, must you choose to a: stop drinking or b: embrace alcoholism? And, if you choose *b*, are you embracing a kind of suicide? If you live to be eighty and still drink bourbon in the morning like my grandmother did, are you suicidal or just committed? My dad died when he was fifty of, I believe, liver failure. He had cirrhosis. But he also had high blood pressure. Could have been a heart attack. It was dark. He was drunk. Maybe he just fell and hit his head. Either way, alcohol? Contraindicated. Implicated. Indicted. Blame the drink, not the man. The man himself was OK. Kind of self-obsessed. Told the same story about making money on an AT&T short-sell over and over again. My mom says that once, out to dinner with friends, after they paid the bill, the conversation lulled for a minute. My dad folded his napkin, stood up, and said, "I guess we've said everything we have to say to each other." He picked up a book of matches, since he collected them, from the front desk, walked to his car, and my mom and he never saw the couple again. No need to keep repeating the same stories, he thought.

He had an insistence on originality. The matchbooks he collected were unique. If he found a duplicate, instead of storing it in the glass jars, he used it to light his Benson and Hedges. Before he died, he told me, "I've won all the awards I'm going to win." When my dad was done, he was done, except with the stock market. It was the one place he allowed redundancy. "You know, I bought AT&T at $20. Sold it short," he told me in the elevator at Ninos and on the subway on our way to visit Columbia University and in the car on the way to the liquor store. He told me that story once a week even after he and my mom divorced and he lost half his 401K to her 401K, after he lost his job and he started selling his stock to live on. He reminded me of the story two weeks before he died. Sold short, indeed. Life may be brief but the stock market goes on forever. Maybe its redundancy makes it unique.

In the mycorrhizal world, capital is food. Mycorrhiza have grown alongside plants since plants began to colonize land. Ninety percent of the world's plants require fungal companions to grow. Mycelia are the vast networks of fungi that live underneath the forest floor. Mushrooms, the fruiting body that through the humus form that vast network of underlying mycelia are one-time stories, "Tell it once and then let's be done." Mushrooms can be sustainable in a lot of ways—if you cut the stalk sharply, leaving the mycelia behind, it will grow more fruit like any procreative dining companion. But if you're interested in the relationship between climate change and mushrooms, mushrooms themselves are not particularly useful. Mycorrhizal relationships—the relationship between fungus and plants is particularly helpful, at least as far as global warming goes. Most fungi release more carbon than they take in but not mycorrhiza. Mycorrhizae form symbiotic relationships with tree roots. The hyphae, the term for individual mycelia, draw nutrients from the soil and comingle with the tiny villa of the tree roots. Shaking hands, sharing germs, or, in this case, sharing food in the form of micronutrients, the mycorrhiza and the root-villa are codependent as any alcoholic and his wife I've ever met. "I'm at the store, dear. Do you need beer?" is always a rhetorical question. Everyone needs beer.

The same year my dad died of complications due to alcoholism, I walked away from a logging road down a hill of moss. That moss unrolled like an emerald carpet. Looking only at the ground for the undulated yellow of a mushroom, contrasting against that floor of green, I got lost. Not lost in all-the-trees-look-the-same-and-I-can-no-longer-hear-the-stream-in-the-distance lost but lost in the I've-never-seen-anything-like-this-is-this-the-same-planet kind of lost. Bewildered by the wildness. Branches on the Doug-firs only began at the height when most of the trees I knew had already been topped out. The trees were as wide as the stream I'd just left behind. This is Oregon. The streams would be called rivers in the rest of the West. Down the tree trunks run channels of bark into which I can sandwich my whole arm. I tried to pretend the bark warmly enveloped me but the bark scratches. Trees like these are not meant for human bodies.

I was looking for chanterelles, apricot-colored mushrooms with an otherworldly kind of sturdiness. You would look and look for them, never seeing anything but huge swaths of Irish moss and crashes of trees bleeding new dirt into the ground. And then, suddenly, you would find one. And then another. And, where you had seen nothing but decomposing tree and moss now were orange umbrella-ed mushrooms everywhere. In this forest, where I had never been, a place possibly never logged before, I did find the undulating caps of mushrooms I was looking for but the ones I found were white. White chanterelles were as mythical to me as old growth forest. I gathered and gathered as if I could take the whole forest home with me. Or, maybe this was home. I could have lived there, eating chanterelles in the fall and winter, eating fiddleheads in the spring, drinking the water that collected on the fat fronds, keeping warm under the blankets of moss like the roots of the trees do, like the mycelia. The trees protect as if flying buttresses of a cathedral. The sun passes through them as if through stained glass. God could live here, if he didn't mind the slugs and the heckling squirrels.

In Oregon, everything seems possible. The forest is full of sequestered carbon. The ferns are so big they are nearly Jurassic. And yet, the temperature is as modereate as a human-loving planet should be. Oregon is the state of moderation. Mycorrhizae even things out. A little here. A little there. Tuck the carbon away for later. It would be awesome if alcohol worked like that. Store the extra in your subcutaneous fat. Don't make your liver work so hard to process it right now. Some of us could use a little ecological help with our addictions. The forest does it for the driver of the Hummer. Why can't the body figure out how to do it with Chardonnay?

My dad, who continued to go out to dinner with me and my sisters, even if he stopped joining friends for dinner, ordered wine for lunch. Sometimes a Bloody Mary too. At the Oyster Bar, my sisters and I would order another round of oysters as my dad ordered another round of drinks. For him. We didn't drink yet. We ate the oysters. He drank the drinks. He slid sideways onto the black vinyl bench seat. We ate our oysters. He kept sliding.

"Eat a bite of your shrimp cocktail, Dad."

"I'm not very hungry."

And he wasn't. He couldn't have been. He sucked all the calories he needed from that glass of Chardonnay. He sat up to take another sip. Never leave anything behind. That would be wasteful. Unless you're referring to the shrimp.

Some people with functional livers can drink that much for brunch. Some people, if they eat an oyster and a slice of bread, can drink that much any time. Excess is only excessive when the scales have already tipped. The problem is, it's hard to know the weight has shifted until you can't calibrate the scale any more. Ice sheets fall into the ocean. Dad lets the vinyl seat cool his cheek.

Dad left the restaurant to lie down in the car. He left us his credit card. We paid for the oysters and the shrimp and his two glasses of wine and the Bloody Mary. We rounded up the tip to the nearest dollar amount, just as he always did. He liked things to end in zeros.

It had been thought that it was trees themselves storing the carbon in their root systems. The trees do exchange carbon dioxide for oxygen but it's the mycorrhiza that take extra carbon out of the system, permanently storing it in the ground, sinking it. The leaves of trees bring in the carbon. The roots suck the carbon toward the ground, but as Kathleen K. Treseder and Sandra R. Holden write in the March 29, 2013, issue of *Science,*

> A portion of that carbon is then allocated to the mycorrhizal fungi, which use it to build hyphae that extend into the soil. Once these hyphae die, the carbon in their tissues could be quickly decomposed by other soil microbes, or it could remain in the soil for years to decades. The longer the mycorrhizal carbon remains in the soil, the greater the potential contribution to soil carbon sequestration.

The mycorrhizae take the carbon out of the roots, bring it into the mycelia. Imagine little hyphae, fingerlike, digging into the soil, like children trying to see how far into the sand their fingers can stretch. Press the carbon in there, tiny fingers. When the hyphae, or mycelium die, the carbon stays stuck in the dirt, like sloughed off alleles or abandoned fingernail clippings. Even if a forest fire comes and claims the squirrels, the owls, the trees, the mycorrhiza, the carbon itself is still stuck in the soil, like a 401K riding out the storm of a volatile but persistent stock market.

My dad never missed a day of work. 6:15 his alarm went off. In high school, I set mine for 6:20. I waited to hear him turn off the water to his shower to turn on mine. We were at breakfast. Cheerios with bananas. Two papers. *Wall Street Journal* and *The Salt Lake Tribune.* I read *Doonesbury,* he read the stocks. In 1988, he was one of the first to have access to the internet but his morning paper still reported the stocks daily. He taught me how to read the stock prices when I was ten but by the time I was in high school, acting interested in whatever interested him wasn't the most important thing to do in my day. I just took a cursory look to see if IBM had ticked up or not. He had some IBM stock. One stock. I could give him that. I loved him that much. I loved him that little.

In 1988, the stock market was recovering from the crash of 1987 when the Dow Jones Industrial Average dropped 22% on one Monday, falling from 2246 to 1738. But my dad stuck it out, not selling when everyone else panicked. By 1988, most stocks had rebounded, even increasing in value. My dad didn't lose a dime. By 1996, the year he died, the Dow Jones Industrial Average had doubled. That October, the stock market neared 6,000. Who dies when the stock market is on an upswing? Of course, these things are hard to time. Just like someone might think the tipping point of atmospheric carbon is 380 parts per million, maybe Dad thought the stock market had reached its heights. Now that the stock market is at 16,000, now that researchers have measured atmospheric carbon at 400 parts per million, who can predict? Maybe the panic can be mitigated with one more drink. To him, perhaps the vodka was a celebration.

"Just one more," he'd say as IBM shares climbed. How do you know you're going down when everything else looks up, up, up?

Fungi and trees have a symbiotic relationship. Fungi deliver nutrients from the soil to the roots of the trees. All this nearly microscopic business of exchange. While some of the mycorrhizae do sink more carbon by storing the carbon in excess of the tree's need in soil, fungi also help decompose leaves and pine needles and fallen logs on the forest floor, producing carbon. The more fungi the better? The more fungi the worse? Even if the fungi have the capacity to sink carbon, they live in forests. Forests are in danger. Can the fungi survive the nitrate run-off from nearby agriculture? Logging? Can I grow mycorrhiza in my backyard? I have some trees. I'll keep them safe. As if one person can keep a vast network of mycelia safe. I have a hard time keeping the fruit tree out back alive, let alone a whole forest.

My sister got married in 1996, a month before my dad died. People who hadn't seen my dad in years couldn't believe how sick he looked. How he tilted to the left. How he slurred. How yellow he was. A friend in for the wedding from New York asked me and my sisters, "How could you let him get like this?" We tried to keep him safe. We kept the woman he'd been seeing from his checkbook. We took him to lunch. We wrote him letters. We asked him please, Dad, stop. We never poured the vodka down the drain though. Wasted words are one thing. Wasted resources are another.

If my dad had known that in 2014 the stock market would be hovering around 17,000, would he have stopped drinking? Would he have wanted to live? Would the benefit of future money outweigh the desire to be drunk right now? Aren't you supposed to live in the moment? How much is money worth anyway? If your wife left you. If your children moved away. If your cousins avoid you. At some point, you reach balance. Maybe that's when you die. The right amount of vodka, the right amount of money. Equilibrium is hard to gauge when the floor is tilting. It's a tit for tat world. The mycelia give you nutrients, the trees give them carbon. The 401Ks contribute cash to IBM, IBM gives you dividends, sometimes splits, continues to grow. The vodka marks, this is a day to remember. The vodka marks, this is all forgotten.

There is sin in not counting the glasses of wine you drink—more than two is too many. There is also sin in the counting—if you have to count, it's already too late. Both not doing and doing will be the end of you. I could no more tell my dad to stop drinking any more than I could tell the Hummer driver to stop driving his Hummer. No matter how many drinks my dad dumped into his liver, no matter how many parts per million carbon atoms the Hummer driver spews into the atmosphere, it's their planet. To each his own. Although the planet is mine too, I guess. In some ways, I have more right to tell the Hummer driver than the dad, really. My dad was a planet unto himself, at least toward the end of his life. A swiftly tilting planet. But we are all mycorrhizal in this forested planet. What I do to you, you do to me. I let him drink. I let myself drink. I let the Hummer driver drive. I drive behind him in my slightly less polluting car, flipping him mentally the hell off.

Balance isn't easy. Maybe the Hummer driver balances out his life by planting trees in the forest, carefully tucking the roots into mycelia-covered ground, singing "Attach, little mycorrhiza." Maybe my dad thought, I raised those kids. I made some money. I swam laps every day. I patented inventions. I bought some stock. Maybe he thought sleeping in the Oyster Bar was enough taxation on his daughters. Get out now while the going's good, he said. Should we have skipped brunch with him? He would have sat home alone, drinking Bloody Marys without the Bloody Mary Mix.

And how am I any different? I balance my three glasses of wine with thirty minutes of running per day. I have no idea if calibration is in the sneaker or the bottle. Is "no" the only proper response? Is not drinking the only way to honor my dad? Is drinking responsibly—saying, "Look, Dad, I can do it." Or is that just chastising him like chastising the Hummer driver—"I rode my bike to work, why can't you?" But no. I don't say no. I do what I want—the addiction to individual choice, to free will—America's fatal flaw and its primary advantage. Does the "I" win out over "you" every time? I look for research on the health benefits of red wine. I ride my bike to work to balance out the beef bourguignon. Cows kill salmon. A herd of cattle add more greenhouse gases than an HV4. I forgive him. Maybe you will forgive me.

I keep my IBM stock. I never sell it. I keep him with me forever. My father. My mycelium. I've invested in the future. Leftover carbon. Leftover wine. Ship my future to me in a mushroom. I'm moving to Oregon to see how deeply I can make this carbon sink.

Love Comes in Waves Like an Ocean

OR MAYBE I can make it work here in Flagstaff, where I think I'm thirsty all the time but know in actuality, that my thirst is well-slaked. I pour one more glass of wine at Erik's mom's house while I say to him, "You have to take all the stuff to the car because I picked up all the toys and did all the dishes," which may be true but is still churlish and beside the point. And yet you take the churlishness to heart and drive it home hard, saying, "So what if you did the dishes? Stop assigning me tasks. I am not your assistant," and I say, "Are you yelling at me?" Which makes Zoë tell me to stop being so mad. If I had a top, it would blow but instead I simmer and storm and think now you've turned the child against me as if children were boats and you and I separate armadas. It is a sea of metaphors, this marriage.

Later, after I've calmed down, Erik says, "Maybe I could be *your* assistant." He wiggles these eyebrows. There's a Butthole Surfers song that says, "You never know just how you look through other people's eyes." Sometimes I get a glimpse of myself through Erik's eyes. It's both what I think of myself and not. I am temperamental. I am right. I am a tempest but my seas calm quickly. Looking at yourself through other people's eyes reminds you that they have eyeballs. That you both have eyes.

It's when we treat each other like children that we get mad. That instead of one sweet kayak of a family, we turn into a fighting navy. I tell you what to do. "Clean up." You tell me what to do, "Calm down." Maybe it's less like armadas and more like splashing each other across our rafts, trying to swamp each other's boat. Either way, we both get wet, wet as in the wet of an Oregon downpour. It took me a time out, a bedtime story about a cat who loves his blue shoes, and the final episode of *Breaking Bad* to stop crying. Erik used to say I had the red wines when I drank too much. Now, instead of saying words, he pulls on the gators and wades around in the temperate rainforest of my raging, silently. He waits. I let it go. In the morning, he reads to me from the *Arizona Daily Sun*. They predict more rain this September. Maybe we'll find mushrooms in Arizona after all.

A Count

SALT LAKE CITY is laid out on a grid. It starts at zero, Temple Square, and moves out North, South, East, and West by factors of 100. Main Street is zero. State Street is 100 East. There are eight blocks to a mile. The story goes that Brigham Young ordered the streets be laid wide enough to turn an ox-cart fully around. It works well for current-day U-turns and for current-day four-lane traffic needs. From my suburban home at 3402 E. 8125 South, I drove, in May, at the end of my senior year of high school, downtown and parked my car at 100 East and 100 South, meaning that to get to the Temple, downtown, degree zero, I had to drive about thirty-four blocks west and eighty-one blocks north. Eight blocks equal exactly one mile, meaning downtown was about ten miles and several generations of Salt Lake City expansion away. My dad bought me a car for my sixteenth birthday, like all over-privileging fathers do. I had to maintain a 4.0 GPA to keep the car and I had to pay for my own gas but really, it was very nice of him. He bought it maybe out of guilt, probably too. It's easier to buy a car than it is to quit drinking, which my dad liked to do, in defiance, he thought, of the degree-zero church's stance on alcohol but in actuality, in defiance of his health and his longevity, which turned out to be not very long.

The Navajo Nation is a semi-autonomous Native American–governed territory covering 27,425 square miles, occupying portions of northeastern Arizona, southeastern Utah, and northwestern New Mexico. In Flagstaff, where I live now, you can drive your car from the invisible "Arizona-USA" border to the invisible "Utah-USA" border in about two hours. In 2010, a census conducted by the Arizona Rural Poverty Institute at Northern Arizona University found that the Navajo Nation population had dropped over the past ten years, by 5.7% in New Mexico, 5% in Utah, and 2.7% in Arizona, leaving 101,835 Arizonan members, 65,764 New Mexican members, and 6,068 Utahn members for a total of 173,667 members of Navajo Nation. Although there are fewer Utah-Navajo-Nation members than Arizonan, when you drive through the Nation in the spring and summer, you drive under the sovereignty of Utah's mountain daylight savings time. Arizona does not follow daylight savings time change. It is an hour later on the Navajo Nation in June although you are still in Arizona. Do the members on the Nation consider themselves Arizonan or Utahn, then? Or, does the land feel truly Navajo-Nation to them? Does it feel semi-USA or semi-Navajo? Does it feel anything 100%? This "Nation" has been theirs since 1868 (not to be confused with this Nation that had been theirs before people trotting out the word *Nation* descended on their Arizona, their Utah, their none-of-these words). Although they were promised one hundred square miles in what was then New Mexico Territory, the actual size of the territory they received in 1868 was only 3,328,302 acres, slightly more than half of those one hundred square miles. Unlike most American Indian territories, the Navajo territory has grown. As members returned to the area by the Little Colorado, the one part of the Nation with a reliable water source, the U.S.

government extended the territory to include where they had lived before they had been interred in prison camps, before the Long Walk, before they had been sent to New Mexico. Now the Navajo Nation covers about a hundred square miles, now that the Little Colorado is drying up. The government is willing to cede non-arable land. The Navajos are willing to cede their Nation and move to regular Arizona where there is running water, piped in from the part of Utah the Navajo Nation does not have any claim.

I parked downtown at a two-hour meter, to buy books at Sam Weller's—a used bookstore near the Temple. The upstairs was dedicated to rare Mormon books but the basement had everything: aisles of fiction, rows of maps, piles of food magazines, whole corners of Utah history, and two short shelves of books of poetry, including mostly white men: Mark Strand and Walt Whitman, T.S. Eliot and e.e. Cummings. I memorized Eliot's *The Hollow Men.* "Here we go 'round the prickly pear, the prickly pear, the prickly pear at five o'clock in the morning." Although Eliot became a naturalized British citizen, the prickly pear secured him in my mind as a man from the American West where the Hollow Men seemed to be made out of tumbleweeds and unsecured dirt. I already owned Eliot's poems. I bought a book of Heidegger's criticism that I would never read and Dorothy Allison's *Bastard Out of Carolina.* I was moving to Oregon for college soon. I looked forward to what it was like to be out of some place.

In 2010, the income for 10,188 of the 43,398 households was less than $10,000 a year. The median household income for the Navajo Nation is $27,389, which is approximately half that of the State of Arizona ($51,310) overall. Thirteen percent brought in $50,000 to $74,999. I made $51,000 at my job at the University in 2010, the same amount my dad made per year in 1988, but that does not account for my capital—my house, my car, my books. I am sitting on a pile of my father's and his father's white luck. I am in Arizona because a job brought me here unlike the native household on the Navajo Nation which was born there, then forced off, then allowed to return, then encouraged to farm, then deprived of water, then told to move the sheep off the land to restore the native grasslands and to make a national park where the Navajo pay entry fees the same as I do even though the Nation is supposedly, semi-autonomously, theirs.

When I got back to my car, the engine wouldn't start. No dashboard lights. No radio. The battery was dead dead dead. I couldn't figure out why. I hadn't turned the headlights on. It was the middle of the day. I turned it again. Nothing. I opened the hood. My boyfriends, both my current and my previous, could fix cars. I helped Monty change the flywheel, helped Darryn install a new carburetor. But their Volkswagens were air-cooled and this Jetta was newer and water-pumped and the engine looked perfectly intractable to me. Perfect as in impenetrable. Perfect as in nowhere to put my hands. Battery dead. Years before cell phones. Sears was on 800 South and State Street. Nine blocks away. I had a credit card. I started walking.

"Poverty rates on the Navajo Nation Reservation (38%) are more than twice as high as poverty rates in the State of Arizona (15%). Almost half (44%) of all children under 18 years of age are considered to be living in poverty, while one-third (34%) of tribal members between 18 and 64 also live in poverty. Almost one-third (29%) of persons living in families on the Navajo Nation live in poverty, twice the rate of families living in poverty in the State of Arizona (13%), for example," cites the Arizona Rural Poverty Institute's report. But those are numbers. My friend Beya, who works with the FBI to communicate with local shelters and children's protective services, knows the numbers are worse than hollow. Isolation. Frustration. Hunger. Thirst. They can make people do things to each other that hit heavier than dust, that whisper louder than a number on a report, that, had that noise and dust not been in your eyes, you might have seen your way clear of not doing.

I walked the nine blocks and asked the salesman at Sears Automotive what kind of battery to buy. He showed me the battery.

"Where's your car?"

"Parked. In a two-hour zone."

"You'll need these."

The salesman handed me a wrench, designed for car-battery replacement, and I started carrying it back to my car. I tried to go fast but the battery was heavy. The wind kicked up. Downtown Salt Lake on a Saturday was deserted, a modern-day ghost town, requisite tumbleweeds and dust devils. A speck of dirt lodged in my eye. I had to stop to rest my arms, put the battery down on the sidewalk, but I couldn't stop for long. My two hours were almost up. The wrench, balanced on top of the battery, slid back and forth. I tried to hold it steady with my chin but that made the muscles in the arms twist in more-than-battery-carrying kinds of way.

By the time I made it back, the meter had expired but there was no meter maid around anyway. No one was around. I popped my hood, applied the wrench. I turned it to the left. Nothing. I turned it to the right. Nothing. I pulled and pushed with the wrench on either side of the battery. I did not make any progress. Zero. Zero. Zero.

The median earnings for male full-time, year-round workers in Arizona is $33,858. For women, it is $28,397. In Utah, for men, it is $33,586. For women, $22,169. In Utah, 60% of the births are to women 15 to 19 years old whereas, for Arizona, only 40%. Does this make the Utah-Nation member more Utahn? In Utah, women give birth young. The Utah-USA women give birth old too, as do the Utah-Nation women members—60% of the women aged 39–50 giving birth are Utahn. As in Utah, on the Nation, Utah women give birth more often than Arizona women. This does not make them less Navajo, just more Utahn.

I tried to apply the wrench to the battery in normal wrench-applying ways. It wouldn't fit. I hit the wrench on the positive terminal. I hit the wrench on the negative terminal. This did nothing but make a lot of noise. I made enough noise, though, to summon a man from around the corner. He was Native American, layered in too-many clothes for this May day, although possibly the right amount for the wind.

"Let me see."

He took the wrench from me. He turned the bolt I hadn't even seen and pulled and lifted the old battery out. He bent over, picked the new battery up, pushed wire to terminal, twisted the wrench only half a turn.

"Try it out."

I turned the ignition. The lights lit blue. The engine roared.

I left the car on and jumped out.

"Oh my god, thank you, thank you, thank you."

I hugged him because this story is yet another example of me overstepping my boundaries. Of my gratitude lacking grace. Of my awkward attempt to get my point across with any sort of subtlety. "Is there anything I can do to thank you? I thank you. Thank you."

I didn't have any cash. I didn't have anything but my Dorothy Allison and the Heidegger and my car.

"Can you drive me to the liquor store?"

I hesitated for longer than was cool or kind.

"Of course. Hop in. It's on the way to Sears anyway. I have to drop the wrench back off. And return the battery. You have to return the batteries. For the environment. Leaking batteries kill the birds."

"It's true. They rot right out of their containers. Leach the toxins into the water. If you have any water."

I left him in the car while I ran into the garage at Sears to return the wrench. The salesmen looked through the garage doors at the man in my car.

"You be careful, now, Miss."

I shook my head at him. It wasn't until I looked at it through the salesman's eyes that I saw what my mother would see: stranger in car. Bad as picking up a hitchhiker. I got back into the car. I have terrible gut instincts but even if I had thought bad thoughts, I didn't care what my gut said. Without my passenger, I'd still be stuck on 100 South and 100 East. Now, I'd made it to the liquor store on the 205 West and 400 South. I couldn't go in with him. I wasn't 21. I didn't have any money. So he thanked me for the ride and I thanked him for the help and it was the very least I could do.

Alcoholism on the Nation runs rampant. American Indians and Alaska Natives die from alcoholism at a rate 514% higher than other Americans, according to Navajo Nation Vice President Rex Lee Jim's address to the New Mexico Senate's Health and Human Services Committee meeting in June 2012. Although the Oglala Sioux in South Dakota have voted to repeal the prohibition on liquor on their reservation, the Navajo Nation says they have no plans to follow suit. It might lead to more crime. There are not enough police on the reservation. Legalization may not be the answer. The towns that border the Nation in New Mexico, Farmington, and Shiprock would stand to lose a lot of business if liquor was available on the reservation. *The Daily Times,* out of Farmington, New Mexico, reports that one Shiprock resident, Laverne, who did not want to use her last name, said that she sees drinkers gathering on street corners and young women getting into different cars every day. She speculates that some people even resort to prostitution to fuel their alcohol habit.

"If they can't get liquor then they drink mouthwash, hand sanitizer—whatever will get them high," she said. "[Legalization] isn't going to do anything. People can talk all they want, but I don't think anything's going to change while alcohol is sold down the road."

The shrinking Ogalalla aqueduct takes its name from the Sioux. The Little Colorado is out of water too. The Navajo Nation is shrinking in population if not by square mile. Their water is gone. When I think about the guy who helped change my battery, I wonder, was he there the whole time? Did I only see him when I needed help?

Another study shows that Native Americans have no more propensity toward alcoholism than anyone else. Circumstances of forced migration, drought, poverty might be inducements to drink, but those inducements don't ride along any tribal bloodlines. We look for evidence where we want. If we see an inebriated Native American, we highlight and underscore our prejudice on our brain, like any scientist who sees what she wants to see. When we see a Native American helping a young girl change the battery on her car, we don't see that at all. It doesn't fit any category so we just drive by, look away. To erase the prejudice, you'd have to erase the brain, and self-annihilation is easier to accomplish on the body.

In my mind, I never really left 100 S. 100 E. Although now I live in Flagstaff, I am still counting blocks, counting books, counting cars as they drive past on Route 66 looking for an America that exists only in jukeboxes. Here, in Arizona, my daughter goes to a tri-lingual school but while the Spanish and English students take turns learning each other's languages together, Diné students are driven in from the Nation to take classes by themselves. There is some attempt to preserve their language but honing their English skills for the standardized tests takes precedence. I'm not sure if the Diné kids' parents are looking for a way out of Arizona for their kids or looking for a way into Arizona or just looking for a way beyond statistics.

I think we should all move to Portland, Oregon, where there is plenty of water and plenty of plenty but the Navajo Nation would probably prefer to keep their Nation, hard won as it was, waterless as it is, as their not-Arizona, their not-Utah. Portland, I'd imagine, does not, if I recall from living there, want everyone in the world moving there. Portlanders use the rain as a barrier but at some point, it will look like nothing so much as an invitation.

Of Constancy

The Peripatetic sage does not exempt himself totally from perturbations of mind, but he moderates them.
—Montaigne

EMERITUS MARKETING PROFESSOR Theodore Leavitt lectured to his students, "The reason the train industry could not compete with the automobile industry was because it failed to recognize that it was not in the *railroad* industry but in the *transportation* industry" (emphasis mine). But how can we expect the train industry to forego its iron beginnings? The heavier the rails, the faster the train—that was how it worked then. It's the opposite thought to current-day, featherweight travel. Fiberglass and super light aluminum—that's the domain of the transportation industry. The train industry knows what it's good at. Ruts. Lines. Permanence.

An online, less-reputable-than-the-*OED* etymology website says that *rut* means "narrow track worn or cut in the ground." First used in the 1570s, probably taken from the Middle English word for *route*. However, the *OED* finds this "improbable." But perhaps it is the *OED* that is in a rut.

Every day I wake up at 6:55. I make my kids' lunch: pepperoni, rice, yogurt, grapes, pretzels, carrots, juice. I eat an English muffin, then check Facebook, Gmail, work email.

Then I check work email, Gmail, then Facebook. I grade student-essay one, check email, essay two, check Gmail, essay three, Facebook, essay four. I hold office hours. I tell students that their Spanish courses will fulfill their cultural understanding block. I teach. I tell students that the difference between dissociation and distance in a narrator is how willing the narrator is to be obviously broken. It is better to be broken. You can see yourself better, like when the bone of an arm breaks through the skin and for the first time ever you see your inside, now out.

I come home. I make dinner—tacos. I have a glass of wine. I watch a show called TV. I go to bed at 10. I wake up at 6:55.

I am in a rut but it's OK because I'm a lover of routine. No disrespect to the *OED* but I love my route. A well-worn route is a rut. A well-worn routine is a life capable of heavy lifting. You can do the work of a thousand boxcars. You are iron track, trains running along the back of you. A rut-lover is a conveyer of speed. My life is going so quickly. My rails are on fire.

People, like my husband, Erik, or his parents, try to convince me to travel. I'm conflicted. I want to go—Napa sounds beautiful. I like wine. I don't want to go. It's far away. I'd have to take an airplane. It will disrupt my route. A self, divided. My father-in-law set up the trip. Three days of wine drinking at Far Niente, Chateau Montelena, Caymus. "We'll get the rooms," he said. "You just have to buy your plane tickets and the wine tastings." $99 companion tickets. $99 a tasting. $99 a dinner. The transportation industry is not always a bargain but $297 is not bad for three days vacation.

We forgot, Erik and I, in our calculations, to include the cost of traffic. It took us three hours to drive fifty-five miles. That night, a tangle of stop-and-go nerves, I lay awake in bed. Too much wine and a too-fluffy pillow triggered trains of thoughts: the flight attendant's eyebrows, the waiter's glasses, the definition of "tasting," plastic water bottles, recyclable or not, the surreptitious reuse of other people's water bottles, contagion, the avian flu, flu shots versus flu mist, wondering if I am a bad parent to say OK to flu mist for one child, a shot for the other, and if I, that same bad parent who left her kids with a babysitter, who is not sleeping in the middle of Napa, sated and spoiled and a little bit drunk, should give up and get up.

I go outside. I walk around. The vineyards layer in rows. The bad parent walks between the vines at five in the morning. It is fall and the leaves of the Cabernet turn yellow like the leaves at home in Flagstaff. I take some comfort in this—I am missing red leaves equally, everywhere—although comfort is not the same as sleep.

In the 1940s, National City Lines, a front company for General Motors, began dismantling light-rail-based trolley lines in big cities. Called the GM Streetcar conspiracy, the rigid rail lines were replaced with flexible, bendable, turnable, carable roads. No longer did the city worker have to abide by the strict rules of predetermined tracks. If the worker wanted to take A Street to work, he took A Street. If he wanted Lexington, he took Lex. If he wanted to turn around and go home, he could circle that car in the middle of any intersection, at least in Utah where the U in Utah means freedom to go in circles on wide streets forevermore, thy will is thy command.

I'd rather drive than fly. Driving is more familiar. I do it every day. My car is nicely beige—a color as comforting as sand. If I am driving, I can stop to pee at any convenient Shell stations along the way. I try not to stop at Texaco because if there's one constancy in my life, it's a prejudice against Texas. The other constancy, because constancies should multiply, is the persistent belief that Shell oil comes from kinder oil places than Texas. I shouldn't drive or fly at all. Global warming. Perhaps I should take the train except Amtrak is the only game in town. They must give way to freight trains. It takes forever to go fifty-five miles on Amtrak. Freight trains are as numerous as prejudices and persistencies. Perhaps, instead, I will stay home.

Like prejudices and persistencies, ton-miles add up. In the U.S., in 1975, freight trains carried 750 billion ton-miles of freight. By 2005, that amount had doubled. Ton-miles by rail release far less carbon than car or plane: Transporting cargo by rail releases far less carbon than transporting cargo by plane: the train releases 0.0282 kg of CO2 per ton-mile, whereas the plane releases 1.527 kg of CO2 per ton-mile. Transporting people by car releases about 1.2 kg of carbon per passenger mile. Transporting people by train releases 0.18 kg per passenger mile, making rail transportation one of the most carbon-economical ways to go. Planes go farther and higher, making the plane the most dangerous to the air. Planes are also most dangerous to routine. When I am on the plane, I need to sit on the aisle. If I don't sit on the aisle, I weep. Mostly for my bladder. Sometimes from my bladder. If there's one thing I must do, it is feel free to pee on a regular basis.

Unilaterally, my friend Rebecca won't fly. In 2010 she took the train from Los Angeles to New York City for her art opening at Ameriger Yohe. She boarded the train at 10 p.m. Having booked a bedroom, she unpacked her pants, her shirts, her dress, her books. Bedrooms are for two and she was traveling alone. Plenty of room to make herself at home. Plenty of time too. It would take three days to cross the country. Three days if all went well. Time enough to establish a routine.

To take the 4 Southwest Chief from LA through Flagstaff, through Albuquerque onward to Chicago takes forty-four hours and costs $1,931. Then you still have to transfer to, and pay for, the 48 Lake Shore from Chicago to Albany to New York City. At five o'clock that evening she called me. She had made it only five hundred miles in nineteen hours. I was in downtown Flagstaff, walking through the square after dinner at Karma Sushi's. We always walk around the block after dinner at Karma's. We stop at Mountain Sports and Aspen Sports and Babbitt's to look at NorthFace and Patagonia gear that we never buy. Max, my son, tries on a hat that reads "Life is Good." Zoë, my daughter, asks if she can have a flashlight shaped like an iguana. Rebecca calls me. She's in the station. I wave to her through the walls of the store, across Route 66, through the metal of the sleeping car. She can't get off to say hello. There has been a delay. A woman walked in front of the train. The train could not, as it never can, stop in time. I tell her, they do that, in Flagstaff. Walk in front of trains. I picture the woman, long blue coat, hair flying out behind her. I picture her pushing a stroller away from her. I don't know if there is a stroller but I see one. Maybe in my imagination, she's pushing her better self away. Maybe she's wishing that she could send the happy part of her to go on and on while the unhappy part could be stopped by the poor train conductor's heavy load. What a great human achievement, even surpassing the invention of the transportation industry, to divide routine from despair.

But Rebecca is stuck with both routine and despair and is thus stuck on that train and there is no way around if she wants to make it to Chicago.

She waited so patiently, since patient is the only thing you can be on a train that goes only one direction on tracks that turn only toward Chicago. Despite her patience, she missed the transfer. To make the exhibition on time, she was forced to take a plane. O'Hare to LaGuardia in an hour and a half. An hour and a half to defy death. To withstand the unnaturalness of flight. To put the fear that you're tearing through God's cloak of safety in some compartment away from you. Now she's done it. She's changed her mind. Her policy. Her beliefs. To change your mind is to kill your former self. Rebecca is anything but suicidal and yet, here she is, torn in two, half on the train, half in New York City.

I am suicidal. All my friends are dead. Or dying. Or will be dead one day. My husband, when I said that I couldn't go on, thought I said, "Do you want chicken for dinner?" I didn't correct him but the poor chicken is dead too. My husband kisses the top of my head. Internal, eternal war: There is purpose in death but better purpose in dinner. I will make fried chicken, chicken cacciatore, chicken fricassee, chicken and dumplings, chicken tacos, chicken in a can. There is purpose in life again. Then, the chicken burns. I want to die. I turn on the radio to hear Maggotbrain's "Can You Get to That?" They sing, "You're going to reap just what you sow." Sow: My daughter and son swing together in concert. There is order and balance in the universe. Life is good and even.

Reap. My daughter, older, jumps off the swing, sticks the landing. My son, before I can stop him, follows suit. He falls to the ground. Cracks his chin open. I should have stopped him, should have stopped them. I have no power. There is no justice. I sowed. He reaped. I remain resolved. I will live. I will die. From the cherry tree, the blossoms fly off into summer heat. They count one more day, one more day. I have never been so happy to be alive. So sad. I shall fight myself no more forever.

What would Professor Emeritus Leavitt have had the railroad industry do? What does he mean they failed to realize what industry they were in? Who is the *they* here? Robber Barons? Getty? Rockefellers? Monopoly? Henry Ford? Does Leavitt mean the railroad industry should have started building cars, divided themselves in two? Should have expanded to absorb all transportation—automobile, aeronautical. The trains should have become cars? Or should they have become more themselves? Is there a way the railroad industry could have kept the trains or the tracks? Is there an America that could have been tracked, where the individual would not want to make his left turn at will, her U-turn at random? Could America have been America crisscrossed by railroad rather than held up high by overpasses and bridges? The railroad industry failed to become the automobile industry. Adapt. The times. The fossil fuels will be gone soon. Use them while you can. We seem to be willing to abide the plane that goes only to the stops already determined, sometimes making us wait for hours to layover some place we distinctly do not want to be. We recover by getting off the plane and quickly finding a taxicab, a Town Car, our mother in her Prius to pick us up at the curb. The train speeds by, empty.

I love my routine of hours but I hate the routine of morning. Same soap. Same contact lenses. Same hairbrush I bought in Portland, Oregon's Aveda when I was pregnant with my daughter and traveling my first time to read to students—at Evergreen State. I was pregnant with the new. Traveling didn't seem so hard then even though I slept on a cot at my friend's house in Portland. Even though I was put in my host's bedroom, in a bed so redolent with graciousness. (Who can sleep in their host's bed while the host sleeps on the foldout?) I slept. Everything was a first time and I crashed into it. Life was a bucket of sleep and I soaked in it but now my pants are so old and my shirts are so old and I'm tired of drying the water off from behind my knees. This face I've looked at before with these old eyes and the old thoughts are dull as a doorknob. I don't want to die. I want a new brain. A neural net with pathways ungrooved. I want some new pants.

The war with the self is the most brutal war. Is there anything more heavy than the recollection of track by the industry that laid them down? Railroad ties resold at the local nursery as landscaping tools. Spikes melted down into wheelbarrows. Tracks themselves pressed into service as dumpsters.

Box car, graffiti canvas. A railroad industry cannibalized by a transportation industry. Pulling up tracks is sentimental. Can you turn old business into a new garden?

After the latest oil crisis, after Iran, Iraq, Syria, Hurricane Katrina, and the Gulf Oil Spill—after the world continued to be its inconstant self—gas prices rose so high that it became less expensive to ship freight by train than by semitrailer. Stopped at the crossing, as I check my email, Facebook, Gmail, brush my hair, the box cars flash by as do flatbed cars topped with trailers normally attached to semitrucks. Boxcar after boxcar speeds by. Rubber-tired trailers filled with freight, one gasoline-fed engine at a time bounce on top of steel wheels, going forward, mostly gas-free. Maybe there was forethought. Or slow thought.

The railroad industry is doing fine. They say they're going to build a train track from LA to Napa. It's a straight shot. Save a lot of gas. Someone in the railroad industry in an industry that doubles as the transportation industry chose that straight line because taking every available turn sometimes gets you nowhere, especially in sunny California, where no one ever wants to die, unless they're trapped in traffic.

Here's a new thought for another trap: Roads are asphalt train tracks. You're still driving where someone else is telling you to go. A new neural net can't be paved. How do you make a new thought? You have to move. It's worse than travel, I know. The packing and the goodbye-saying and the finding a new grocery store. But you have to go. The tulips you see in Michigan are not the same tulips you see in Phoenix. That tulip, eaten by a javelina, will break your mind. Inside that broken mind, on the edge of a gnawed tulip, you will find a reason to live. It's called yellow. You have never seen a yellow like this before. Keep looking at it until you have to move again.

Or maybe you have never seen a tulip. Maybe you should get out of your car. Leave it by the jangling railroad stop. The noise will go away soon enough. The other cars will find you. You'll be surprised how smooth the ground next to the tracks is. Don't worry. You won't trip. The tracks are dangerous but the weeds alongside never are. It's a route that's been taken a million times but never once by you. You might think it's suicide for a flower to grow along this route—from Flagstaff to Los Angeles is mostly Mojave. But the Utah penstemon grows there. You're from Utah. It survives. So can you. Indian paintbrush survives everywhere, even here, in between the oil-dipped lumber and the steel spikes, between the Turtle Mountain Wilderness and Barstow. You are willing to take note. You take comfort in color. Even desert dandelion seems surprising, in the desert, even though it looks as routine as the dandelions stuck in your hard dirt at home. Desert larkspur is as blue as your coat and owl's clover is pink for the owl that is calling you to go ahead. This rut is less of a route. You're going so slow you might actually get somewhere.

Everything grows more slowly in Flagstaff. There is a fruit tree of some sort in the backyard that is the same eighteen inches tall as it was when we moved here. We water it. Occasionally. The monsoon keeps it wet when we forget. But it doesn't get any bigger. Erik has planted flowers he calls maguerites. We have yarrow. Creeping thyme. Black-eyed Susans, echinacea. I keep geraniums in pots. I forget to water those too.

Erik is the water rememberer. And the water gatherer. For Father's Day, I bought him a rain barrel to harvest water from our roof. He tucked a gutter into the lid and waited. Two hours of rain filled the barrel. He bought another one. He spent all of June dunking a five-gallon bucket into the barrel and hauling water to each individual plant. It takes him two hours to water with the barrel compared to twenty-six minutes with the hose. When he's done watering, his clothes are covered in dirt from bending into the barrel to get the last bit of water, his shoes drenched, his fingers pruny.

Our water bill showed half as much usage as last year's June although it rained only twice. The yarrow is still alive, as are the marguerites. That little fruit tree—whatever it is, grew its first inch. It's something different—touching the stuff rather than keeping it at a remove—hand against rubber hose, hand pointed away, water touching rock but not touching hand.

The Grass Is Always Greener

IT IS A Thursday afternoon. The sky is blue. It rained a couple of weeks ago but now the trails in the woods are dry. There's not a single cloud. No storm on the horizon. I can hear the dry creak in the branches of the pines.

Erik gets home at 4:30. I wait until he has opened his beer.

"Oregon State called. They invited me for an interview."

"Wow. Congratulations." But unlike his beer, his delivery was a little flat.

"We've always wanted to move to Portland."

"You always wanted to. Move back there. I never lived there. Plus, Oregon State is not in Portland."

"You want me to say 'no'?"

"No. Go. See what they say. It will be hard though. We can't go backward."

I don't know what he means backward. Oregon is always forward. Go west, Young Man. Drink from their rivers. Eat their salmon. Go to their Tillamook and buy cheese! Collect blueberries and blackberries and raspberries spring through summer. There is not a month without a viable vegetable.

"I have a job here. You have a good job. You'd have to give up tenure. My parents are here."

In my mind, I think, I need a job in Oregon. Dungeness crabs for the taking. But then again, I remember Oregon. I remember why I left Oregon. Not everything is as free as it looks.

"Think of the property taxes," Erik says.

"Taxes? We're not going to go because of taxes? That's one reason we should go. Stupid tax-free Arizona. That's why they're going to close the university soon. No taxes. And then neither of us will have a job."

I don't mention that with the lack of snow this year and the fact that I just read Timothy Egan's *The Big Burn,* I have been having dreams of the largest ponderosa forest in the world going up in smoke. Erik has called me histrionic before. I stop before he ventured into other "h" words. Hyperbolic. Harpy. Hysterical.

In one of my roles in my current job, I am the energy mentor at my university. When I went to the training, Nick and Avi, the Green Initiative Leaders, told the group—of which I was the only professor—everyone else was a graduate teaching assistant or a student—that to make progress in a community, you can really only tackle one or two green initiatives a year. This year, the campaign is "reduce the juice." Avi tells us that vampire energy, the kind of energy that a computer or a TV suck even when it's not turned on, costs the university half a million dollars a year. $500,000. We haven't had raises in five years.

Nick took us over to his energy demonstration. A cup warmer, a coffeepot, a blow-dryer, and a lamp lay on a table, plugged into a power strip. Holding an energy meter called "Kill-A-Watt," he turned on each individual appliance. The meter showed the coffeepot drew 8 watts. The hair dryer on high drew 1400 watts. But it's Flagstaff. The wind sucks the moisture out of your everything. It doesn't take very long to blow dry your hair, but in those few minutes, you could run a computer for two hours. I had never heard of a coffee warmer but apparently people use them all across campus. The cup warmer drew 200 watts. As energy mentor, it's my job to remind my colleagues to drink their coffee before it gets cold.

After the demonstration, the mentor leaders served us lunch. Avi and Nick ate their vegetarian sandwiches. I know. Meat is the problem. I ate the turkey on my sandwich guiltily. I always eat turkey guiltily, but less guilty than I eat steak (and with less pleasure). And yet guilt is not the same as change. They gave us pens made out of corn to distribute, which I warily took back to my people in the English Department. English Departments are good places for skepticism but not such great places for change, especially when it comes in the form of small steps, goofy slogans like "Reduce the Juice," and pens made of corn.

In the next faculty meeting, I argued my case. "Reduce the Juice." I had a hard time not giggling. Juice. Hot juice. Sex. Instead of giggling, I told my fellow faculty that although our building had been renovated to cut down on energy waste, including automating lights in our offices, we still had switches in the classrooms. I demonstrated by turning the lights off and on. They seemed attentive. Like they remembered, as if in a past life, that switches moved up and down. And then I told them about the vampires. Even turned off, their computers pulled energy from the grid. The pointy canines of the power outlets drew electricity through the night. All they had to do was turn off their surge protectors and $500,000 a year would be saved.

At this point, I expected rolled-eyes. I expected talking over me. These are English professors. To me, this means a) they already know this, b) they have enough work to do, or c) what is a surge protector? But instead, everyone nodded when I said it took me only a minute to get in the habit of crawling on the ground of my office and digging behind the desk to turn off my power strip but now I do it every day. Maybe they listened because of the promise of salary bumps. The $500,000 might be enough to make them crawl on the ground. Maybe it's because I was first on the agenda and so it sounded important. Maybe because my friend Angie piped in to say we'd no longer be bringing bottled water to meetings. Maybe it's because I promised them a pen, made of corn by-products. Maybe they were just nodding to be polite even though as English professors, they know that politeness will not save us from inevitable doom. But maybe, as we sat in that Room 346 as we do every month, every year, they thought, we share custody of this building. Maybe that's enough to make anyone turn the lights off. Maybe, too, they can hear the crackle of the static in the forest. Nine percent humidity and dropping.

Jill had been my OB-GYN. She delivered Max. She's kind of a hippy. She walks to work. She's a vegetarian. But she didn't care that I watched *Survivor Man* while I contracted hard with the Pitocin or that I watched three episodes of *Modern Family* while I zoned out after the Pitocin proved too much and the epidural proved just right. I had wanted a natural childbirth but, just like I wanted to be a vegetarian, these things are great abstractions to me. When push comes to shove, I will eat a hamburger with bacon on top of it. I don't mean to be so weak. I am just not very good at suffering for a long time. Four episodes of *Survivor Man* is about all I can take.

Jill and her husband, Chuck, were Flagstaff icons. Jill delivered half of the people's babies. Chuck played music for those babies when they grew up and attended sing-alongs at the library. He played guitar at the *Hullaballoo* and guitar at the Concert in the Park. He hosted sing-alongs and bonfires and they both were featured at the Viola Awards in 2013. I saw them there. They told me they were moving to Portland. I felt in my gut the way I always do when someone tells me they're moving to Portland. My umbilical cord unravels, stretches toward the leaver and tries to lock in to their Portland-heading uterus. Flagstaff would fall like a circus tent without a pole. What would they do with their house?

They were serious about sustainability. In Flagstaff, they walked to work. Chuck had a car for gigs but he rode his bike to the grocery store, the kids following on their bikes, carrying groceries back on their handlebars. They installed solar panels on their house for electricity. Most expensively, they had forced air gas heat converted to radiant heat. Solar-heated water warmed their house. But to convert from forced air gas heat to radiant heat meant you pulled up every floor to install tubing through which the water could run. It was a huge investment. Six evac tube panels provided hot water to heat the house. Sometimes, the solar panels were covered in snow and they had no way to heat the water that heated their house radiantly, through the floor. At least they had a wood-burning stove, like most everyone does in Flagstaff, for backup. The contractor hadn't been great. He said he was going to handle the permitting. He didn't. Cost more to get the permits after the fact. Jill and Chuck thought they'd be in that house forever. It's worth $80,000 to be sustainable in Flagstaff if you're going to stay. It's a little less economically sustainable when you move to Portland.

They moved to Portland because Jill would have whole days off. Whole lives without on-call shifts. Chuck could move beyond the local festivals and libraries, play big shows in the big city. Portland's the sustainability capital of the world, at least it would like you to believe. I called Chuck to see how he liked Portland, how it compared to Flagstaff, if they were able to live as sustainably there as here. Chuck said he can be vegetarian now because every restaurant has a vegetarian option. But the house they found with the good school district was in Lake Oswego, which meant Jill had to drive. And Chuck needed a car to take the kids to school and to make it to shows.

"Plus, there's not a lot of sun for solar panels," I pointed out. I'd lived in Portland. I wonder if they loved the rain.

"Rain is not the problem. It's assumption. People assume it's too rainy so they don't look into solar panels. A little irony, when we started researching it in 2010, the best model was a home in Schenectady, New York. One of the least sunny places in the country."

"Do you think you'll get solar panels there, then?"

"If we can find a way to afford it."

"One day. Solar voltaic shingles."

We both were quiet for a minute. Imagining.

"We have access to tons of locally sourced foods. But we moved our chickens," he said. "That was probably one of the least sustainable things we did. A whole new coop." A truck of their very own to get them there.

Chuck and Jill had loved Flagstaff. They had tons of friends here. They were known here. Visibility is a kind of sustainability. If people can see you, you know you're alive. In Flagstaff, you're within a two-hour range of nine national parks. But they also love Portland. Olympic Peninsula. The coast. Music. Their friend Desiree from *Bookman's* moved there. Flagstaff is not so sustainable job-wise. Unless you work for the university or for Gore, you look for other places to move. "In Flagstaff, you could live an environmentally sustainable life, but, practically, work wasn't very sustainable—driving to play at libraries for no money, Jill working at the clinic more and more."

"The only downer about Portland is the drug use," Chuck said. He is surprised by the obvious drug problems in Portland. People always bumming everything. Chuck doesn't even smoke but people are always approaching him for a cigarette or some weed. There is a bleakness to Portland, underpinned by the mood-setting gray skies. Perhaps the abundance of water, locally sourced foods, and bike paths make you believe everything, including drug use, is sustainable.

I'd left Portland for a job. I had worked at the Oregon Humane Society as the computer manager. I loved Oregon and I wanted to be Humane but I could only fake managing computers for so long. I wanted to be a writer—the least sustainable job dream of all. Which is how I ended up in Flagstaff.

Maybe we'll stay in Flagstaff. See if we can buy Jill and Chuck's house. Believe in their dream. It will be just like moving back to Portland, but without as much water. Or any water. Forty days and counting.

How do you get to live where you live? First, you dive into darkness. Make the jump. Face the facts. You read the news. The bark beetle approaches. The fire has grown to 25,000 acres. A dog was shot because a hiker thought the dog was a wolf. Your sister and brother live in Montana. Your brother-in-law tells you that in Montana, it is legal to shoot a wolf if you feel at all endangered by that wolf, even if you think that a dog is a wolf, even though wolves are on the endangered species list. I think of my job at ORLO, that environmental arts organization I used to work for. We had another bumper sticker that read "You Enddanger," meaning you are the enddangerer but also as in "You End Danger," meaning it's up to you to save the wolves and the salmon.

I say, "Same as humans shooting humans in Florida. Any sense of danger, it's your right to kill."

"Yes. 'Stand your ground' for wolves."

Your brother-in-law puts an orange vest on the dog.

No one shoots his dog but a man killed seven people in Isla Vista because no women would sleep with him. You wonder how deep you should go, thinking about how evil people can be, how myopic, how everything looks like it's all about you through the sights of a gun.

Instead of thinking about evil, you wonder how can you make the place you're living in a viable one. You ask your brother-in-law, "What about the bark beetles?"

"Stapling pheromones to trees has been shown to convince the bark beetle, 'there is no food here.'"

"What about the West Fork trail? The one where you walk in and out of the stream under a canopy of oak, pine, and red rock?"

"The fire is burning low and slow," he says, "in the manner of fires of old that burned the brush and sustained the tree."

I don't ask, but think, "What can we do about the men and their guns?"

To yourself, you respond, "You still have a word. Say it." The word is not "no." Is the word "yes"? Or is the word "speak." Maybe someone else will say it. Maybe we'll say it together. In the days after the shooting, YesAllWomen had 500,000 hashtagged tweets after the Isla Vista shooting. The most Twitter has ever had. Some people are speaking as they are tweeting. Some bark beetles are moving on. Some fires burn themselves out. The wolves are coming back.

Once, after a bad breakup, in Portland, after I stopped drinking gin out of a Mason jar, I made a list:

1. Go on a walk.
2. Eat blueberries.
3. Volunteer at the animal shelter.
4. Get a cat.
5. Swim.

I went to swim at Oxbow Park on the Sandy River. This river too is shallow enough to grapple through. The current is strong as it pushes you downstream but your arms are stronger than Mason jars full of gin should allow them to be. You hook your right hand onto a deep-set rock. You pull yourself up until your left hand finds another stuck rock. You pull and pull until you look upstream and two river otters are spinning in a deep pool next to you. On the bank, someone has left a disposable diaper but you ignore that as much as the otters ignore you. You are swimming with otters. It is summer. It's still America. Not even Oregon is perfect but you are swimming.

The campus visit was magical. Camellias blooming in February. Three distinct rainbows. Butterflies. Flocks of birds. River after river after river.

There were some downsides. I couldn't see the hills that surrounded the university. The clouds had socked them in. I remembered that in Oregon, you can't leave wet socks, wet towels, wet bathing suits on the floor to dry. Unlike in Flagstaff, when you wake up in the morning in Portland, they're still wet. And, Oregon is not necessarily Portland. When I flew into Portland for the job interview, I went straight to the beer store and got Erik beers. I went to Laurelhurst market for some smoked duck and pate. I did not go to the wine store because Oregon makes Pinot noir and I can drink Pinot noir no longer. Maybe I'm not thirsty for Oregon and water, I thought. Maybe I'm just hungry for charcuterie.

When I stopped on my way to the airport to visit my friend Misty, as we ate mussels and clams with our glasses of not Pinot wine, she reminded me of something I'd said a long time ago. "It's hard living in Oregon because it's too easy. There's nothing to fight against."

"And," I mentioned to her, "all I write about is wanting to move back to Portland. If I get this job, what will I write?"

I hate to move. You have to find a new doctor. A new dentist. A grocery store. I love the sun. I also love the rain. I am lucky to see the sun and to hear the rain. If only there were two of me although two of me would then probably like to be four.

Pipeline

MAYBE ERIK AND I drink too much. Maybe we drink too little. Maybe we do everything a little too much and a little too little. Maybe there's a little too much. Who doesn't want to whittle down the too much? Maybe there's a little too little. Who doesn't want to build up the thin and dire?

It was February and there was no snow. Not only was there no snow, but it was warmish. I wore only my Gortex jacket. The Gortex was just for show. There was no precipitation forecast. Erik wore his flannel. We have thirty coats between us. He, I think, more than I. He has his grandfather's wool winter coat, his dad's lumberjack flannel, his Marmot parka from KUTV, his green Northface from REI, his peacoat, his new yellow windbreaker, his ski coat, his fishing coat, the coat he wears to shovel snow. What if he needs those coats no more? What if the word *shovel* applies only to food?

Because it is not snowing, we leave the kids with his mom and step dad. We go out for a date. I want to go to Tinderbox because I like cured meat. He wants to try Majerus's because it's new. It is new. And sporty. The restaurant is empty but the hostess seats us at the precarious two-top in between the server's station and the bathroom. I order a glass of wine. I see the bottle they pull from underneath the bar. Magnum. Castle Rock. It tastes as purple as it looks.

I sit with my arms folded.

Erik folds his arms. He's copying me.

I can only fold my arms so hard to make him take me seriously. I unfold them and then refold them. I think I'm making my point.

"Did you taste this wine?" I ask him. He has a beer. Sierra Nevada. Opened right in front of him. Beer is always safe. "It tastes like mop water."

"But it has legs."

"It's not the wine that's crawling. It's the glass trying to escape."

"You drank the whole thing."

"Well, I'm not sitting at this crappy table without something to drink."

I fold my arms. Erik mimics my arm-folding. It is hard to drink bad wine with your arms folded. It is even harder to drink beer.

Philip Seymour Hoffman died with a needle in his arm. Five empty bags of heroin surrounded him. If this were a movie, he would have been the man who had seen too much. In the movie, his mother couldn't afford a wheelchair so her neighbor carried her around on his back, in exchange for sex. Hoffman, the character, had walked in on them. His mom was squeezing lemons to increase blood circulation. She needed to work what muscles she had left before they all atrophied. Philip could tell by her eyes, because carrying-man doesn't stop his sex-having, because she needed some help getting to the grocery store later, that she wanted to provide a bit of flesh for him. But she was all skin. Her eyes made wide by the flesh falling in skinny skin all around them.

The lemons made Hoffman remember his kit. He carried his own for times like these. He promised his mom he will bring her some milk next time, so she doesn't have to be carried to every grocery store, every time. Then, because he can't afford to buy his mother a wheelchair and because he saw sex-haver on top of his mother and because he wondered if she went to the store only for the lemons, he taps some of his powder into his spoon. Maybe she wanted the lemons only. Maybe she wanted to be carried on the back of the sex-haver. Maybe the sex itself was good sex. Maybe Philip Seymour Hoffman didn't want to think about it so Philip Seymour Hoffman took out his syringe and turned his powder into liquid with the heat from a match. And he didn't think about it any more. Well, five bags later, he didn't think about it anymore.

Or maybe Philip and William Rivers Pitt, senior editor of *Truthout,* whom Philip probably know well, were having coffee in Brooklyn at Tillies. William had a coffee. Philip ordered chai. William tells Philip about a coal company that had just dumped tons of 4-methylcyclohexane methanol in the Elk River in West Virginia. 300,000 people were told not to bathe, let alone drink, the water that came from their tap. Philip told William he would have to humanize the story to get people to care, to add some narrative, some character. So William told him that a child living in Elk River snuck out of his bed at night, went to the faucet, turned the handles, and poured himself a drink. The child's esophagus is as thin as a seventy-five-year-long smoker's.

Philip said, That's the ticket. I will play him in my next film.

Philip wouldn't live to hear about the 50,000 and 82,000 tons of coal ash polluting some 27 million gallons of water with heavy metals and other poisons, near the towns of Danville and Eden in North Carolina, but he had lived through droughts in California. He rubbed his hand over his parched skin, rubbed his scraggly beard. He breathed in. The dry air burned his lungs. He is currently missing the wildfires in Los Angeles. It is May 15th and Southern California is on fire again. Williams tells Philip the fracking and drilling might be causing drought in some of the states that use the Ogallala. They use so much water to get the oil out of the ground. Ninety-seven billion gallons that is lying heavy in some pools, heavy and undrinkable. Philip both cares and doesn't. Although he once lived in California, he feels deeply depressed, like Oklahoma.

"The state department says there are no serious environmental concerns about the Keystone pipeline," Philip, sipping his spicy latte, told William.

"Yeah, if you don't count the fact that like fracking, you have to infuse the tar sands with water to get it to come up out of the ground."

"Canada's going to mine it anyway."

"Canada used to seem so promising."

"At least it's winter," Philip said, pulling his coat tighter around him.

"I used to love the snow. When I look at it, I think how beautiful it is. How it transforms everything. And then I remember that it is being wrecked, poisoned, denuded, and ruined for money and I want to go outside and sit in the snow and listen to it as it buries me until I am gone from this country that would do such harm to itself, brazenly and without restraint, for profit."

"Well," said Philip, "we probably shouldn't go killing ourselves over global warming."

"Well, what should we kill ourselves over?" William asked.

Russell Brand said in *The Spectator* that drugs and alcohol were not his problem. Reality was his problem. In the movie of Russell Brand's life, an actual documentary of him shooting up. "I sit wasted and slumped with an unacceptable haircut against a wall in another Hackney flat (Hackney is starting to seem like part of the problem), inhaling fizzy black snakes of smack off a scrap of crumpled foil." And in a movie of your life, reality is your problem and drugs are a very good solution. Russell Brand, who has long hair, now says that drugs are not, in reality, a very good solution to reality but what solution is?

On Facebook, after Hoffman died not only in the movie of his life but in his real life, someone said, addiction is a disease. Someone else countered, it's a choice. Someone else said, it's not a choice you can make if you have children to raise. It's selfish.

Hoffman had children. As any good parent, he was slavishly devoted to them. He apparently, although twenty years sober, was still a slave to addiction. But we are all slaves to choice. It seemed like such a good idea, free will. Mr. St. Augustine said that man was not born evil. That it was only through the fall of man, his bad choices (woman, sex with lemons), that evil came into the world. You can choose God or you can choose evil. But even if you choose the Grace of God, you still have to stop in hell for a time to purge yourself of sin—purge yourself of choice. Hairshirts and flagellation. Heroin is a good way to get to God, to beg off reality for a while, skip purgatory. Close your eyes to your mother and her squeezing lemons and you tie a rubber chain around your arm. As you squeeze a lemon in your fist, you're choosing against choice. No kids, no planet, no saints, no hell. Just a quick ride to heaven. We have to miss out on heaven to save our kids? Yes, maybe. Because heaven is not a verb, just a distant, annihilating noun.

What do we have to do for our children? My friend Justin emailed me a report that said the Antarctic ice sheet is breaking up. "It's pretty much over." I emailed him back, "We had a good run." But sarcasm only staves off the terror so long. I don't care about me. I could evaporate today. But my kids. Why did I hand them this misery? Why did I let this coastal shelf collapse? The air is shifting. The ice sheets are tilting into the sea. Step on it, make it flat. Or at least stand up. Philip Seymour Hoffman. Please stand up.

Did my dad have a drinking problem? Or did he have a standing vertical problem? When I visit him in the condo he bought after my parents' divorce, I see there are no lemons. There are the vestiges of a home as made by a kitchen—plates, bowls, cups, but no spices. No flour. There is no reality of a home without at least the pretense of baking. My dad leans against the counter, approximating sobriety. He cups his chin in the crotch of his hand and nods while I tell him that although Drew and I broke up, we might get back together, even though he's started dating Rashna. She is from Singapore. Why would he choose me from Utah over Rashna from Singapore? I have all these hang-ups. Boring sex. No lemons. My dad is a drunk although maybe not today. He seems like he's hearing what I'm saying. He likes Drew. He reminds him of himself as a young man, as all older men say of all younger men, especially those young men who can hold their liquor. Drew's an expert. Straight gin, three olives. No vermouth required. Like my dad could once but now, liver-challenged, cannot. But maybe my dad has quit drinking. Today's the day. Here he stands, in the kitchen, nodding about my boyfriend, seeming vaguely interested, seeming like this is the story that might make him stand all the way up straight. Perhaps he has an opinion. Dump that guy. He's not good enough for you. You can hold your own against any Singaporian lemon sexer.

But my dad doesn't say that. He says, "*Ars seemila*."

If only my dad knew Latin. Then I could convince myself of his sobriety. Maybe he's talking to Augustine. This is my punishment now. This liquor that is my God and my hairshirt.

Ars seemila: It is seamless. It does seem like this. *Ars seemila* means it's good to see you. *Ars seemila* means I could care less you are here. *Ars seemila* means bring me some lemons. *Ars seemila* means this house could look like a home if I could stand up straight. I will bake for you. Lemon bars. Lemon bars go very nicely with gin.

I could be mad at him. How selfish. How uninterested you are in others. How lacking in willpower. How sick. But really, I just think, I hope it's better in there, Dad. Out here, it's kind of rough.

I want to have opinions about addicts. I want to say, as Russell Brand says, 90% of people can have a drink, even smoke crack, and not be an addict. But 10% of us, we have one sip and we can't go back. But I don't get that. Reality is everywhere. It can't be only 10% of people who are trying to avoid it. Is drug and alcohol addiction fundamentally, Augustinely, worse than watching TV all day, playing video games all day, reading all day, shopping all day, avoiding the fact that those stitches in your clothes were sewn by a five-year old girl in Zhang Zhou, that the big box store just cut the hours of the cashier so no healthcare, that the plastic of your credit card is made from petroleum sucked out of the ocean next to the last swimming polar bear? Or worse than the anorexic whose mind shakes with hunger or the bombastic loud talker who can't stop making noise or he'll disappear or the football player who keeps ramming his head to make the singing stop or the member of the NRA who shoots so many holes in his backyard tire swing that he forgot that swings were for swinging or the mom with her lists, so many lists, that she's papered over the wall of reality and the nondrinker so proud, he pats his back, makes a percussive sound. What's there to hear over the deep boom of self-satisfaction? We're all trying to get out of here, it seems, through guns or lists or heroin. Everyone addicts every day.

It's not that I like being in a room with an addict. I like people who can stand up straight, on their own strength, of their own free will. People who need a counter to lean upon seem ungodly and unwilling to do the good work of choosing a healthy choice. But I don't know many people who can stand up straight, all by themselves, and look the world in the eye all day long.

I could have told my dad what Russell Brand wishes he had told Amy Winehouse: Don't take a drink, don't take drugs, one day at a time. But who am I to tell my own father what to do? Don't people get to make their own bad choices? If I said (which I did say), "Please Dad, stop," and he didn't stop, is he just now choosing drink over me? If I'd never said anything, I never would have thought his drinking had anything to do with me. But now that I've asked, I've been denied. The sound of vodka drowns out the pleading voice of a child. Be quiet, child, maybe the gurgling will stop. The mind of an addict, like anyone's mind, is a confusing place. Maybe it's better to get out of there. Get out of here. Maybe here and there are the same place. Then what do you do? Where do you go? God. This child is breaking my heart. I need a drink. I don't mind dying if I don't hear her say "stop" anymore.

Humans like to name things. Put a label on it. Tie it back. Keep it away. Name it *other.* Addiction. Selfishness. Slow suicide. Bad. All those words are "not me," "not me," "not me," "not me." But drugs are just a way, more destructive than most, but more effective too, to deal with what is sometimes a bad reality. It takes a lot of work and a lot of imagination to make reality good.

The same day the *New York Times* ran a Philip Seymour Hoffman story advocating widening the distribution of an opiate antidote, Naloxone, they also ran Porter Fox's story called "The End of Snow." A depressing, off-the-wagon-throwing article about how in a few years, there may be no more ski resorts. And, while ski resorts may sound frivolous, the water the ski-resorting mountains produce from snow is not. Without snow, predictable water resources disappear. Irrigation methods become obsolete. Agricultural systems dependent on run-off disappear. It's enough to make anyone suicidal.

And yet, one of the nice things about the end of the planet is that it does not feel like the end of the self. As I sit here and read about this not-too-distant future, I'm thinking, at least it's not me that's a mess on the news today.

I am a mess. I didn't get that job I thought I wanted. There's a typo on an expensive flier I just made. My colleague just emailed me in all caps. I keep trying to explain to my son Max that to play walkie talkie, he has to hold the button down to talk, let go to listen. He does not listen. I'm trying to work while he's yelling, "What you say?" from the other room. I cannot type while I hold down the walkie talkie button, which is pointless because now my son is standing right next to my ear, still asking, "What you say?" It's twelve o'clock and while I do not want a glass of wine right now, I probably will want one tonight. I will count my glasses. One. Two. I open a seltzer. I slice a lemon. It'll be five o'clock soon enough.

But this planet! It's a bigger mess than me. There is no water in California. California's on fire and it's too cold to ship natural gas from the Midwest so there is no heat there either. California on rations hot and rations cold. It is not snowing in California. California has the intelligence to be two things at once but neither can it remedy. California forgot to verb.

This is the reality, but not the kind that makes you want to die. The only death reality is the reality that the wolves are dying and the tigers are dying and the polar bears are dying all because you, addict, should live.

So I should do something. I should look at this from the point of view of a wolf. From the point of view of the hawk. From the POV of the worm. From the rabbit. This reality out there is more interesting than the reality in here. Paul Ricoeur, *The Rule of Metaphor*, says of the ability to see is the ability to do something.

> On the one hand, the mass of images is behind all voluntary control, the image arises, occurs, and there is no rule to be learned for "having images." One sees or does not see. The intuitive talent for "seeing as" cannot be taught; at most, it can be assisted, as when one is helped to see the rabbit's eye in the ambiguous figure. On the other hand, "seeing as" is an act.

To understand is to do something.

And while I would like a lemon tree to grow in my backyard, here at 7,000 feet, here in the mountain desert, here in America, I would also like water to go with my lemon. Snow, let it snow, snow.

What's cool about snow? Cooler than lemons? One flake at a time builds a whole watershed. Is it foolish to imagine that little changes can have significant impact? Porter Fox argues that "Nothing besides a national policy shift on how we create and consume energy will keep our mountains white in the winter—and slow global warming to a safe level." That's like they say in AA, you have no power in the face of your addiction. Submit and you shall be saved. Your purgatory will be over soon. But that's not likely. Submission only makes you thirsty. If you wait for a National Policy Shift, you will be skiing on sand, under the hot flap of palm fronds.

If you're going to change reality, you're going to have to go outside. First, maybe you should pick up some garbage. Go down into the ravine in your hometown. Pull some tires up the greasy slopes. Step on plastic bags tucked under rocks. Pull them out. Pick up yogurt containers and water bottles, trucker bombs and ice cream wrappers. Put them in a bigger, more responsible plastic bag. This won't stop global warming but notice how, after all this plastic collecting, there is no rubber tie-off wrapped around your arm.

Then stand up. Straight up, even if you've been drinking all day or shooting heroin all night. Fake it until you make it. What can you see as? See as an owl? See as a worm? See as a bear? See as the night? See as. Make it seem real. As an actor in the movie of your life, you can see through the point of view of a lemon tree where "squeeze" means something new again.

When I said to Erik, "You are an asshole," I was wrong. He, who plants milkweed for the monarchs can never be a noun. If I am so limited. If I am so shortsighted. If I am so mad because he sat on his ass while I cleaned up the Legos, then where will we be.

I read a poem-essay about manta rays. How their angel wings are cut off, lined up on the dock, "So neatly laid out and carved up were the mantas that they resembled a squadron of charcoal-gray stealth bombers seen from above in a vast assembly plant, wings beside fuselages. After the gills are removed, some of the remaining cartilage is sold as cheap filler for shark-fin soup in Asia," Greg Wrenn writes in *23rd Century Poem.* I don't know where we will be in two hundred years. Wrenn hears the poem of a boy writing a poem for the last dying orca. I hear my voice with its sharp words. It drowns out the poem even now.

Greg Wrenn doesn't think our canvas shopping bags will save us. He suggests we need a paradigm shift so great to change our behavior that it would be akin to nuclear holocaust. Beauty without truth won't get us there. He writes, "I'm increasingly turning away from a certain kind of poetry that idealizes the natural world while photoshopping out any hint of our current crisis. Such poems may no longer be defensible. They might be Beauty, but they aren't also Truth—are they perhaps pretty fabrications, ones with life-and-death consequences?" My friend Rebecca reminds me that in debate, their topic for their senior year was "ethic."

The debate students would argue this plan: To make everything worse faster so the apocalyptic moment came faster. But she said to me, "You can't do it that way. You can't get big good out of little bits of evil." Wrenn doesn't think beauty, or poetry, is going to save us. No. But saying "asshole" aloud isn't helping either. If I could sew the wings back on the manta ray. If I could take back my words.

But I go forward. I take my cloth bags to the grocery store and pray the canvas pays some kind of alms to a god I don't believe in. My sewing skills are not good. Words don't go back in my mouth. You can only get to big good through tiny good.

To appease, I make Erik soup. I avoid both shark fin and manta ray. It does nothing. It does something. "To cook" is an infinitive verb.

In the End, We Will Fight Over Cheese

I SPEND A lot of time in a bubble of self-righteousness. You left your car idling when you dropped your kid off at day care. One thousand tons of carbon against you. You drink bottled water. One thousand tons of garbage patch swirling in the ocean thanks to you. You buy clothes made in China. I am so good. I buy my clothes from the Full Circle Thrift Store (not even the chain store Goodwill). I turn my car off. I drink out of an unwashed Nalgene. I hang my towel up. I do the laundry. I make lunch for the kids. If righteousness were awarded with cheese, I would have a cave full of gouda. I'm just as bad as a self-righteous Christian. Supercilious. At least the Christians have a bible to fall back on. I award myself cheese based on my own prejudice and proclivities. I like cheese, therefore, cheese is good. I don't approve of plastic water bottles so plastic water bottles are bad. It's like my own God-setup in here.

Thinking you are good turns you mean. Such high standards. Can anyone live up to you? One good thing about becoming an asshole? To fail puts a hole in your bubble of goodness. When I published that poem that hurt my colleague's feelings, I stopped picking on people for shopping at Dillard's. I am imperfect. You are imperfect. I have failed. I may as well be Swiss cheese—and not the expensive Gruyère type. I am softer now. Not only like I got punched in the gut but that I am all gut. I hurt someone's feelings so badly they won't take my apology. For the sake of art, I flattened them. Now, flattened in return, I push the cheese toward you.

"No, go on," I say to you. "You have it. It's not that big of a deal. I don't need so much cheese. I've been taking this idea of goodness too far without ever actually being that good."

After the hollowing out, the public shame of hurting someone's feelings with something I wrote makes me walk stooped over. The same snow that in the nighttime makes me shiver shows the lines on my face in the day. I die by lying. I die by telling the truth. The pressure of lie against truth was meant to bring news but instead, it just brought toxin. By saying that she was getting divorced even though I wasn't sure of that fact. By bringing up her mother's cooking. By taking the story of her friend's death and making it mine. By turning it into a story about the dying of the bees, I grow older. I grow fatter too. I have eaten all the cheese. Cut the fat off with a knife.

It is possible that it's just me. That I am the one who should stop. What kind of person fights over *The Sound of Music*? Erik seemed crazy, yelling at me from the bottom of the stairs that Italy was not safer than Austria during the war. I said, maybe just a little. Hitler was from Austria.

He said, "No, *The Sound of Music* takes place in Switzerland. That was safer."

And I said, "Maybe the Swiss were taking the easy way out."

He said, "How could the Third Reich have a Navy? They're landlocked."

And I said that's what Slovenia's for—although it wasn't. My knowledge of naval battles of World War II is limited but Primo Levi was Italian and I knew that. I shouldn't have said anything about Italy at all. Mussolini. I didn't wish him on anyone, not even the Von Trapp family as rerendered by Carrie Underwood who is as sweet and Aryan as a bubble. If she hadn't been singing so much about happiness and whiskers on kittens, maybe Erik and I wouldn't have seized upon geography as our fact-Issac to split in front of our real fact-Zoë who cried "no" at us. Stop fighting. It was late. She was tired. She didn't want me to say "go." She didn't want Erik to say "stop."

I stood on top of the stairs. Erik stood at the bottom. Somewhere between we should have been able to stop. There are normally fourteen stairs on a staircase. If he took seven and I took seven, we could have met in the middle, somewhere safe, like Switzerland. I speak a little German, a little Italian. Erik speaks Spanish. You'd think we'd figure out how to say, "I don't really care about the ways you can say goodbye." *Auf wiedersehen, adieu.* Egos are mountains, snow-covered, crag-ridden mountains. Ice-picks and crampons. We saddle up. I walk you to the door. Nobody is saying "no" except our daughter who was singing just a minute ago.

I regret this fight. I regret *The Sound of Music.* I regret every time I've said "no." What will I regret more? Telling Max to be quiet because I'm working when I'm writing a book for kids about being lost in the forest? Yelling at Zoë for not keeping up when we go running even though she didn't want to run, she wanted to be in the forest with just me? Thinking I'm in the forest and that Erik is the forbidding darkness, a rabid bat, an ill-fed bear when he really he is mostly a man in boots and a hat, walking his dog, looking at the moon, wondering if I see it too?

There's a crazy river that runs through me. In this fight, I am meat. I see wolf everywhere. I am easy with metaphor and not so good with canines. I'll give them my steak and then yell at them for taking it.

Regret is a kind of dissociation. You see yourself, in the past, wishing you could, puppet-like, steer yourself in a different direction. For every regret, you create a bigger gap between you who you think you should be and who you really are.

I lash out, hiding from the embarrassment, the shame of fighting. How do I hide? With some additional, if misdirected, fighting. "Are you going to leave me any of the cheese? That's my cheese," I say to Erik. Now, cheese can become our World War II.

Shame is actually hot. I like to be cool. I will do a lot to avoid shame. It comes most often at night, when the difference between you and the ambient temperature is greatest. The moon flashes against the snow. You. Interrogated. Hot and wrong. Your shadow nuclear blasted against the sheets. You will not escape it this time.

Shame on you. You are a forest fire.

It's one thing to have a premise about art—a right to lie. A right to absorb and repurpose. A right to make a story out of another person's life. It's another thing to take the art and make the subject read it. No one wants to see themselves in your two-dimensions. You've evicted them from full-blown animation and ironed them out onto a piece of paper. To get their life back, they have to cut themselves out of the paper, make a hole, and blow.

Some people are not awash in regret. Regret makes you want to fight about cheese, ever trying to correct your mistake. One day, I'll get this cheese thing right. Erik, having forgotten about regret or cheese, pulls butterweed out from the roots as we walk down the hill in the forest behind our house.

"You're not supposed to pick the flowers," Zoë reminds him.

"They're not flowers. They're a noxious weed."

"Like obnoxious?"

"Kind of. But worse. They grow and then the other plants can't grow."

It's true there is no Indian paintbrush, no lupine, no Utah penstemons where the butterweed grows.

Erik's allergic to the butterweed. It makes him sneeze. And his hands smell bitter as coffee, stained with the ropey butterweed stems. He leaves the plant, root and all, in the middle of the trail. It won't reroot itself in the tamped-down path.

So when we fight about paper towels, I shouldn't say that he doesn't care about the planet. Obviously, Erik doesn't want a treeless and garbage-filled planet for our daughter, a world made of unrecycled and unrecyclable paper towels. Perhaps he picks his own battles. Perhaps he is good without trying to convince others to be. Perhaps he realizes that looking at the future Zoë, standing atop the garbage heap, coffee-soaked towels at her feet, wondering in which pile will she find something for her child to eat is probably creating pre-regret, not actually helping her have a good life with us now. He loves Zoë and her future. He doesn't want her life to be hard. He turns the lights off. He doesn't let the car idle. He'd recycle the paper towels if they weren't already soaked in coffee.

He watches when I show him how to open a can without a can opener. He is not worried about the end of the world—the kind where we have one can of food and no can opener. Or, if he is, he is not going to let the end of the world ruin his day. But still, he pays attention. It is good to know stuff. I saw this on the internet. I take the can of tomato paste, turn it upside down, rub the ridges back and forth on the concrete sidewalk until the metal on the top of the can is smooth and flat. The can has lost its rigidity. The metal is no longer sustainable. I crush it with my hand. The top pops off and tomato paste oozes out. I am covered in tomato paste.

"Everything can be flexible. You just have to learn how to wear the edges down." I'm proud of myself even though Erik, tomato paste-free, twirls the obvious can opener in his hand. He brings me a paper towel. I offer to go to the store to buy some more cheese.

Sustenance

MY MOM MADE tacos. My sister's boyfriend had killed himself earlier in the day and we ate tacos. We ate many tacos. As if the tortilla would sustain us against collapse. As if the lettuce, tomato, onion would keep us from falling apart. As if the shredded cheddar cheese would help us keep it together. And maybe it did. It didn't bring Garrett back but it kept anyone else from leaving. My sister Paige's friends, Garrett's friends, stayed at our house until the middle of the night. Suicide is as contagious as gonorrhea. My mom's tacos were prophylactics slipped over open wounds. She heated tortillas in the microwave. She added another pound of ground beef into the pan, the chili powder, garlic powder, onion powder. The kids decimated even the vegetables spread out into neat thirds: Tomatoes. Lettuce. Raw onions that burned their mouths, distracting their mouths from the words that they couldn't say.

What does a fourteen-year-old boy need to sustain himself? A girlfriend. A parent. A sister. Another parent. A girlfriend's parent. A sweater. Curly hair. A girlfriend who will probably have sex with him. A girlfriend who loves Jane's Addiction and Cat Stevens as much as him. A girlfriend who plays the guitar for him. A bunch of friends who, at least when he knew them, didn't eat onions. A bunch of friends who hang out with him at his girlfriend's mom's house. Access to the mountains. A trip to the mountains in a car he borrowed from his parents even though he was only seventeen. A picnic. A treat when he got home. Tacos.

This was the late '80s in Salt Lake City, Utah. Avocados were hard to find. Jalapeños came pickled in a jar. My parents ate nachos—tortilla chips with slices of cheddar baked in the oven—with those jarred jalapeños. That night, my mom didn't bother with the chiles. The onions did their job. You can ask why only so often until it begins to sound like your own problem, the equivalent of onion breath. Cover your mouth. Your breath warms the room.

•

There are so few choices that don't affect others. If I take more lettuce, there is less lettuce for you. If I eat this pear, the worms will have one fewer pear to turn to dirt. If I drive my car in St. Louis, there will be less water for you in Nairobi. One would like one's own life or one's own death to bother no one but it doesn't work that way. Everything affects everything. You think you can eliminate yourself but you can't. Your self echoes not only metaphorically but literally through everything you touched, alleles on bathroom doorknobs. Your own mother has copies of your DNA in her body. In an article published in *Scientific American* December 4, 2014, Robert Martone writes,

> Microchimerism is the persistent presence of a few genetically distinct cells in an organism. This was first noticed in humans many years ago when cells containing the male "Y" chromosome were found circulating in the blood of

> women after pregnancy. Since these cells are genetically male, they could not have been the women's own, but most likely came from their babies during gestation.

You think you are on your own but you are not. You are with your mother at all times. You think you can keep the tomato separate from the onion but everything gets folded together, in a proper taco.

•

Tacos are great emblems of free will. You can choose your own fillings. My mom is a strong believer in choice: When she makes tacos, she serves them with the chopped onions arranged in a third, the tomatoes in a third, the lettuce in the final third portion of a big plate. The taco meat, always hamburger then, was frying in a pan. You can choose a corn tortilla. A flour tortilla. Even a hard shell corn tortilla. You can put hamburger inside. Or, if you are feeling veg like my sister, like her later boyfriend, Kurt, the one who didn't kill himself, who instead sang "Meat Is Murder" along to the Smiths, then you can just put cheese in your taco. If you're me, you can put a little hamburger, a little cheese, a little lettuce, a little onion in the corners of your plate, mimicking the serving dish. Nothing has to touch. You're free to choose. You're free to call this plate of condiments a taco. Perhaps this is what everyone loves about tacos.

•

There are a lot of canyons to choose from in Salt Lake. It is one of the things that makes the city attractive—the possibility of so many routes of escape. Parleys, Millcreek, Red Butte, Little Cottonwood, even Neff's or Ferguson, although the last two you can't drive, only hike. The road up Big Cottonwood canyon lay between our house and Garrett's. He could have chosen to cross the canyon road and drive to our house. Instead, he turns onto Big Cottonwood Road and drives toward Brighton and Solitude Ski Resorts. It is too early for snow but the leaves have changed. Canyon walls slice the day in half. By three o'clock, it is near dark, especially in November. There are plenty of privacies in the canyon. Pull one curtain shut after another. City. Sun. Change. Choices. Fourteen years. Close them shut.

The car that drove him up the canyon was a cloud of sorrow. The engine, desperation. But free will steered. Free will is exuberance. It's American. It's nobody and stop me and I'll turn the car left if I so choose and right if I so want. I'll stop here and park here when the sign says no stopping November 1 to May 1. It is November 4th and I will stop my car.

The car in its many colors, makes, and models emblematizes American individualism. If I want to drive all night along Wasatch Boulevard or down Highway 26 toward Canon Beach or on Highway 180 around the Arizona Snowbowl, I can. If I want to get stuck for three hours on the Dan Ryan Expressway, or Highway 37 East on your way to Napa, or on 179 from Phoenix to Sedona, that is my prerogative. Or perhaps I never want to get stuck in traffic again. My car only drives up the canyon, never back. That choice is up to you but it will take your mother a lifetime to remember to set the table for three instead of four.

It is his car. It is his life. He owns it more than he owns misery. He owns it more than his own failed attempts to get his mother to notice he was slipping behind a cloud, more than his calling out in the night or listening to the Moody Blues or Suicidal Tendencies, more than his mother's soft crying at late in the night, and his dad's quiet simmering, his father's rage against his job, the calls to sell Armstrong ceiling tiles, as if ceiling tiles are worth persuasion, against the lack of promotion or raise and that rage that ended up in his fist against his face, only once, twice, enough to know that he chose that as much as he chooses this. The world is dragging him down. It's a bad place, he thinks. People shoot each other. Pull each other's fingernails off. They beat up homeless people and leave dogs chained to posts, unfed and unwatered. People profess to love him and then when he's on the phone with them, they answer a call on the other line. He hangs on hold for an hour. They never click back to his line. Even his mother hangs up on him sometimes. She is her own person. But she always calls him back. She is her own person and he is a little bit she. Maybe it's a little bit of self-protection, always taking his calls. Robert Martone continues,

> It is remarkable that it is so common for cells from one individual to integrate into the tissues of another distinct person. We are accustomed to thinking of ourselves as singular autonomous individuals, and these foreign cells seem to belie that notion, and suggest that most people carry remnants of other individuals.

The chimera, in Greek mythology, is a monster, composed of the parts of three animals—a lion, a snake, and a goat. Usually depicted as a lion with the head of a goat arising from its back and a tail that ends in a snake's head. It does feel monstrous, worrying about your mother, your kid, your husband, your students all the time. Their perspectives weigh heavy like goats upon your back but you would not be yourself without them. It is hard to juggle these diverse needs of carnivores, vegetarians, and mice-eaters but you realize that thanks to their stomachs, you are rarely hungry.

For Garrett, I think it was not so much about showing his parents, his friends, his sister, that it was his life, he could do what he wanted to with it. It was about revealing his separateness—I am not you. It's about choosing difference.

His note could have read, although I don't know, I never saw it: I am sorry this will hurt your feelings. I am sorry this will ruin your night, or maybe your life. But I have tried to do other things—I wrote you letters and made you a mixed tape, I ate your soggy pancakes and I took you to the Jane's Addiction concert and I played dolls with you because you were my little sister but no matter what, no matter how many walks up Ferguson Canyon or how many hours cut from school to order fries on the Training Table's table telephones, I did not feel like I was choosing. I felt like I was a country being mapped, playing a part, following the obvious choice that was really not a choice at all. I was a nice guy. I had curly hair and a soft mouth. I am choosing to hold the gun in that mouth and to make a bloody mess out of that curly hair. Please forgive me for being me. Not being.

It was as easy then to get a gun out of your parents' closet as it is now. You go to their bedroom. No one is home. Your mom works in a doctor's office. At your dad's work, Armstrong ceiling tiles aren't exactly flying off the shelves. Your dad keeps calling Industrial Prime, developers who build office complexes in Murray. Rumor has it they're going to start building near the mouth of the canyon. In other cities, this might be cause for alarm—business complex at the opening of this sensitive environmental point, this canyon where water for half of the city flows out, where half of the tourists drive up to ski, where half of the forest, Ferguson's canyon, is designated "wilderness." Not in Utah. Business is best. Your dad hopes to cover all the ceilings across the whole Salt Lake Valley with tile. Your dad doesn't think about the water. He doesn't think about the place where you and your girlfriend hike, taking a blanket and a water bottle, where you are the one who lets your naked ass bear the cold of the forest floor. She moves on top of you so determinedly, you feel like a girl. Now that, your dad would mind.

But you're moving by halves already. Half a foot in their bedroom, half still in the hallway. It's not that you're unsure. You just don't want it to go wrong. If someone walks by. If the gun is not under the bed in its shoebox. If the gun is not loaded. There is an image in your head. You walk into the room. You bend your knees, not dramatically, as if in prayer, you don't have any questions, just so you can drop to all fours. You lift the dust ruffle. You reach your hand toward the Nike box. You pull it toward you. If you hit your head, the image will be ruined. The spell will be broken and maybe this you will not be the separate you that does what the mother-bound-you can only imagine. If you pull the box toward you and the gun tumbles out, the image will be ruined. If you stand and have to pull your pants up because you forgot your belt, again, the image will be ruined. You are in a tunnel. If anything interrupts that tunnel, the image will be ruined. The tunnel might open. You might be able to see differently. You might be able to think about things in a new light. But you don't bump your head. Your pants stay up just fine.

Your girlfriend didn't choose this. Her name is Paige. Your mother didn't choose this. Her name is Teresa. Your sister Mindy didn't choose this and the act of naming them suggests they are distinct from you. But you know they each died that day. It's not the same as dying entirely. The metaphor breaks down just like free will breaks. Free will might be a lie. Family bonds are like chains of DNA. They are heavy. They are not free. You take them with you wherever you go. They reach deep into your mother's DNA. You are dragging your mother up the canyon with you but you don't know this. *Microchimerism* isn't a word you know. You can't imagine all the beasts your mother has living inside her: lion, snake, goat, taco. You can't tell anyone what it feels like. You have no metaphors. Your car is not a metaphor for American anything. Your gun is not a metaphor for anything but free will, which we have already established is a lie.

Garrett wore a sweater vest. A white shirt. His curly hair. The only tunnel he was crawling out of was the tunnel of the barrel. His lips opened like a kiss. His lips opened like when he was one and his mom fed him sweet potatoes, like when he was two his mouth shaped into an "o" for mom, when he was three and he fell off his bike, his teeth hitting concrete harder than this barrel, when he was four and his little sister fit her whole fist inside his mouth, when he was five and he bit the kid in kindergarten, when he was six and he fit seven marshmallows therein, when he was seven and he won the rope-tying contest by pulling the slack end with his teeth, when he was eight, at the beach, cleaning shells off with his tongue, when he was nine, Jeff punched him in the mouth, when at ten, he punched Kyle in the mouth for calling him a girl, when at eleven sang all the Beatles' *White Album* while he picked away at his guitar, at twelve, first drag of a cigarette, he loved the way it pulled air down inside him, made visible what once was in, at thirteen, first kiss, my sister Paige, how he loved her lips. Her lips were bows. His were an arrow. He did not want to suck her in. But in she went.

At my mom's kitchen table, into Paige's mouth, no tacos go. She goes outside to smoke a cigarette. She's thirteen but no one stops her. My mom stands in front of the stove, turning bits of cow upside down. She feels sorry for the cow but she feels sorry for everyone, for Paige. For Garret's mother. His sister. Even his father. If you can't distinguish between your pities, well, you might as well eat the meat.

She cuts more onion. Why not? She doesn't put it in the tacos. She serves it on the side. It should be your choice to burn your mouth, to ruin your breath, to inhale the sour air but it's important that Paige eat something. As she picks up the taco shell and puts it onto the plate, my mom's alleles migrate onto the taco shells. Paige gives in, takes a bite of taco, thereby swallowing her cells of my mom, of the taco, reminding her cells it's her mother's cells that made her. Microchimera—they are two bodies in one. It's one thing to kill yourself, another to kill your mother. My mom is Paige, Paige, my mom. Tied together by tacos and DNA, neither can escape the other but then again, neither drives the car up the canyon alone.

You Never Know Just How You Look in Other People's Eyes

THERE ARE SEVERAL ways to get to Siena, Italy. For Erik and me, to get out of Lecce, a town notched in the heel of the boot of Italy, and into Siena, where, if these boots had laces, you would tie the knot, we had to take a car, then a train, then a taxi, then a plane, and then another train, and then walk straight uphill to the medieval city that is like Florence if Florence had not become heart-of-the-Renaissance-Florence. We took our first train from Lecce, through Brindisi, to Bari.

We are competent train-takers. We take the subway when we're in New York. We know you can sit forward or backward. We don't get motion sickness. We can walk up and down the aisle. We know it is not like a car or a plane, but, admittedly, even though the Burlington Northern and Amtrak make us wait at the crossing in our Flagstaff hometown twice a day, we know trains as occasions, not everyday transportations.

The train from Lecce into Bari was late. We got into the cab to head to the airport. I told the driver, "We are late," in whatever pretend Italian I knew then and have since forgotten. We were blond and carrying rolly suitcases. In Lecce, no one pretended to know English like I pretended to know Italian. But in Bari, the cab driver pretended to understand. Maybe I showed him the plane ticket. It was 11:40. Our flight left at 12:15. The train station is nowhere near the airport. I know he understood me because he spoke the international language of late-for-the-airport. He drove on the sidewalk. He took a left in a lane marked "right turns only." His tires scraped curb. He stepped on the accelerator to speed around a bus to turn in front of it, bus honking, brakes squealing.

Now might have been a good time to tell the cab driver I was pregnant. Being pregnant shifts your perspective. Suddenly, your life, as protector of fetus, becomes much more precious, even if it's a pregnancy you're ambivalent about—it's hard to be pregnant in wine country. Unlike normal times, making the plane on time seemed less important than surviving the cab ride. But I did not know the word for *pregnant* and, although my perspective had shifted slightly, I didn't want to bug the driver who was concentrating very hard to make a third lane for the taxicab where two lanes only existed.

•

We thought we missed our flight. But then we read the arrivals and departures wrong. We had time to make it to the gate where we had prepaid for assigned seats. In Europe, people who fly Ryan Air rush like Barian cab drivers across the tarmac, suit coats flying, hand holding hat, to get their seats. Erik and I fly in America where our seats are assigned, and we board as soon as possible because sitting in a too-small seat ensures on-time departure. In Bari, I walked to my seat like a pretend-calm person even though I did not understand why there were two staircases leading up to one airplane. The flight attendants had opened the back door of the plane to let us board. I did not know planes had back doors although I did know, thanks to my desperate attempt to keep the plane from crashing by listening attentively to the safety speech at the beginning of every flight that "the nearest exit may be behind you." That an exit can also be an entrance is a very European idea.

After that, easy peasy, as Max, who was then only a two-month-old fetus, would say as a five-year-old now. He lived. We lived. The flight. The cab ride. I did not know how dangerous knowing only iPod Italian might be. When we arrived in Siena, our host spoke English. The knot that had been in my stomach, squishing fetus Max, unwound. I would give anything for a host for forever, someone to take me to a foreign country, find the airport on time, speak Italian to the taxi driver, explain why Americans don't use two staircases to board the airplane from the front and the back.

•

It's impossible to know how high the seas will rise. Maybe they won't rise much at all. Maybe we'll tuck the carbon back underground somehow. But some maps predict a bleaker future. In *Grist Magazine,* Greg Hansom describes pictures of sunken cities, newly named reliefs like Sea of San Diego and Archipelago of Bainbridge. San Joaquin Peninsula is all that's left of Orange County. The coast we know now probably won't disappear in our lifetime but in the next or the next or maybe sooner if the coal keeps burning and the cars keep driving.

I say "the coal" as if I am not sitting in a house, typing on a coal-burning laptop as the heater kicks on and pours naturally gassed heat upon me. As if "the cars" means I won't drive my Honda CRV to pick up my kids from school. Another article in the same magazine claimed that it's liberals as much as Republicans who are the problem. We blame them for denying what we believe is there. But somebody else's denial is necessary for us to believe that we liberals are doing the right thing, which is a whole lot of nothing. Nobody wants to be blamed for the Santa Monica pier falling into the ocean, but no one also wants to turn the heat down to fifty-five degrees in the winter or the air-conditioning to eighty in the summer. Heck, I have a dream to drive Route 66 all the way from Santa Monica to Chicago, Illinois. I wish I'd driven my car to Italy. Cars are a host country, like a planet. Every gum wrapper and seat print is our own. Our dreams are our cars. They take us out of here without it having to feel the pain of the unfamiliar. But, as the seas rise, perhaps we should get familiar with the boat.

•

In Siena, the Palio happens twice a summer. Around the Piazza del Campo, horses race. Men, called Camparsa, in medieval outfits parade flags from their district through the streets toward the piazza. The streets, lined with nearly black cobblestones, are bordered by tall, connected houses from the 1300s, red flags, black stone, a Duoma, the Siena Cathedral.

The food in Siena was not the food of Puglia, which was dominated by broccoli rabe and orchiette, a whole-grain pasta. Siena had pizza. Pasta ragout. Risotto with truffles. It had gelato. It had the food of the American Italian Vacation and it had wine I couldn't drink. Like a proper tourist, I bought a scarf for ten euros. Like a tourist full of regrets, I should have bought a hundred. We stayed in a hotel that overlooked a garden. The piazza formed a circle where, during the parade, the horses rode around and the centuries swirled around and everything was stone, which is how you make a city last—make it stone, make it circular to keep the art inside and the pillagers out. You keep the Renaissance at bay by keeping Florence down the street. You keep nature managed by turning it into a vineyard called Tuscany. Italy is a land of circles made by square painting frames and plots of grape and tomato vines. In Siena, you can't see far because of the tall houses and the circling streets. It is easy to get lost although most of the time, the Duomo is in sight but the middle of the Duomo too is round and so if you end up on the wrong side of it, you might never know.

And I didn't know, when we were on our way back to Lecce, to return to Zoë, the already-born kid, who was being watched by her attentive but window-opening grandparents who didn't know about the Vape that you plug into the wall and emits some mosquito death vapor—and who could know of them? They, like we, are from the United States where we have deet but no Vapes and so invited a thousand or so mosquitoes into their cottage to feast upon our already barely alive daughter. She wasn't really barely alive, but she had the Bad Lungs and the RSV and the inhaler broke the minute we plugged it into the wrong wall adapter. We adapt less well to the foreign world. We have made mistakes. We repeat them. Mosquitoes can sting more than once.

•

The mosquitoes are getting worse. The Natural Resources Defense Council reports that mosquito-borne diseases are already spreading more rapidly. In the regular times, like the eighties, at 7,000-feet elevation, people are safe from mosquitoes carrying Dengue fever. Dengue-fever-carrying mosquitoes once didn't travel higher than 3,200 feet. But it's getting warm up here. Mosquitoes don't suffer from altitude sickness, just the cold. Which it is not. Not even in December. *Scientific American,* in a September 27, 2013, article notes that incidences of Chikungunya, a disease carried by the Tiger mosquito, which causes high fevers and rashes, is on the rise in Western Europe. *Zanzara,* Italian for "mosquito," was a word we all knew when we left Italy. *Chikungunya* is a word we do not know but maybe experienced that long night in Lecce when Zoë couldn't sleep.

•

Erik and I wouldn't be late for the plane this time. We made it to the Siena train station early. I read the schedule. Or, I tried to read the schedule. Pisa CSE, Pisa Centrale. Trenitalia. One stop in Empoli. Isn't there a nonstop?

Erik and I peered through the glass, the train schedule old and blurry. Our phones didn't work then, in Italy. The computer, as the nebulizer adapter died when we plugged it in, died on the plane in from Rome. If it were 1960 and Erik and I were on the platform, perhaps then things would have made more sense. We would have studied the book harder, not being so lulled into submission by easy info access on our smartish phones. We would have taken trains more often, understanding that Centrale and One Stop were the same idea. Perhaps, in the 1960s, when the mosquitoes were happy at 3,200 feet and San Diego was confident of its shores, we would have been more versed in chivalry. Perhaps it would have been a time when Erik understood One Stop and Centrale to be the same destination, I would have trusted him. Perhaps if all our verses had been written in 1960s chivalry, he would have waited for me while I was in the bathroom instead of getting on the train without me. Perhaps I would have trusted him and his new British friends as they all waved to me to get on the damn train. Perhaps my 1960-self would have been more credulous. But Erik made new British friends and boarded a train without me. If only we could go back in time and then, again, in time, because it keeps coming, time, perhaps I would have jumped on that train, full of belief and trust in trains I did not know and toward the only Pisa that could have been waiting for me.

•

We use the word *believe* when we talk about climate change. Fox News doesn't believe it. Members of the National Resources Defense Council do believe it. Readers of *Scientific American* mostly believe it. *Belief* is the word you use when you cannot be sure about the future. And the scientists aren't sure how high the mosquitoes will fly. They aren't sure how high the oceans will rise. Belief, though, whether you do it or not, only worries about the future. When you believe in God, you pray to him to make good things happen. When you believe in climate change, you believe that maybe good things don't. One of my mentors believes science will save us—big carbon scrubbers in the sky. How is hope different than belief?

•

Instead, I did not get on the train. Erik did not get off the train. I stood on the platform as the train pulled away. Erik stared at me through the train window. *Incredulity* is another word for stubborn. I sat down on the concrete platform, underneath the schedule that predicted when Erik would come back. I'd figured out the train schedule by then but not my husband. I figured out that he might have been right about all trains leading to Pisa but that didn't necessarily make me wrong. I waited as one train came back. Two trains. Three trains. He was not on any of them. I figured out that maybe sometimes it's important to just go with the person you are with rather than let your butt get cold on the concrete platform of the Tranitalia Empoli station. *Longing* is another word for not knowing what to do next.

•

If I had a house on the Olympic Peninsula, built fifty feet behind the neighbor's property, which reaches out to the shore of the Puget Sound, how long would I have to wait until I could claim millionaire status for my now-oceanfront property? When the water swallowed the neighbor's strangely suburban lawn? When the water lapped at my neighbor's duck-dotted welcome mat? When the country duck hanging as a welcome sign is as wet as the doormat? When the roof of my neighbor's house makes a nice fishing dock? You are silly to think oceanfront property will mean anything when you have to stay indoors to keep the mosquitoes from injecting their malarial parasite near the now-warm waters of the Puget Sound.

•

Eventually, I got on a train to Pisa. Eventually, Erik came back. Our trains must have passed each other. When I got to Pisa, he wasn't there. I went back to Empoli. He wasn't there either. O'Henry, the Italian version.

•

The seas have risen far enough to turn Queen Anne into an island at least once before, Jurassicly. They can do it again. Of course, the pretend house I built on the Sound will be under water by then, but, then, the sea doesn't mind the taste of human constructs.

•

Finally, our flight back to Bari, back to our mosquito-ridden daughter, back to our flight back to Rome that would get us out of Italy nearly departing, I rode the train back to Pisa. I had the plane tickets. He had to be there. And he was. He stood at the edge of the platform. If this had been a movie, I would have run to him. He would have run to me. Open arms.

•

I am a good swimmer. If not a good reader of schedules or husbands. I am ready for you, warm waters of the Puget Sound. I know it would be too much to ask for you, dear ocean, to leave me any oysters.

•

But this is not a movie. His arms are folded. Crossed. I'm so happy to see him. My heart thrills. I am home. But still. I cannot believe that he left me behind.

He says, "I cannot believe you."

Which I take to mean, I cannot believe in you.

But I say, "You can't believe me? I can't believe you!"

I touch my arms. My hair. I am here.

"You're the one that left me," I say.

"You never trust me," he says.

"I'm the one who speaks Italian," I say.

"You cannot read a schedule," he says.

"I came to you. Twice." I say.

"I went back for you," he says.

We each folded our arms because no one wants to believe they misunderstood a schedule, a wave, a bathroom break, a pregnancy, a train trip to somewhere so beautiful so badly. If this were an O'Henry story, this would have been a love story. But this is not O'Henry. Erik was raised by a single mom who did everything by herself—made peanut butter and jellies, went to work, paid the mortgage, bought a car, hiked in the desert, took the kids to the dentist, mopped the floors. He doesn't believe that just because I had to pee, just because I was pregnant, just because I wanted to be convinced by the signage, that I shouldn't have just gotten it together, got on the next train, and met him in Pisa. A feminist is the guy who figures his wife will figure it out. His mom could have done it herself. And, on my side, I don't believe I should have just trusted him, just gotten on the train just because he said so, without even talking to me. I'm a feminist who doesn't believe anybody should tell me what to do, even if that means I wait on the platform for two hours to be rescued by some chivalrous husband who does not believe in chivalry. Two stubborn faces staring through the window. There's no way to know how to go back. I sing a version of the "Charlie on the MTA" song, "Did he ever return, no he never returned / And his fate is still unlearned / He may ride forever 'neath the streets of Pisa / He's the man who never returned."

Erik doesn't laugh. And then he does.

•

You can know a few things. You can know this: No one is going to rescue us. We are going to miss our flight from Pisa to Bari. We are going to miss seeing our kid, with her mosquito bites, harboring a virus we cannot pronounce. We are going to spend the rest of our lives passing our traveling companions on the train from Pisa to Empoli, from Empoli to Pisa. But we won't know what it feels like until we open the windows and actually touch the water of the Puget Sounds. Until then, all we will see is our warped faces, reflected back at us. Duck decorations can't swim. I should have believed Erik instead of staying put and hoping he'd come back to save me.

They say with time, you look back and laugh. For Erik, that's not so long. For the island of San Diego, it's too soon to know.

Thumbs

THE FIRST THING you should know about being an artist is that there's a chance you will kill yourself, either deliberately, with a gun, or pretend-accidentally, with pills and alcohol. My whole life is a list of artists whom I loved, suiciding: Sylvia Plath and Anne Sexton. Vincent van Gogh and Mark Rothko. Virginia Woolf and Kurt Cobain. Jim Morrison and Ernest Hemingway. Jimi Hendrix and John Berryman. David Foster Wallace and Janis Joplin. On the Wiki, there's a great list of suicides, no way comprehensive, dominated by people with great access to phenobarbital and/or shotguns.

Does suicide come from the same place as art? As with art, with suicide, there is a great ability to dissociate from the self. If you can see the self acting as if from above, like watching yourself in a movie, scripting your movie, making your hair cover your brow just right, making your voice shrill or sultry depending on the adjectives at hand, doesn't it follow that you would like to be the director of your final scene, the author of your final words, the couplet of your own sonnet?

In 1948, Sir Fred Hoyle said, "Once a photograph of the Earth, taken from the outside, is available, a new idea as powerful as any in history will be let loose." The first astronaut to rise above the whole planet Earth as one coherent ball, to look back upon it to say, "That is us." All of us. He will for the first time see how fragile we are. And also how "of-one" we are. How small and how big. The whole of humanity in his lens. Is Earth a reflection of himself? Can he imagine each of the seven billion people? The astronaut will try to hold all the humanity in one hand, to capture it perfectly and steadily with his Nikon. Earth will seem so permanent to him. So perfect. A marble to cup in his hand. But this marble is not inviolate. The pictures of Earth taken in 1969 will not be the same as the pictures taken in 2014. You can see the Kennecott Copper Mine's swath cut into space. You can see brown where the once green Amazon rainforest used to be. Where once were sheets of ice, now blues of sea. He should have held that marble more tightly. Blew some cooling breath upon it like a wish.

That ability to dissociate—to look from above. You think it would make us save ourselves, seeing the planet from afar, feeling like with one hand, maybe you could fix it. Maybe you could see yourself as part of it. But like the art of the suicides, maybe the picture postcard was just that. Some way to abstract the self from the self—distant, literally, a two-dimensional postcard. A memory trapped by a stamp. Something made, distant, other. Although for the first time, we could see the whole of us, now we felt in control of it. We could mold it like clay, sculpt it like marble, mix the colors like paint. Once you can see yourself as separate from yourself, you want to meddle with it. Even if it means you might kill it. Once you see yourself from beyond yourself, you are your own god. Choose the ending, artist. Choose the ending, astronaut.

Not all artists kill themselves. Some live for a long time. J. D. Salinger and Mick Jagger. Cher and David Hockney. Eudora Welty and Paul McCartney. Presumably, they saw themselves apart from themselves and yet did not feel the need to sound the final chord. Did not want to experiment on the self as apart from the self. Maybe they could see the separation, the image of themselves and still feel part of themselves. Maybe the smell of their own body, their hair, their armpits, kept them tied to themselves the way the astronaut is tied to his spaceship, which is tied, via radio transmission, back to Earth. Maybe they write and sing and paint strings of lists for themselves to keep them tied to themselves. Maybe everything they see becomes part of them—there is no opportunity for abstraction. I am he as you are he as you are me. I am the eggman. Of eggs and men. But if it's an artist's job to paint distinctions, it can be difficult to see the egg in the mirror.

I don't think it counts quite as empathy, being able to imagine David Foster Wallace's suicide. I read about it like everyone else, in *Rolling Stone* magazine. I told the students in my undergraduate nonfiction class that he had died. They were sad. They didn't know who he was but they empathized with me, which is more than I successfully did with Wallace. I pictured myself as Wallace. I tried to buck up even though I was failing. My (Wallace's) parents called me. I called them back. I told them I was looking forward to Christmas. My girlfriend brought me a philodendron. She knew how I hated flowers, already dead sitting on the table, in a vase made out of already dead sand. I told her I would water it. I promised I would find a good place in the sun but philodendrons are easy to trick. I put it in a shadowy corner. I didn't water it for weeks. Still it grew. At night, after we went to bed, I told her, I am not a philodendron. Maybe a daisy. A Gerber daisy. But what girlfriend would take warning from this statement?

I see myself (my Wallace self) walking up the stairs. The polished banister. I would remember this banister forever, the way it felt smooth against my hand as a dolphin. I would remember the dolphin forever. Each step up the stairwell I would remember. I, Wallace, will remember forever, forever.

This is the first time I ever felt like I would remember everything. I can see myself, my foot in my tennis shoes, the shoes I actually played my last game of tennis in that I knew then would be my last game of tennis because I am a Gerber daisy not a philodendron. Each step is less painful than the previous. I am swimming up those stairs. Everything is smooth sailing forever more. Every step is a step forward and up to a forever that will last until I make the noose. Even the noose was beautiful. Life goes full circle. I saw the future and it was as long as a rope. I never told anyone how much I loved the future. As long as I knew what was coming, nothing could stop me. I could see myself, swinging into the future.

Shuttle and International Space Station astronaut Ron Garan said, "When we look down at the earth from space, we see this amazing, indescribably beautiful planet. It looks like a living, breathing organism. But it also, at the same time, looks extremely fragile." What does fragility look like? Fear, I suppose. Breathe carefully. Take the right steps. Fragile is smooth. You think of bulls in a China shop. Humans are all bulls. Even ballerinas break their toes. Fragile is a super kind of desperation, when you can only see from a super position. Supra. Inside the thing, the thing looks tough. I stomp on the ground, the ground pounds back. I breathe out on a cold, cold day, the cold takes my vapor to freeze. I dig a hole in the sand, the ocean sweeps it flat again. The earth seems to push back. The humans seem to push back. On a one-to-one basis, feet on the ground, we both seem tough. But then we climb the stairs. Then we make a circle out of a rope. Then we write a sentence with an "I" in it and forget a direct object. Then we venture out to space. With each inch away from the ground, the porcelain begins to crack.

"Anybody else who's ever gone to space says the same thing because," as Ron Garan also said, "it really is striking and it's really sobering to see this paper-thin layer and to realize that that little paper-thin layer is all that protects every living thing on Earth from death, basically. From the harshness of space." Paper-thin, the atmosphere. Crack it. Crack the porcelain, a crack in the continent, a crack between self and self.

I remember when the band Hole played Reed College. I don't remember Nirvana playing Reed but maybe that's because they were not NoMeansNo, the only band I cared to see, besides Slack and Lovebutt. My difficulty to predict what is art and what is fame explains a lot about my own ability to see myself, imagining the phone call that says, "You won," and parsing the reality of the form rejection letter. Kurt Cobain knew fame, I think, but fame on the inside never looks like fame on the outside. On the inside, you still have to find your phone. Your kid, Frances, has toys. You have to look for them. You're the parent. Your girlfriend, Courtney Love, needs you to adjust her shirt. It's a complicated one, the kind where you sometimes put the armholes through the head holes. You think that would make you live forever, the image of Courtney, with her head where her armpit should be. You, Cobain, are still laughing, even in your greenhouse, with the memory of it. You can see Courtney with Frances Bean on her hip singing, "Take everything. Take everything. I want you to." You can see her covering Fleetwood Mac's *Gold Dust Woman.* Each song is about the future. You see yourself taking permission from Stevie Nicks. Stevie dances around you like the Gerber daisies in the greenhouse. She, too, tells you to "take your silver spoon. Dig your grave." You didn't really have a silver spoon but you had a gold record so that has to count. All you ever wanted was respect from the people who sang as beautifully as you. If they could feel the gun in their hand, they could feel the magnet. They wouldn't blame you. They would understand that the future is always the future. Metal has its own pull. It leads you away from yourself.

From satellite images, an astronaut sees Super Typhoon Haiyan swirl toward the Philippines. Winds of 200 miles per hour hurtle toward the tiny islands. If an astronaut saw the typhoon from outer space, he would push his finger forward toward Earth—reach out to help. He would, like a daughter helping her mother tape Christmas packages, put his finger right there. He would press lightly against the storm, with just enough pressure to make it stop. He would, if he could, dispel, like a God, the winds and water. But his arm is not long enough. His finger not really the size it appears. Parallax confuses. The astronauts, all eight of them, in the International Space Station, sit in their ship and watch the planet swirl, melt, burn, sink, strip. They put their fingers to their lips. They ask the planet to settle down. Quiet itself. But what can the planet hear? The thin veil has no grip for ears.

Dickinson's poem "My Life It Stood a Loaded Gun" is the song I sing to myself at night. You can sing all of Dickinson's poems as hymns. You can also sing them to the tune of "Yellow Rose of Texas," which I do, but by the time I get to:

> To foe of His—I'm deadly foe—
> None stir the second time—
> On whom I lay a Yellow Eye—
> Or an emphatic Thumb—

I have stopped humming. I hear the actual Emily speaking to the mountains in the voice of a gun. She is yelling to the ducks, who she, acting as gun, shot, and to the deer, who she wounded. She's telling them to listen to her and to be silenced by her and this is Dickinson's best gift. To be herself and not herself at the same time. The poem ends,

> Though I than He—may longer live
> He longer must—than I—
> For I have but the power to kill,
> Without—the power to die—

This gun carrier—God, willing her to live, animates Emily-the-gun like a Pinocchio. Emily, the powerful shooter who cannot shoot herself. Emily, who may not be Emily at all. She's a gun. She's an eye. She's a thumb. She's part and parcel. Separate. Giving up free will is deadly to others but not to the self. Giving up free will might be the thing that saves you. The Master can still shoot the gun. The power is there, in his finger. You gun, extend him. You gun, carry on. He must live longer than I, dear God, or I will live forever. In the equivocation—"though I than He may longer live, He longer must than I," the "may" hangs upon the "He." The "He" can't live forever. The "He" will die; the gun will live. The loaded gun eternity. The loaded gun is as god as the god does live. An inanimate, animated God. And if he's not a God? Just a guy out on a walk, finding a gun, becoming a hunter? Then who lives so long? And even with the full power of the gun, forever is a very long time, especially if the "Yellow Rose of Texas" is stuck in your head and no thumb parallactic enough to blot out the sun or no way to stop the specter of God, your master, coming into your house (did you remember to sweep?), picking you up. Now you are the guard, one consonant heavier than God. It's a heavy life, protecting your God's interminable head, which you must do, without will, but alive and a part of the world, with thumb, doe, and eider-down.

The phrase "Physician, heal thyself" is from the New Testament, Book of Luke. As in the Dickinson poem, who is speaking to whom? The subject becomes its own direct object. There's separation between the third person—a schizoid bit of advice-giving. The distance from speaker to self, self to speaker conveys a distance. Who is talking? I'm always mumbling to myself in the grocery store, extra firm tofu? Filet or ribeye? I really should give up meat. The cows. They step on salmon. They trample the desert. They add methane and carbon dioxide and suffering. These decisions make me desperate. Maybe I can compromise. Are tofu and steak a good pair? What kind of sauce? Didn't I just see the tarragon? Béarnaise is all I ever really wanted. It's crazy to talk to the self but at the grocery store, who else are you going to talk to? The vegetables? That's crazy.

Nearly four hundred physicians kill themselves a year. Some because they now have diseases they've tried to cure in others. They know that the cure is worse than the disease. Some because they have good access to phenobarbital. Some because they, like all of us, are depressed. Some because med school is hard. All of them do it because as constant lookers at the body, and therefore death, and therefore, their own death, they see themselves as apart from themselves, and simultaneously as themselves. They point to their shoulders, their heads, their hips. That is they, they say. Who ever wanted to be a they? Who wanted to see themselves as a separate planet? Not even a vegetarian. Not even a vegetable.

Writers look at their own hands. They watch themselves type. The fingers curl around a pencil. An age spot between the thumb and forefinger in the webbing of the hand. Rub the dry skin from the knuckle. Peel the fingernail. It barely hurts. Fingernails are as separate from the writer as their words. Hunter S. Thompson wrote a suicide note that appears to be talking as much to himself as anyone else.

No More Games. No More Bombs. No More Walking. No More Fun. No More Swimming. 67. That is 17 years past 50. 17 More than I needed or wanted. Boring. I am always bitchy. No Fun—for anybody. You are getting Greedy. Act your old age. Relax—This won't hurt.

You have to talk yourself into suicide. It takes external means. Something has to come between you and yourself—most likely a gun but sometimes pills. Elliot Smith stabbed himself in the stomach, hari kari. Wallace's rope. The implement is between you and yourself. You use it to come between you and yourself. Come together, he who wants to live. Stay apart, he who wants to die. You are always bitchy. You aren't as fun as you used to be. You and I cannot live together. I will take the pain away. The gun is the only one left talking. Ask Emily Dickinson.

Unlike Dickinson's one emphatic thumb that can erase only one gun-sight object at a time, from space, you can obliterate Earth with one thumb in front of one eye. All seven billion people gone with one parallactic gesture. All the frogs. All the movies. All the bears. All the 7–11s. The remaining ten tigers. All the hot dogs. Both of the wolves. Even Iceland. Move your thumb away and Earth and its frogs and the now-only-one wolf come back. Magicky, Magic, Zoë would have said when she was three. The whole planet returned to you through the movement of a finger. Magic. Is that powerlessness or power? Your fingers. They move. Intransitive verb. No need of a direct object, the subject is everything. They, the humans, the wolves, the Zoës, move stuff. Transitive verb. Transfer the power from the thumb to the wolf. Unlock the trap. Humans. Do something. Let the animal lick his own wounds.

Here's what the suicidal astronaut should do. Go back to Earth. I know it looks bad from up there from above, you can locate the trouble—like a writer in revising mode, you can see what's wrong with the sentences. The white tops of the blue planet are smaller. You can choose to sit in front of the control panels, analyzing the distance of star and planet to contemplate the vast unknowns. You can measure the world against your finger. But maybe you can turn that ship around. Full speed ahead. You might have to quit eating meat. You might have to give up your car. You might need to learn to love direct objects. You might have to chain yourself to the redwood tree or the last undammed river or the locked gates of the oil refinery. To get back to you, you're going to have to put your feet on the ground. Do not let the noose lift you off the floor. You might have to remember verbs are your best friends. Do keep walking. Walk not into the river Thames. Walk not into the oven. Walk on regular, non-sinkholing ground. Land your ship on the oil-drilling platform in the middle of the gulf. Obscure the platform with your space station. Down on Earth, the refinery and your craft are about the same size. Find that oilman. Measure your thumb against his. Yours is not bigger. Nor is his. Thumb to thumb, you can put some ice back on that shelf. The you and he. You share some DNA. You share some of the particles of the big bang. You share the ground you're standing on just like the lilac bush and the bats and the oil, the spaceship, the refinery, and the polar bear. It's nice to have thumbs, but it's not everything. Everything is a verb and we nouns swing around like electrons around a nucleus. Give him a postcard of Earth. Hang on. See yourself in the mirror that is the mycelium under the forest dirt. In the plankton in the ocean. Borges wrote,

> I wrote a story once about a man who began a very large picture, and therein was a kind of map—for example, hills, horses, streams, fishes, and woods and towers and men and all sorts of things. When the day of his death came, he found he had been making a picture of himself. That is the case with most writers.

To heal the suicide, you have to stop speaking to yourself in the third person. Speak in the second person. The second person point of view will take care of you: Come here. Bring yourself to me. I will cradle you like a baby. I love you so much, you say to me. You have been too set upon swimming. You're a protester, I know. You're against the melting planet. You're against the bombs. You are against life as it so dumb. You say, life is boring. Life, friends, is boring, said the also-suicide John Berryman. But your thumb isn't boring. The writer keeps looking at his own hands but they are still your hands, even if you use them to blot out the sun. They keep typing as if without you. The split is inherent. You were born already reading what you once wrote. It's hard to reconcile the self with the self as you see yourself inky against the white paper. How does the you get back to the you? Move the thumb. Put it to work. Put the gun down, release the thumb. You need it for the space bar. You need it for perspective. You need it to play thumb war with the oilman who matches you pound by pound, inch by earthly measured inch. You need to be both you and your someone else at once.

To help those with phantom limb syndrome, therapists hold a mirror facing the remaining limb. The patient moves their leg or their arm and their symptoms decrease. The pain lessens. The need for opioids diminishes. Even the sense that the missing leg is there begins to go away.

Look for the total. All joy now. Tether. Foot. Space station. Face. Artists hold up a mirror to Earth. There it is they say. What seemed unseeable is now seen. Now, artist. Try to get yourself into the mirror. Hold it at a kind of angle, so you include a picture of an oil rig, a tree, your spaceship, your typewriter, a train, and a side of your face. There you go! You are simultaneously marble and holder of the marble. Patient and therapist. Image maker and image taker. You wrote your memoir while you showed the world the world. Keep your face tethered to that mirror. Who is that mirror? It is you. All joy now. Save the planet by putting a blueberry in your mirror. And every time you save the planet, you save yourself. You are you, planet. Tug the tether. Come back here.

"Are We On Fire" May Have Been an Indigo Girls Song

WHEN I WAKE up in the morning, I can smell smoke but I can always smell smoke. So many smokes: The smoke from the slash pile that you can smell before you see while driving on Highway 6 on the way from Portland to Tillamook. The smoke from the Purina Factory due east of town that you can never see but know horses are being made into dog food today. The smoke from the cigarette that makes a slash pile of your lungs. The smoke from the campfire, which somehow smells different than the smoke from the forest fire. The campfire smells cold and sharp and the forest fire smells hot and wide. The smoke from toast, whose burn smell lasts for longer than a cigarette, almost as long as a forest. The smoke from the forest, whose mychorrizal systems begin to force its mushrooms into the bark of a 300-year-old tree that fell of its own accord, which now begins to decay. A slow burn. The smoke this morning is forest. Prescribed burn. But in case it isn't a prescribed burn, then what? A real fire, nearby. Will the evacuators begin calling? Who are the evacuators? Do they know I only have a cell, not a home, phone? Will they knock? The picture of someone at my front door makes me look at myself. I'm not wearing a bra. I look around the house. The butter scraped against its wrapper. The bowls on the floor for the dog to lick clean. The box of cereal, the cherries, the four coffee cups? Why do I have four cups? I am only one. I see my kitchen as the would-be evacuators see me. I see myself cleaning up hurriedly so the evacuators, who are not actually on their way, don't see the mess I've left for the fire that will devour my house.

The video in my head of my morning doesn't stop playing. I watch myself walking back and forth between kitchen and back door. I stop. Check email. Bend over to pick a Lego off the floor. I watch myself do dishes while I thought, so, this is what I do now? Dishes and Legos? I put a load of laundry in the wash. Think how deeply I will resent those pants once they are dry and in need of folding. The silence in the rest of the house. There was no email. No IM. No Facebook. No phone calls. No texts. The sound of the keyboard is zero. I haven't heard from you or you or you for a long time. But then Erik called. The tether jerked. The mirror tilted wide to accommodate another face. Yes. We should either have pizza or go to dinner and suddenly I am no longer watching the top of my head while looking at my computer. I'm just looking at my computer, typing "Pizza sounds great" to Erik.

Erik isn't a poet. He doesn't send me postcards from his office to my office testifying his love. He doesn't bring me pledges of his love in the form of found sketches or wildflowers. He doesn't paint pictures of me standing next to trees in the nude. But he does sing. His best song is "My wife hates America," which goes something like, "My wife hates America. She says no sparklers. No mustard on her hot dog. No marching bands for her." He has another song called "My wife likes chafing," which he sings because I bought Scott instead of Charmin. I think the Scott toilet paper produces less waste and uses less paper. Erik thinks it's rough and demeaning. He doesn't pack picnics or plan surprise parties. But he does watch with me and Zoë and

Max the trains as they plow through town. He stands closest, knowing how near you need to be to feel their power, to feel how far they could take you, to hear how the trains lost a battle but keep on driving. He also knows how far you should stand back. How powerful the engines are. How the engines can, like life, crush you. How you would never win a battle with a train. He holds his hands flat against Zoë and Max's chests, holding them close, holding them back.

Surfaces, Depths, and Plentitude

THE HUMPBACK WHALES travel over five thousand miles toward Antarctica's short summer in pursuit of a paradox: a tiny plentitude. They are hungry. They are huge. At fifty tons apiece, they consume more fish than all the teenagers in all of Utah must consume Big Macs. The food they're looking for are tiny fish called krill. Fortunately, even in these times of scarcity, there are still a lot of krill. Krill mass exceeds that of all human life. Even the mass of all the Big Macs.

Krill-collection is an orchestration worthy of the kind they teach at Hamburger University where would-be McDonald's employees learn to work as cogs in machines. Like the combined efforts of the drive-thru cashier, the guy on grill, the woman with hair net on the fry basket, the humpback whales use their individual jobs to create a perfect system, together. One whale exhales to create a net made of oxygen bubbles that startles the krill. Another whale sings loudly to create confusion. Another whale herds the krill upward. All the whales blow together to make something researchers call "bubble net." Together, they package the krill into tightly wrapped filets of fish, quarter-pounders, and french fries. Once the krill are at the surface, the whales open their mouths wide and eat them, like McDonald's employees eat french fries on their breaks—with no thought of the future. Worrying about cholesterol is for old people, not McDonald's employees or whales.

There are about 30,000 to 40,000 humpbacks left in the wild. Each one eats nearly 1.5 tons (3,500 pounds) of krill, meaning humpback whales alone consume nearly 105,000,000 pounds of krill per day. McDonald's sells 75 hamburgers every second, 6,800,000 hamburgers per day. Each hamburger patty is an eighth of a pound, meaning they sell 10 pounds of hamburger every second, which equals 864,000 pounds of hamburger a day, which comes from 5.5 million head of cattle a year, just in the United States, just from McDonald's. Recently, scientists have discovered that whales help sequester carbon in the atmosphere, which is handy, because beef, in the form of cows, adds to the gases that help cause global warming. Ironic that this almost-extinct but returning species is here to help us, and our hamburger-loving ways, out.

The whales, while coming back, aren't quite keeping up. Americans eat almost a ton a food per year, 185 pounds of meat. That's 600,000,000,000 pounds of food eaten by Americans. Whales may provide an antidote to beef eaten at McDonald's but they have a lot of recovering to do in their own numbers before they can compete with the appetite of hungry Americans.

•

Using online calculators, you can measure how much carbon you use to travel by car (1.2 kilograms per passenger mile), by plane (1.57 kilograms per passenger mile), or by train (0.18 kilogram per passenger mile). Please ignore the mixture of standard and metric measurements. To stop climate change, you're going to have to do some fancy math. For instance, even riding your bicycle produces some amount of carbon dioxide but then so does breathing, which is, I think the point of this story. There's only so much humans can do until they stop being humans.

Methane, after carbon dioxide, is the second most prevalent greenhouse gas. CH_4. That's carbon with four hydrogen atoms instead of carbon dioxide's two. You would think it would be twice as harmful as CO_2 but you would be wrong. In 2012, CH_4 accounted only for about 9% of all U.S. greenhouse gas emissions from human activities. Still, at the bottom of the carbon calculator it notes that quitting eating beef would make a more significant impact on reducing greenhouse gases than would buying a Prius because people like hamburgers. Some people even like McDonald's hamburgers. Not everyone likes a Prius but seventy-five people like a McDonald's hamburger every second. What if seventy-five people gave up a hamburger every day?

•

It is a massive amount of food, eaten by whales. Usually, this kind of consumption is frowned upon. Gluttonous whales. Fast Food Nation, deep-sea version. But consumption isn't always bad. Consumption is a kind of mirror. A sonar scan of the deep ocean shows an image of krill so wide and vast it looks like the visage of a whale. Shape and shadow make a flat mirror. The fry cook for lunch is a customer for dinner. He knows the value of Supersize. The cashier can see it in the jowls of his customer. The cashier scratches his own jowls, no receipt necessary. Do you have to probe the shadow any further or can you take it for granted that you can see yourself wherever you look? Hello, tree, your bark is as wrinkled as my forehead. Hello car, your dent is my pimple. Hello, Pendleton blanket. When I fold my hands together, I feel as woven into the world as you.

•

As a guest writer at a conference, I was invited to be on a panel about the ethics of nonfiction. I made my fellow panelists nervous by telling them I was going to read an essay from this book about suicide, creativity, and sustainability. The panel leader looked at me with tall, pointed eyebrows. Her head shook back and forth, no no no. There has been a strong urge in the writing community to distance itself from the idea that creativity breeds depression or that depression breeds creativity. The colleague to my right said, "It's been a myth for a long time that there is a coincidence of suicide among the writers." And, I said, "There has been a coincidence of suicide among the living. But writers kill themselves too." An article in the *LA Review of Books* was willing to broach the taboo subject. Nancy Spiller wrote in the December 30, 2014, edition: "Regardless of the scope of its success, demanding creative work done so fully and for so long by the likes of Plesko and Williams requires an extreme and extremely draining sensitivity on the artist's part. This hyperawareness of both the miraculous and miserable in human existence can prove life threatening."

I remember my mom asking my friend Jeff Chapman how he could be so happy and still be a writer.

I was like, "Mom, I'm happy,"

She looked at me with eyes caustic enough to strip the veneer off of my super-smiling surface face, then rolled them high up into her head, to write me and her look off.

Jeff said, "It is a myth that you have to be depressed to write."

But she wouldn't have any of it. "Depth comes from sadness. To have anything interesting to say about the human condition, you have to go very deep. And low is deep."

"Maybe deep is not bad," I said. "Maybe sadness is good, if you make something out of it." I'm a diplomat, at heart. But isn't it worse to be sad and to not write or paint or dance? At least the artist exhibits her work (you can't see much under water), like the whale who has to surface.

The looks of a mother are multiplex. The surface of an eye rolls and your stomach churns preternaturally, in the depths like some amoeba in the primordial forest. Our mothers shape us with approving eyes, exasperated eyes, eyebrows raised, like, "You know better," and eyes so soft you know she'll forgive you even if that lemonade spilled on the floor is sticky and ubiquitous. Theses looks you can take to the bank—turn into something in the mirror of your bathroom and the shape of your kids. Who is the krill? Who is the whale? Who takes the minimum wage she made from her job flipping tens at McDonald's and gives it to her daughter so she can buy more lemonade? My mother's eyes go down and then up again.

As I suspected, no one killed themselves during my panel talk. I talked about dissociation, the way writers sometimes look at themselves as apart from the world. They have to find ways to stitch themselves back in—by using research or focusing closely on the pattern of ferns spreading across their thumbs. During the panel, we discussed using other people's experiences in your nonfiction. Is it OK to use other people as fodder for essays? someone asked. I said, "People are a mirror to the world. They not only pull you to the surface. They fill you up."

The mirror the world provides to the self is filling. Robin Williams said, "When you have a great audience, you can just keep going and finding new things." Your audience reflects yourself back to you. You pull out of them a new joke and they laugh as though they've never heard it before. If everything is a vicious cycle maybe we should take the vicious out of it. Cycle is about as good as it gets. Me in you. You in me. Me in the reflection of the metal of a car. In an audience feeding you, the jokester, jokes. Even whales. Even good news in whale poop. You get more out of more.

•

There is good news in all this consumption, this seemingly untoward amount of krill being eaten by these come-back whales. What goes around, comes around. The whales, consuming so much krill, must then poop so much digested krill. The shadow of a plentitude. Krill. Whale. Poop. Through the eye of a sonar, all three are the same.

The whales force the krill to the surface. The whales follow them to the near surface of the ocean. Before the whales breathe, they open their mouths wide. More lawn mower than cow, these big mouths cast their shadow. And then the shadow is gone. Light is returned to the ocean, darkness to the belly of the whale. Whale and krill are a cinematic project. Light and dark. 105,000,000 pounds of krill gone in a flash. Who knew the ocean could bear such weight? Who knew the ocean could bear such loss?

But not all is lost. In fact, something is gained. The krill makes its way through the stomach of the beast. The whale strains the krill through his baleen like a sieve. The water slides out. The krill stay in. Whales are swallowers and they swallow this tiny fish whole. In their stomachs, the whale begins to digest 100 million pounds of flesh.

Digestion is a mirror and therefore, a compensation. Entropy and the second law of thermodynamics and ecclesiastics have all gathered together to say, what goes around, comes around. What was once krill, became food, which became poop, which became food for the plankton. What the whale poops, the plankton eat.

Plankton is not one. They are multiplex, as multiplex as locations of McDonald's. *Plankton* comes from the Greek word *planktos,* which means "wanderer or drifter." To be a plankton means you drift. You could be a jellyfish and be plankton. You could be an algae. You could be a single-cell organism. To plank means to not really have too many goals, as Erik might say about certain football teams that seem to want to win but never quite make it happen. You don't want to set your sights too high. Perhaps there is something useful to the drifting. The easiness of a life. Some of these plankton, the phytoplankton, photosynthesize as they drift. Instead of working the depths of the ocean for krill or working the grill, flipping 1/8-pound patties, singing songs about special sauce, lettuce, cheese, these plants work by floating. They make progress by drifting. Plants do seem to have all the luck; like house cats, they lounge around, absorb the sun. The soil, or in the phytoplankton's case, whale poop pushes its enzymes and minerals into the cells through chemistry. A stoichiometry that feeds the algae and cyanobacteria with not a single cell opening its mouth. Shel Silverstein's *Lazy Jane* would have made a good plankton. Lazy lazy lazy lazy lazy lazy Jane. She wants a drink of water so she waits and waits and waits for it to rain. Or in this case, for it to rain sunshine.

Whales rise to the near surface of the water to poop. As the poop begins to descend, the phytoplankton absorb it. The carbon in the poop is changed to oxygen, in the regular photosynthetic manner. As the number of whales continues to climb, the amount of krill they digest and exude, the more carbon the phytoplankton take in.

The phytoplankton eat the whale poop. Wait. Reword. They consume the nutrients because they eat the sun. Think of whale poop as the soil of the sea. Drifting by the whales, the phytoplankton run into good luck. The sun at their back, the macro nutrients absorbing through osmosis.

•

When I was a sophomore in high school, my English teacher tried to steer me away from Anne Sexton. I knew what he was thinking, even though he didn't say it aloud. He gave me a collection of Margaret Atwood's poems, which were beautiful but beside the point. I said, "I needed to get lower." Anne Sexton: "Fi fie fo fum now I'm borrowed. Now I'm numb." Anne Sexton: "Oh woman, say what you mean. This baby that you bleed." Anne Sexton said, in "Wanting To Die":

> Balanced there, suicides sometimes meet,
> . . . .
> something unsaid, the phone off the hook
> and the love whatever it was, an infection.

That same suicide and art article published in *LA Review of Books* reads, "The conventional thinking is that creative people have more psychological problems than the rest of the population," says Dennis Palumbo, a former screenwriter (including the film *My Favorite Year,* and episodes of television's *Welcome Back Kotter*) turned author and licensed psychotherapist specializing in creative issues. "What they have is more access to their feelings." Those in other lines of work like lawyers or bricklayers, who don't have to dig within themselves for their raw material, can suppress their emotions, including "the more intolerable ones."

Dig deep. Deeper writing tends to bring out the maudlin and the earnest in me. Better perhaps to skip across the surface of the water like a perfectly flat stone, making shallow investments in the thick layers of plankton, oxygen, carbon, scum. But without the depth of the pond or lake or ocean, the stone would not skip. The weight of the stone must be matched by the depth of the water. You cannot make a stone stay aloft without knowing how far it could sink. The muscles in your arms bend in proportion not to distance but to pull. *Proprioception* comes from the Latin *proprius*, meaning "one's own." Individual perception is being able to recognize the relative position of neighboring parts of the body and the effort it takes to move those body parts. Your whole self needs to understand the whole of the body of water to skip the rock across the water. This is how Jesus managed his miracle. He knew the water was very deep. He understood how his walking was a kind of suicide. He would drown by the cross eventually. The water was his body. Such perspective, such proprioception, such depth, kept him afloat, for a time.

These bodies of water, these reflections of our bodies, these metaphors, we are water, water is we, keep us tied to the world by the word *is*. *Is* isn't a state of being. It's a moving back and forth like the water when the waves make a concentric circle when the stone touches the surface. Then it hits again. Concentric ring against concentric ring until the ripples reach the shore like waves. Or tongues. Brains may go down to the bottom. Hearts may go down like blood pressure or pulse rates but tongues stay on the surface. The body keeps itself in balance. Head above water.

Ordinarily, down is bad. There is an up. You should go toward it. If you get up there, stay. If you don't, you will be going down. And down is bad.

Erik is standing on one of the barstools, the wand attachment of the vacuum in his hand. Zoë stands below him, her finger on the power button.

"Now," Erik tells her. She pushes the button. The vacuum whirs. Erik shoves the corner tool in the space where wall meets roof.

He sucks up two of the ants. Carpenter ants. The ants were purposefully coming out of the ceiling, heading down toward the floor. To the ants, this is success as is any progress they make toward eating the frame of our house and helping our house fall down. This up-sucking-by-vacuum is good news to us but is not such uplifting news to the ant who has now effectively fallen all the way down. The ecology of vacuums. The ecology of ants.

Whales, as they try to save the humans, do additional service when they die. Their bodies, heavy and full of carbon, sink to the ocean floor where the carbon cannot escape into the atmosphere. Whatever carbon happens in whales, stays in whales. Even decaying, the whales do the hard work, scraping down the grills, draining the fryer. McDonald's uses clam-shaped Taylor or Garland brand grills. Between each run of meat or vegetables, a crew person scrapes any carbon or food residue off the surface of the grill and pushes it into the grease traps. Some kind microorganisms take the grease apart, sink it further toward the bottom of the sewer. If krill is a mirror to a whale then maybe the grill master is a mirror to phytoplankton. Scrape the carbon off the sky, phytoplankton. Get to work, drifter.

•

I have no stable opinion about suicide. Some days, I think humans should get off the planet and let the frogs go back to their regular business. Some days, I think just I should get off the planet and get out of the way of my own bad ideas (concentric ring against concentric ring keeps me alive. Everything is paradox and everything hypocrisy). Some days, I think guns should have imprinted on their barrels: "Shoot self first. Others second." Some days, I think of Garrett's, my sister's boyfriend who shot himself, mother and wonder how her face survived. Is it still beautiful? As beautiful as my mom's? Maybe a few more wrinkles, even though she's younger. Shouldn't I be able to see the deep tear in her ocean? Inside those wrinkles, deep as they may be, you can find her laughing.

•

When I looked at the image of Sylvia Plath with her feet sticking out of the oven, I almost threw up. I'm not sensitive but the picture felt real. Real in the way the words *suicide* or *transform* or *sustainability* never seem real. The sandals strapped. The buckles pointing outward. Her skirt hitched high. Her calves thicker than her thin frame suggests. No head. Just legs and a door.

Could this really be a dead woman? Sylvia of the darkness who seemed always so much grumpier than Anne, even more sarcastic. "Dying is an art. Like everything else, I do it exceptionally well." And then, in the array of Google images, are the imitators. Actors with heads in the oven wearing different, less perfect shoes. Fake or not, one problem with geology, one problem with oceans, one problem with the Philip Larkin poem "man hands misery on to man, it deepens like a coastal shelf, get out as early as you can and don't have any kids yourself."

Sylvia Plath's son killed himself. Mother hands misery on to son.

When I scroll through the images on the Google search "Sylvia Plath Suicide Images," I start to feel less bad. Sure, there are pictures of Anne Sexton and Virginia Woolf. Gwenyth Paltrow playing Sylvia in the movie. Marilyn Monroe. But there are also pictures of plastic daisies in a frying pan. There are images of Sylvia smiling in a swimming suit. There is a picture of a woman giving birth to a baby in a hot tub. The feet are still in the vagina but the baby's head is being brought to the surface. What this has to do with the Googled "Plath" is beyond me but the drift of images soothes my upset stomach. What does suicide engender? Just like anything, it can't stop bringing more—more suicides, yes, sometimes, but more of everything else. Such a nonstop burgeoning all these bodies are.

•

When a tree falls in the forest, soundless or not, it begins to decay. *Decay* and *falling* and *down* all seem like bad words but like the whale, the tree does work as it falls apart. George Wuerther writes in "Praise the Dead: The Ecological Value of Dead Trees,"

> If you love birds, you have to love dead trees. If you love fishing, you have to love dead trees. If you want grizzlies to persist for another hundred years, you have to love dead trees. More importantly you have to love or at least tolerate the ecological processes like beetle-kill or wildfire. These are the major factors that contribute dead trees to the forest.

I saw a tree in the forest, its bark turned into stringy pot roast. Ants worked between the strings, bringing food in, taking food out, making food of the tree, making the tree into food for the mushrooms. Mushrooms grew under that tree, decomposing that tree, fixing its nitrogen. The nitrogen fed the soil. The soil fed the tree. Later, after I was gone, perhaps a bear came by to eat the ants. A deer ate the mushroom. The next-door neighbor trees ate the soil. Cannibal trees grew tall, their new needles sucking up all the carbon dioxide their little strings could absorb.

•

The point of falling down is to come back up. Robin Williams fell down and then he got back up. Then he fell down for good. David Foster Wallace. Anne Sexton. Virginia Woolf. Some people stayed up for the long haul. Some people seem all surface but the anchors of their jokes run deep. Think of Joan Rivers falling out of favor with Johnny Carson when she was offered her own show on Fox, leaving her guest-hosting spot with Johnny Carson. Joan Rivers' husband, Ethan Rosenberg, said he tried to call Carson about the move. Carson says neither Rivers nor Rosenberg even bothered to tell him. Carson and Rivers never spoke again, Carson punishing her for this betrayal by never inviting her back on *The Tonight Show*. But Rivers survived, although her show didn't. Her husband killed himself. Rivers even made a joke about him killing himself: "My husband killed himself. And it was my fault. We were making love and I took the bag off my head."

Rivers made a plentitude of jokes. A McDonalds' worth. A sea-full of krill plenty. An antidote to loss. Eighty years of joke-making sequesters a metaphorical kind of carbon. Push the dark into the depths. Dig for it when you need to go on stage. Surface to depth, depth to surface, these whales, the McDonald's, these Rivers stitching the planet back together.

She made jokes about growing old: "My breasts are so low, now I can have a mammogram and a pedicure at the same time." Can you imagine Sylvia Plath or Anne Sexton getting a mammogram?

About plastic surgery: "I've had so much plastic surgery, when I die, they will donate my body to Tupperware." Turning carbon to silicone. That's one way to save the planet.

About happiness and depression: "I think anyone who's perfectly happy isn't particularly funny." Rivers made surface happiness and depth-digging part of her routine. "I have a wonderful psychiatrist that I see maybe once a year, because I don't need it. It all comes out onstage." If only Anne Sexton and Sylvia Plath had been funnier. Or become famous for their senses of humor.

She even had a joke about McDonald's: "Don't you hate McDonald's? I heard you can't get a job there unless you have a skin condition." Although that one is not very funny. She's wrong, too. My boyfriend who worked there when I was fourteen had great skin. Not one pimple. Still, McDonald's is as ubiquitous and plentiful as krill. We should keep it in our mind, in our jokes, and in the reflection of our face in the mirror, good skin or not.

She fell down with Carson and her husband fell down and even she fell down the subway stairs. Diagnosed with osteoporosis in 2002, she could have broken her hip. She didn't. Instead, she went back up the stairs, had some more plastic surgery, made so many jokes, lived another twelve years.

My friend Rebecca, the painter, said to me, one day when she didn't feel like getting out of bed, "Don't hate me if I give up art and just make cupcakes and casseroles."

I said, "Your casseroles are art."

It's OK if you go someplace dark as long as you bring something back. Like cupcakes. Or casseroles or a good joke.

The etymology of the word *transform* is *transform*. Add a bit of Latin-y business to the end of the word and the word *transform* hasn't transformed since the beginning of the word. It is constant to change. We're all always turning into something. It is good for the planet, this changing. An exchange really. Oxygen into carbon. Death into jokes. The more there is the more there is. Ask Ovid who wrote rarely about McDonald's or whales but spent a lot of time turning women into trees. But if he knew what a hundred million pounds of krill turned into, he'd be impressed, maybe even inspired enough to let Daphne transform out of her tree into a whale, or at least let her tree age, and die, fall and rot into the soil where she can be the bearer of baby mushrooms and carbon sequesterer.

Inner Resources

WAYS TO STAVE off suicide:

- Borrow somebody else's neural net.
- Write a love letter to someone, maybe your dead boyfriend.
- Eat blueberries.
- Go outside. Even if it's winter and there is snow on the ground, you will think of green.
- Make yourself laugh by telling yourself it will all be OK.
- Try not to be so sarcastic. It's corrosive, this sarcasm.

There are several ways to stave off apocalyptic global warming:

- Stop using so much fossil fuel.
- Unplug your computer from the wall socket.
- Take shorter showers.
- Ride your bike.
- Don't travel by airplane.
- Don't buy plastic.
- Don't use plastic bags.

- Don't buy blueberries from Argentina in plastic clamshells in November.

But sometimes these things are impossible. The shortening of showers. The riding of bicycles—all these hills. The laughing. The finding of non-Argentinian blueberries even in June. The antidote to sarcasm is sincerity. Sincerity feels like such a layer of bullshit.

What might be a layer of bullshit is the prospect of geoengineering, a backup plan to save the planet. Or at least to save the atmosphere. Geoengineering is the deliberate, large-scale intervention in Earth's natural climate systems to counteract climate change. It's a last-ditch effort in case humans don't change their climate-altering behavior. Scientists have devised ways to artificially create more cloud cover by adding sulfur to the atmosphere to cool the air. There are drawbacks to this plan but it is a potential, albeit last-ditch effort, to prevent self-destruction.

The oceans will still become acidic. And the ozone layer might disappear entirely. But if crops continue to burn and tsunamis continue to drown and humans can't stop themselves from their humany ways, then perhaps something less humany must be done. Something with big machines. Or big guns. Big molecules. Americans like things big and the small changes to live sustainably are even smaller than they are.

Smaller than the gut microbes they destroyed in their stomach by overdoing on antibiotics and now they can't eat anything but rice. No blueberries.

One way to stop the greenhouse gases from turning the planet into an ever-hottening greenhouse is to whisk up the ocean to create more cloud cover. That sounds easy and simple enough. Not too troubling, unless you're a fish. The size of the machines would need to be alien movie-sized like the ones in *The Abyss, War of the Worlds,* the new Superman, *Man of Steel.* A turbine or a generator or a big fan spins and spins the water, makes a ruckus. The molecules, not liking this busy-ness, separate. The O's say goodbye to the H's and flee to the sky. "Here, humans," the O's would say. "Here's our gift to you. A big fat cloud between you and that thing you claim to love so much, that indomitable sun. We broke up, me and the H's, just for you and still you curse the rain."

To stop yourself from killing yourself, you stir things up a bit. Change your basic weather patterns. Find the ocean inside of you. This will require self-awareness, which, being suicidal, you think you have too much of but actually you have too little. You need to get away from yourself. Stop bothering your poor mother. She's had it up to here with you. What you need is a new personality. You have to do the thing most uncharacteristic of you.

Let's say you are usually a friendly person on the outside, "Hi, how you doing?" but on the inside, you're saying to yourself, "My god, that is a stupid coat." Change it around. Make yourself alien. Go ahead and say aloud, "My god, that is a stupid coat," and think to yourself, "Hi. How are you?" You might make an enemy. You may even get punched in the nose. But you're at the beginning of changing your neural net. Even better, you might realize you've been being a jerk in your head all along. Maybe you'll shut up about people's coats. Maybe you'll stop being a jerk in your head and in your mouth. You might even find a way to like rain.

Once, when I lived in Portland, I claimed to love the rain in the same way people who live in places it snows claim to love the snow. But lying to yourself is only a temporary means of survival. No one likes her feet wet. You tell yourself it's beautiful but frostbite is a killer and gangrene killed my grandmother. First you lose your footing. Then you lose your actual foot. Then the infection spreads like depression. Like carbon dioxide. You are not a tree. You cannot breathe in all these combined H's and O's. All this carbon. All this anti-air. You need regular oxygen to live. What is oxygen? It is rain coupled with blueberries.

They grow lots of berries in Oregon. Grapes are a kind of berry that you make into wine. Wine is a big industry. People like to drink, not usually to death, at least not on purpose. The grapegrowers don't want the grapes to die either but in Oregon, it is awfully wet. It is moist most of the time. Powdery mildew is the enemy. To prevent the moisture from growing fungus on the grapes, you just apply sulfur. It's an easy machine—kind of like a potato gun or a portable humidifier. The sulfur prevents mildew from growing, protecting the planet of the grape, letting it survive until harvest and crush. It's so harmless, wine with sulfured grapes can still be labeled organic. Still, the sulfur must interfere with the sun to some degree. Some wines taste like sulfur. Some people are allergic to sulfites. And sometimes, sulfites stick grape fermentation, which means the wine remains grape juice, and the world ends nonalcoholically.

There are other ways, besides the spurring on of cloud-making from the ocean, to man-make a fix to this carbon problem, to this greenhouse effectively turning our planet into a desert-zone. You can spread a layer of sulfur dioxide along the atmosphere, like a layer of protective Vaseline. The sun does not like sulfur dioxide—it's a mirror to its vampiric self. The sunlight bounces off the sulfur. Deflection. Rejection. Take that sunlight. Try not to hotten us up so much. Our planet is not an old two-liter bottle of Squirt, capped and trapped. We are a can of Zima. We are going to dance all this heat away.

This geoengineering is good for the kind of humans with a lot of luck and a little forethought. To coat the atmosphere in sulfur dioxide, you (not you in particular, you in general, like you and your mother) send giant balloons that rise up, like clouds. The balloons rain down sulfur upon the atmosphere. Smear it on like a salve. The hope is the sulfur dioxide stays up in the sky instead of collapsing into the ocean, turning it to vinegar. That the ozone layer doesn't take offense and leave for a better Venus. That the sky turning whiter wouldn't make the swans disappear. Humans have always been an experiment. Bleach is their favorite color.

Suicide is the greatest rejection. Dear Life, You are too stupid. Please go away. When you kill yourself, it's the one big, fuck you, everyone. The last one, but a good one. In suicide, hutzpah. I do not need you, you dirt, you air, you soft animal flesh. You want it all gone. Bleach kills everything.

It takes technology to kill yourself. Death by self, unless you can manage to starve or not breathe, requires tools and apparatus. You need a knife. An electrical cord. A hose for the exhaust pipe. A bottle of pills. A gun. A razor. A train. The fact that it takes something human-made should be a sign it's no good for you. Can you kill yourself with blueberries? No you cannot. They grow by rain and by sun. A reasonable combination of both. Be like the blueberry. Breathe.

They say that the art of deconstruction is to find the flaw and, therefore, the key to any piece of art. You are art, made, constructed. Bleached and grown, twisted and loved. What is the most *you* thing about you? Your dirty looks? The way you quote Oscar Wilde? That you sleep with one hand down your pants? That you consistently see yourself in the eyes of others? That you see through the skin of others, like Superman, and see all their flaws. Their flaws are your flaws. Stringy and elastic. You feel your own muscles stretch like a rubber band. Now we're onto something. Their sadness crushes your soul because you know it crushes theirs. You know how desperately they're trying to hold on. It makes you suffer. Their flimsy skin. The way they say, hey, that's cheating, when you place your Scrabble letters on the board, let go, for a second, and then change your mind and pull them back. It's fine, it's fine, they say but you've already seen their insides. You've decayed them like plutonium 135. Half-life half-life. The fingers on the Scrabble letters are the only things holding them together. You are made of carbon. You keep spewing yourself into the atmosphere. You remind them, by letting go, by coming back, how fragile everything is. And now, by seeing them, you've reminded yourself. You are blowing apart like hydrogen and oxygen, abandoning your letters, going back to them. You wanted a second chance. The word *beloved* was better than *valuable*. What will it take to turn you into a protective layer of Vaseline. Compassion. To save them, you have to save yourself. Maybe grow some local blueberries. Give them to your friends. Live.

If you and your mother do not have any balloons, you can fire the sulfur into the atmosphere with heavy artillery shells. The suicidal aren't supposed to have guns but this is an opportunity to save the world, save yourself. The corn you grew this summer only made it knee high. Then the sun came on too strong. There was no cloud cover. There was no rain. There was just you and this cracked plant looking desperate at the sky. Corn is good for many things: soda pop and bread, candy corns and potato chips, Aunt Jemima maple syrup, popsicles, Eggo Waffles, and polenta. Without corn, you are lonely. No one, not even your mother, understands you. How do you stop this sad story and make the corn stalk grow? You find a bazooka. Maybe a tank. A cannon might do. Pack a bullet with some sprinkling of gunpowder and a pinch of sulfur. Send your last hope into the sky. Shooting upward is dangerous but not necessarily deadly. Spread the word. Be careful of the bird.

With the atmosphere fully lathered in sulfur, what happens to the sunlight? Shame spiral? The solar flares turn inward. The sun, rebuffed and rejected now looks like you when you were feeling your worst. What if the sun takes it to heart, undoes himself, goes supernova? It is hard to feel sad for a sun that one million of your Earths could fit inside of. But you are its people. It will miss you. The sun won't even turn into a red giant in 4.5 billion years. That's a long time to go on with all your good efforts returned. Maybe the sun will shrivel and die without the humans who once loved the sun.

Balance is the most useless verb. If you can balance, you're already doing it. You don't need to say it. If you're telling someone to balance, then obviously, they can't. Just balance the amount of sulfur with the amount of cloud. Just balance the amount of sun with the amount of artillery fire. Just balance the amount of carbon you release with the number of trees you plant. You always wanted palm trees in Cleveland. Just balance the good things with the bad. Just wait another day and balance will come. People are the worst at balance. That's why the oceans do it for us.

On the top of the staircase is where you need the most balance but have it the least. You could just throw yourself off the balcony, off the deck, out the wind, down the stairs. The moment is unbalanced. Everyone can see your insides. You are a mess of wires and propulsion. If life were a teeter-totter, you'd be on the ground with the snakes. If life were a teeter-totter, you'd be stuck in the air with the clouds and the bombs. If you knew how to balance, you would have stopped driving your car long ago.

Bicycles. The solution to suicide and global warming. All you need is for it to stop raining. One very unlikely prediction of global warming is that it will lead to less sun, more clouds, naturally. We won't need the sulfur. The carbon will heat up the air. Hot air will heat up the oceans. Hot oceans will make more clouds. More clouds will mean more rain. The sun will not be rebuffed. The sun believes in clouds. He's already been to Venus. And, we can live on in the everywhere that is the Portland, Oregon, of our dreams where everyone already rides bicycles, even in the rain, and everyone lives in balance with their oxygens and their hydrogens, mixed, shaken not stirred, their corn and their mothers. The bicycling may be wet but isn't too full of hills. All that even breathing, the in and the out, the oxygen balancing the carbon as you balance on your pedals and balance you're just glad you have a coat, even if it's ugly.

And on those sunny days there is no conflicted feeling about the sun. You are one hundred percent certain. You don't need any sulfur protectant. The sweat on your face reflects the extra bit of sun the layer of carbon trapped in here. You are your own Vaseline. It doesn't worry ozone and it doesn't worry shame. Do I love you or hate your coat? It doesn't matter. Take it off. The sun has arrived. Oh, sun, it's OK. It has been too long. Thanks for just a little of you. June in Oregon is for blueberries, enough for everyone.

You Can't Love One

JOHN MUIR, NATURALIST, conservationist, and founder of the Sierra Club wrote, "When we try to pick out anything by itself, we find it hitched to everything else in the Universe." I mostly understand this in a Karmic way—if when I'm driving, I pull in front of you and make you put on your brakes so unto me will I be forced to brake severely for others. But I can, when I'm reading, or when I'm sitting on the ground and the dirt is made hot from the sun and I crush balls of dirt into their constituent grains and rub them into my hands until my skin cells and the grains of sand fall back into the dirt to be reheated by the microwaves of the sun, I get this "oneness." I understand Walt Whitman when he wrote, "My tongue, every atom of my blood, form'd from this soil, this / air."

I like this idea of being one with the world, with the forest. Being one with the forest seems easier than being one with the humans. I love those impressive ink drawings of human feet as roots of trees, seaweed as hair. But there's a problem with this metaphor, everything is collapsed human into the point of view. The seaweed loses itself. Feet cannot suck water up from the ground to quench the thirst of the leaves. Still, I, human, like to lie in hot sand. I like to float on the waves. I like the idea that there is less between me and the world but I don't know how to stop the world from always being a direct object to my "I." I like to believe that if it wasn't for this big, boxy brain, maybe me and the snow could get together. Maybe the snow could come first. Maybe the sand could crumble me. Well, I guess it will, one day. Maybe the bats and I could really understand each other but whenever I try, it's always, me, me, me. "I'm so cold," I say to the snow. And the snow is always so silent. There are barriers between us and it's hard to blame the snow.

When I was pregnant with Max, I took a walk with Erik and Zoë in the forest. Fall in Flagstaff is nicer than spring, almost as good as summer. Not windy. Not hot. Full of mushrooms. Most of the forest is third or fourth growth. The trees had been logged long ago. Most of the trees now growing had been planted by humans. You can tell by the way they grow so closely together—as if someone should have harvested them by now. But there are a couple of old growth trees, one that is at least 150 feet tall. Its branches are as big as most trunks of trees. How do you love a tree? The older ponderosas get, the redder their bark. Unlike redwoods or Douglas firs, the ponderosas seem as interested in growing wide as they are in growing tall. This ponderosa is as wide as a garage. Its branches perfectly spaced for a super-sized monkey to swing right up them. There are no monkeys here. Not even a squirrel is harassing this tree. He's just wide and tall and old and if I weren't so afraid of hyperbole, I'd say I felt, pregnant, very much like this tree.

I took off my shirt.

"What are you doing?" Erik wondered. I used to undress outside more often. I'm surprised that it perplexes him now.

"Take my picture."

Zoë takes her shirt off too because who doesn't want to be mostly naked in the forest? I remove my bra but leave my pants on. I don't hug the tree. I just stand by it. Zoë stands in front of me. Erik obliges and takes a couple of naked-pregnant-wife-by-tree-with-daughter pictures. I touch the tree. I know I'm being ridiculous but this tree is bigger than me. I would like to be that tree. Taking my shirt off was the only way I could think to let it know. Before the breaking birth, it's a good idea to feel a little whole. What were the pictures for? To ask who looks more at one with the tree? Is being at one the same as being at ease? Who looks more at ease? Who looks more long-suffering? Me, my husband, my daughter, or the tree? If you suffer long enough, making everyone else suffer with you, do suffering and oneness become the same thing?

It's not just Tupperware that's disorganized. Erik and I each have a side of the closet but I've crammed my long dresses on the rack that's supposed to hold his shirts. He can only access his shelves that hold wrinkly shorts and wrinkly pants by reaching through a rack of my shirts. Shoes pile on both sides. Sometimes his flip-flops end up on my side, sometimes my tennis shoes on his. Hangers hold clothes we've had since before we got married. Neither of us spends money on new clothes although he bought my favorite skirt. I bought him four shirts that I promised to iron if he would put in a new vanity in the downstairs bathroom. It took me four hours to iron all his shirts. He's still painting the bathroom. He's a perfectionist. I am not. There are still some wrinkles in his shirts. There will be no splotches of paint on the new vanity. That's why I'm a writer and he's a film editor. I can fudge the lines, move the paragraphs, make a transition appear natural. He spends whole hours making sure the cut from one image to another is perfectly spliced.

On the one hand, we could get divorced. Our drawer spaces are generally separate even though our books, CDs, and bank accounts are not. On the other hand, we could never get divorced. Who would perfect my measurements? Who would flatten his shirt with her hand and say it looks just fine as it is?

Emerson, in *Nature* wrote,

> Philosophically considered, the universe is composed of Nature and the Soul. Strictly speaking, therefore, all that is separate from us, all which Philosophy distinguishes as the NOT ME, that is, both nature and art, all other men and my own body, must be ranked under this name, NATURE. . . . Nature, in the common sense refers to essences unchanged by man; space, the air, the river, the leaf. Art is applied to the mixture of his will with the same things, as in a house, a canal, a statue, a picture. But his operations taken together are so insignificant, a little chipping, baking, patching, and washing, that in an impression so grand as that of the world on the human mind, they do not vary the result.

Erik and I are art and nature to each other. Baked and chipped, space and leaf. Can you separate mind from world? Who is the mind? Who is the world? Even in a relationship, a partnership, a marriage, you are the subject, the other is the direct object. Erik is nature. Unchanged by man. I am art, changed my mind by man. We sit in the living room. Alex is in town. We only sit together in the living room when there is company. Instead of arguing about inches of rain or Tupperware, we argue about names.

"I love the Mountain Goats album," I tell him.

"Which one do you like best?"

"*Pale Green Things*."

"You mean *Under the Sunset Tree*?"

"No. *Pale Green Things*."

But I'm feeling awkward. Maybe that is not the name of the album. Erik doesn't even like the Mountain Goats anymore.

Alex chimes in. "Erik's right. It's *Under the Sunset Tree*. Their good album."

I'm swinging over the man-made canal with a rope tied to a tree by boys who don't think I will jump. And they are right. I don't.

But later, Erik pulls me over to him.

"What's the line about the rodeo one in 'Angel from Montgomery'?"

"Make me a poster of an old rodeo."

"What does that have to do with angels?

"Even angels come from somewhere, maybe," I offer.

Why I Did Not Ride My Bike Today

MY FRONT TIRE is always flat. I live on a hill. A very tall hill. I live at 7,000 feet elevation. It is snowing. It is raining. It is hot. It is far. There are no bike lanes. I am late. I am tired. I am not sure if I can make it all the way to work. I am not sure if I can make it home. I ran over my helmet with the car. I am hungry now. I might be hungry later. How can I pick up the kids? What would I wear? Where are my bike pants, my bike lock, my panniers? Have you seen that hill? They say Flagstaff sits at 7,000 feet but I wager my house lies somewhere near a million.

Sustainable Garbage

MY FAVORITE BIN is the blue bin. The blue bin is for glass. For $3.95 per month, a special glass recycling truck comes by and picks up our mixed colored bottles. The truck rattles noisily. The bin shakes out its contents. Unlike our paper or cardboard or plastic recycling, each clink signals to the neighborhood an element of our consumption. The clinking goes on for a while at our house. I expect the neighbors to step out onto their porches to find out what the racket is all about. I hope the truck moves on before they associate blue bin, bad noise with me. I'm a living, breathing PSA. Drink a lot of bottled drinks. Recycle your glass.

The late '70s was the heyday for the Public Service Announcement—Smoky the Bear's "Only You Can Prevent Forest Fires," the most famous. The best ones though were set to music: School House Rock: "Interjections show excitement / or emotion / and they're generally followed by an exclamation point, / or a comma if the feeling isn't quite as strong," and that egg dancing with a bottle of mayonnaise trying to convince you: "Don't Drown Your Food." I was with the egg. I ate my mac and cheese without the cheese. Salad without salad dressing. I don't think I even tried mayonnaise until I was seventeen. There was also the Woodsy Owl song with the very good slogan "Help Keep America Lookin' Good." For the first measure, extend the second "a" into the future. Quickly tuck "lookin' good" onto the end as a quick punch. No one likes to be told what to do but if you sing your imperative, and if you are patriotic, and thus can hold the "are" sound in "The Star-Spangled Banner," then maybe the catchy tune will inspire you to pick up your wax-coated paper cup from McDonald's and find a trash can. Maybe if Woodsy Owl adorns the can, you will even bother to throw away your straw.

We were the first on our street to order the new, blue bin. Dog walkers and runners stopped in front of it. They patted the bin on its lid. The blue bin was so small compared to the big brown garbage bin and the big green recycling bin. We named it R-2.

Our across-the-street neighbors wanted to share ours with them.

"We'll give you two bucks a month to use your bin."

Erik and I shook our heads.

"It's only four dollars a month," Erik said.

"We would never fill up our own," the husband said.

These people, they teach with me in the English Department. They have tenure. I do not. I do not want them to see what is in my glass recycling bin. I don't want them to watch me fill it. Garbage is private, even if it is glass.

What did people do with their garbage before Woodsy Owl and his song, "Give a hoot, don't pollute?" I would like to believe people put their garbage in the garbage can at home and at the park when there was a convenient trash bin but I've seen the edges of riverbanks. Rusted Coors cans of whatever metal held beer before aluminum. The old pull tops—everyone just expected you would toss those on the ground. Hundreds of tiny feet sliced open by the silver shells of discarded pull tops that covered the beach. Reflective. Like solar panels but without the photovoltaic cell. Thus, the invention of the stay-on tab. America was looking not-so-goodish before the stay-on even if "stay-on" isn't as sing-songy a word as "pull-top."

Erik is often threatened with becoming my not-husband when he leaves his bottle caps from his beer lying around. Sierra Nevada and Full Sail caps. Deschutes. Fat Tire. Epic. I pick them up off the counter, the table, the nightstand. I pull them out of the washing machine and also sometimes out of the drier. They tumble onto the floor and I chase them like a cat chasing a moth. But cats like moths. I don't like bottle caps. When Erik visits my mom's or either of my sisters' houses, he stashes the caps in their coffee mugs and their jewelry boxes. In the butter and the soap dishes. In DVD holders and in their empty wine glasses. They would divorce him, too, if he didn't look at them a little guiltily and point out that with the Full Sail caps, you can play rock-paper-scissors. They look at the cap. He ducks out of the kitchen before they can make him take his caps to the garbage. Perhaps we should collect them all like my mother collects wine corks. And then we can throw them at him in celebration. A kind of confetti but more pointed.

In the '80s, people drank Coors, not craft brew. They drank Tab. They did not drink bottled water. At my local Fry's grocery store, you can buy a twelve-pack of water in plastic bottles, topped with plastic bottle caps, wrapped in plastic packaging for $3.55. I find a cheap sticker manufacturer. I ask them to print a thousand stickers of an image of a dead seagull, guts on display, guts full of rubber bands, milk jug lid bands, plastic packaging, and plastic bottle tops. This image appears in every essay and article written about the garbage patch that swirls in the Pacific but it is not yet on every case of water at Fry's. I plan to take my stickers and cover the twelve-packs as thoroughly as any 1970s pull-top covered beach.

Erik objects to my plan. "Sometimes that's the only water some people have."

"It costs like $1 for twelve ounces. About a thousand times more than water from the tap."

"People on the rez don't have taps."

I see that I am being an asshole.

I settle for putting stickers on the Evian but when I get the stickers, it's hard to see what this picture of a dead gull is trying to represent. The image is too small. It looks like a picture of hair swimming in the ocean. It is beautiful and my stickers are coated in some kind of plastic anyway.

Even a few months after the city offered the new service, only a few people on our street wheel their R-2s out on the once-a-month Wednesdays. According to the *Arizona Daily Sun,* Flagstaff's local paper, no one is convinced the glass is getting recycled. The glass was just being crushed and used as landfill cover. To me, that's fine. The landfill does need cover, otherwise, all the light garbage just blows away, putting Woodsy Owl's efforts to waste. The forest re-covered with flying plastic bags from Fry's and straws from McDonald's. But recently, a Phoenix company has volunteered to come get the glass, drive it to Phoenix where it will be picked up by Fevisa, a company in Mexicali, Mexico. There, it will eventually become glass for Corona, Budweiser, and Coca-Cola bottles. The circle now cycled, if with an inordinate amount of transportation fuel to make it so.

We never fill our blue bin all the way but there are enough wine bottles and beer bottles to make a loud sound to bring the neighbors to wonder. We don't drink it all ourselves. We have some friends. My family visits, bringing Erik's bottle caps back to him where they then hide them in his shoes. When he puts his shoes on, the bottle camp imprints its edges on the bottom of his foot as jagged as any Lego.

I like to believe that were we to live in Europe, ours would be a usual amount of alcohol detritus, that America is particularly Puritanical when it comes to liquor and not nearly so Puritanical when it comes to waste. But then the Europeans like individually wrapped soaps and tiny bottles of Perrier, which, although French, are still bottles of water, glassed instead of plastic. And Evian? The perfect Swiss invented the bottled water. Do they have R-2 recycling bins in Switzerland?

In Portland, you return your glass bottles to the store. The five-cent deposit guarantees it. Or, you donate your glass to an entrepreneurial homeless person. Either way, it's a pain to take all your glass in. Glass is heavy. Unless you go daily, you have to take the car. In the '90s, you had to find a baggage clerk to take your glass from your shopping cart, your sticky bags, your soaked-through cardboard cases, your hoppy-sweet boxes and watch him count. Four hundred bottles once. That's a party of money returned. You buy more beer in more bottles. Like any cycle, this one is predictable. You'd be back in the glass line next week. Now they have machines that will take your bottles for you. Brown in one slot, green in another, clear in yet another. Separated glass is worth more. It's easier to recycle. People expect their Corona in clear, their Budweiser in brown, their wine in green just like they expect a trashcan, Woodsy Owl emblazoned or not, on every corner.

What would the world look like without the Woodsy Owl campaign? Cigarette butts and hamburger wrappers. Tab cans and Coors cans mixed with Diet Coke and Budweiser plastic mixed with Red Bull and Full Sail glass bottles. Gum and plastic wrap. Chicken bones and bottle caps. Sheaves of paper. Boxes of cardboard. Rubber bands. Floss. Hair. Birds. Stickers. Maybe it would have been better, rather than moving it away, out of sight. Maybe we should have to step on it. Smell it. Sit on the grass with it. Swim alongside it. Because although we keep the garbage tightly lidded under recycled glass, neé sand, in landfills, there the garbage continues to seep and soak into the groundwater. And, from the top of trash bins, dumped from bin to truck, trucked from Flagstaff to Phoenix to Mexico, the garbage escapes, flies oceanward. Somewhere far away, our garbage, made tiny by rock and water and wind but not disintegrated, swirls outside our vision. Maybe Woodsy was wrong. Maybe we shouldn't keep America lookin' good. Maybe America should do something besides look good. Maybe all our garbage should surround us. Our lawns adorned with floss weaving between blades of grass. Our marigolds blooming next to waxy, McDonald's cups, the *Mc* shining as orangely as the flowers. Cans and bottles commingling with stones in rock gardens. Coffee grounds lining driveways. Toilet paper stuccoed against walls. Garbage in our front yard holding us accountable the way Erik's bottle caps hold him accountable. One, two, three. Rarely more. It's not nothing. The neighbors might raise their eyebrows at the loud crash of beer bottles by the time Wednesday comes, R-2 filled at least halfway—but it's a limit and one less than one quiet wine cork a day. Like the paper towels rolling down the highway like tumbleweeds, the bottle caps are a reminder of what he takes in, what he leaves about, and a reminder to keep count.

Teeth

I FIND A flossing tool in the middle of the trail in the forest behind my house. The handle is made of blue plastic. The floss is regular flossing string wound tight. Flossing with regular dental floss is tricky. You have to stick whole hands into your mouth. Winding the string around your fingers cuts off blood circulation. My mom uses these plastic doohickeys to floss. She buys whole buckets of them.

"But all this plastic, Mom. I mean, string versus petroleum-processed garbage. You used to love regular floss."

"I recycle them," she says, which I feel is both sweet and a little gross. Bus-benches made from recycled plastic (and some stuck bits of carrot). I feel for my mom. She loves to floss. She's been doing it for years. She probably wants to switch it up a bit.

While I'm walking through the forest, finding plastic flossers, I'm listening to an episode of *This American Life* dedicated to drug use. The episode is billed as an irreverent look at drug culture—everyone is doing it, your waitress, your bartender, your doctor, your rabbi. A producer at *This American Life,* not Ira Glass, interviews his own father, who smoked pot all day every day while running a top advertising firm. This surprising and generally irreverent story turns ordinary and "Just Say No" as Alex remembers a moment as a kid on the beach with his father. On a vacation, the family stops at a pristine, private California beach. They set up a tent. Get changed into swimsuits and the producer remembers his father saying, "But first. A little Berkeley Gold." The father had stopped at his friends' house in Berkeley the day before. His friends gave him the gift of weed. And the producer asks his father, "Why weren't we enough?" because even adult children must be the sole important thing in a parent's life. "Were you putting something between you and your feelings?" he wonders because he found the ocean so moving, the moment so perfect—as if the producer's experience was the accurate experience. Maybe his father was tired of driving all day. Maybe his dream was to smoke pot on the beach while his kids bounced in the waves. Maybe the kid was not the only beautiful moment in that father's life.

The producer has totally put the words in the father's mouth. The father has to say, "Yes, I must have been distancing myself from the moment." But what does this kid know? Maybe the pot put him more in the moment. Maybe the pot made the father's experience all the sharper. Maybe it made the father feel more like a kid and therefore at one with his children, the beach, the day.

The show made its point: they are they, we are we, straight is straight and fucked up is fucked up, an us versus them mentality. At the end of the show, in a different act, a recovering alcoholic and comedian replayed a bit from when he first stopped using: "I really think straight people are the losers. They don't know what it's like to really want something. To really want something and then to get it and to get it and to get it again." But the comedian has recovered, is recovering, is not *that* anymore. He sees it differently now, sober. The straight people win. The users are the losers. It's smart to choose the winning side. But the comedian still believes in that *want*. Want is a substance all its own.

In America, white people usually get what they want. We want a plastic tool to floss our teeth so our hands don't get dirty and our fingers don't turn purple? Here's an oil field and a factory and some extra plastic to wrap the plastic in. You want paper towels to wipe down the counters? Here's a tree. Would you be interested in a car that gets nine miles to the gallon? It seats eight even though there is only one of you. Everything is plastic, or paper, or Styrofoam. Some people eat dinner every night on paper plates. There is a twelve-step for almost everything: alcohol, narcotics, love, depression, codependency, eating disorders, chronic pain, cutting, divorce, food addicts, gambling, hoarders, infidelity, internet addiction, kleptomania, liars, marriage, methamphetamine, narcissists, procrastination, PTSD, sexaholics, TV, texting, technology, video game addiction, and workaholics. We are a nation of addicts. We want. We get. We addict. We enroll. We admit. We undo our wants in twelve easy steps. We are our wants and we don't want to be us anymore.

This is not the sixties. *The Doors of Perception* by Aldous Huxley have been opened and shut. Psychedelic mushrooms are not going to save the planet. LSD isn't going to bring on the paradigm shift that will stop wars, feed the hungry, and bring rain to the desert. Drinking yourself to death isn't going to help anyone either. The twelve-step programs make you admit your problem. Then you have to give yourself over to a higher power. You must apologize. If you slip up, you must start over at zero.

If we were going to give up our addiction to modern life, first we'd have to admit we used the plastic flossers. Then we'd have to stop using them. Then we'd have to give ourselves over to a higher power, possibly our dentists. And then we would have to apologize to the forest trails, which we have besmirched with our blue plastic, to the air, which we have steamed toxins to make the polymers, to the air, which we have riddled with carbon, by firing up machines to melt the plastic, mold the plastic, transport the plastic to our stores. If, one day, at a restaurant, eating your gigantic carbon-footprint-making steak, you get a piece of meat stuck in your teeth, you might ask for some floss. Someone might give you a plastic flosser. And wanting it so badly, to get it out of your teeth, you may insert that flosser into your mouth. You will have to begin the steps all over again. One. Admit you have a problem.

May 6, 2014, the *New York Times* reported that climate change is already here. Where it rains only a little, it has stopped raining. Where it usually rains a bit, the rains have become torrential. Last year, Colorado received more rain in a week that it usually receives in a year. Nashville suffered from devastating floods after 20 inches of rain fell in two days. The *Arizona Daily Sun* reports that the southwest has seen the most dramatic changes. We've lost 20% of our forests since 1984, due to wildfire and warm-weather loving insects. David Breshears, a professor at the University of Arizona, helped write the forest section of the National Climate Assessment Report. "Increases in temperature have a dramatic effect on forests in terms of wildfire," Breshears says. "We really see that now." If the study of the mycelium is right, and the symbiotic relationship to mushrooms and trees helps pull carbon out of the atmosphere and sinking it into is true, then maintaining healthy forests is imperative. And even if the soil doesn't hold as much carbon as we might hope, it holds some. Burning forests and unleashed sands can't mitigate climate change at all. It's not so much we're in denial, all that's certainly part of the problem. The real problem is I see it as the tooth flosser's fault, the paper plate user, the driver of the SUV. I am preaching from my self-righteous perch but it's also a hypocritical perch. I've got the natural gas blowing in my living room. I have not committed to the solar power gods quite yet. I live in the Southwest. You live over there, where you're complaining of a bitter-cold-global-warming-can't-come-fast-enough Midwest. I should move but that will leave you and you and you behind and no matter where I move, even to Portland, the rains will change.

Instead of dividing addict from non, user from teetotaler, indulger from abstainer, Portlander from Flagstaffer, environmentalist from climate change denier, perhaps we should indulge in the pleasures of intoxication. Perhaps recognizing the positive aspects of indulgence will let us equate many kinds of intoxications, undermining our tendency toward singular addictions. After my walk in the forest, there were lilacs. Lilacs in the southwest and I know there are lilacs in Utah. Lilacs in Maine and lilacs in Alabama. Obviously, there are lilacs in Portland. I put my whole face in the sex of that bush. I nuzzled it like it was a bear, like it was a dog, like it was Erik's pubic hair. I nuzzled it like I nuzzle Max's neck or Zoë's elbow. It was a trip.

All indulgences and intoxications at once is not a mental health issue, it's a planet health issue. If we can't get drunk off the weed and the grapes and the hops and the smell of lilacs, we'll lose any sense of needing this place. Or that place. Our places.

If everyone has access to a lilac, they have access to a metaphor. If they have access to a metaphor, they have access to knowing what it's like to live where it's too hot, so ride your bike, where it's too cold, hamburgers from McDonald's taste like soy burgers anyway, too rainy, solar panels don't put you in more debt than a car.

Metaphors can elide the differences between us, the Southwest is not the Northeast, Arizona is not Maine, but metaphors can make the case for connection. They can let you believe, for a minute, that you can see what it's like to have a bird's perspective. A cat's point of view. I am like you in that I like lilacs. I'm a little drunk on lilacs. I'm swinging on the swings. I'm running through the forest. I'm dancing for the rain, in the rain, because of the rain. I'm dancing around the living room with Max in my arms and Zoë in the lead. Erik plays the guitar and you are singing along in Anchorage, you are singing along in Salt Lake, you are singing along in Denver, in Nashville and in New York City. You are singing in Dubai and Nepal and Nairobi. It is raining it is raining it is raining and perhaps there is no divide at all.

Sustainable Lies, Sustainable Statistics

MY SISTER PAIGE, fourteen, around midnight, put the transmission into neutral and rolled the minivan down the driveway, not starting the engine until the car lulled to a natural stop at the bottom of the hill. The sound of a car in the driveway would have been enough to awaken my parents. The question was, how did she open the garage without alerting either my insomniac mother or my insomniac father? Simple. She had opened the garage as they were getting ready for bed, hours earlier. The sound of the water running and the spitting as they brushed their teeth covered door rattling open. At midnight, she knew they'd most likely be asleep. It was only at three a.m. that they lay awake in their beds, silently, together, my dad rubbing his knuckles, my mom biting her pinky finger, wondering where they'd gone wrong.

In the morning, when they found the car home but the garage door wide open, my dad asked us as he made crepes for breakfast, "Does anyone know how the garage door got opened?" Val and I shook our heads. Paige offered, "Maybe you forgot to close it." Paige had a strategy. Deflect blame. Remind the parents of their flaws.

In a TED Talk, where all research is boiled down to one succinct argument, Allan Savory begins with the old thinking: Grazing livestock on grasslands kills the grass and kills the soil. The understanding had been that cows graze and graze on native grasses, eating the grass to the root, stomping out soil microbes with their hooves, turning tall-grassed plains into desert. In his talk, he showed pictures of what looks like Arizona desert to me. A few spindly bushes in waves and waves of red sand. He says that he once believed overgrazing was the problem. In fact, he advocated the killing of 40,000 elephants in his native South Africa. The ground had been overgrazed, overtrampled. The elephants had to go. His face looks unbelievably sad. "I love elephants," he said. He had them killed. He had been wrong, he admitted. The science was flawed.

Paige had been fourteen when she stole the car. I was thirteen when I eluded my parents' kind control. Monty and I couldn't find the cabin. I was supposedly at my friend Shannon's for a sleep over. My mom had dropped me off at her house. I'd gone in, waited in the foyer with my real-story-covering friend. Her mom worked at a real estate agency. No need to explain my presence to Shannon's mom. She wasn't there. Monty drove up twenty minutes later. We waved goodbye to Shannon, not really considering that her mom would be home eventually and that my mom would be back to pick me up in the morning and that one and then the other would find me not there. We headed toward Brighton ski resort in his Volkswagen Fastback as the sun squeezed dark between canyon walls. Night skiers parked alongside us, carrying their boots and skis toward the mountain lit up with streetlights. Monty and I walked the other way. It was cold without ski gear. I had only my rain jacket and my backpack full of regular sleepover equipment. Pajamas. My blanket, fluffy, nail polish. I had a granola bar and an orange my mom had packed for me in case I hadn't liked what Shannon's mom made for dinner. I shared it with Monty. We hadn't brought anything else to eat. We looked for the cabin Monty's friend had offered to let him borrow so Monty and I could spend a whole night together. To find the cabin, the friend had said look for a blue front door. It started to snow. We looked and looked for blue doors. How many cabins were up Big Cottonwood Canyon? More than we knew. None had blue doors. Monty had his hoodie on. I didn't bring gloves. When my teeth started to chatter, Monty took me and my frozen hands home.

About the elephants and overgrazing, Savory said, "We were wrong then, and we are wrong now." He argued that for soil health, you need the upset of hooves, the eating down of plants, and the fertilizing capacity of grazing animals' manure to keep soil, and therefore plants, healthy. *Scientific American* in March 2013 described Savory's thinking.

> So Savory decided to mimic the great herds of old, which have died out in many regions or persist in far reduced numbers, with managed "strategic" herds of grazing vegetarians. The sheep and cattle picked for the project, if managed properly, would theoretically bring nature back to its normal cycle in semiarid regions where rains for part of the year are followed by long dry spells.

You have to manage the herds carefully, argues Savory. Letting them on the range for a short while. Then move them on before they chew the grasses down to the nubbins or kick so much of the soil up that it kicks up carbon too. Using animals to graze down patches of grassland, then moving them off quickly would put a stop to clearing lands with fire. The grasslands would return to the time when great herds of antelope and pronghorn sheep, gazelles and elephants, grazed the land. Carbon would sink into the soil. Grasses would heal over desert. Greenhouse gases levels in the atmosphere would be returned to preindustrial levels. Save the world and eat steak at the same time. Our prayers have been answered.

Monty and I had nowhere to go. It was too cold to sleep outside. His mom loved me and was permissive with her own kids, but she would not have let me sleep over at her house—maybe out of respect for my mom, maybe because she did really love me, differently than she loved her own sons. Maybe even she, like my mom, thought thirteen was too young for sleepovers with boyfriends. So Monty took me home even though taking me home meant that I would have to admit I had lied. My mom shook her head at both of us. Told us to sit down. We were in time for tacos. I was grounded for two weeks and I could never have a sleepover again but Monty still joined us every night that week for dinner. My mom was a good cook, she liked Monty as much as his mom liked me, and, with Monty in the house, at least she knew where her daughter was.

If you Google "good news, grazing, ted talks" the first hit is to Savory's TED Talk itself. The second hit links to an article on Slate.com debunking the theory. This "holistic grazing plan" succeeded only in Rhodeisa (Zimbabwe today) in the early '70s, *Slate* claims. You'd need to increase livestock by 400% to sink all the excessive carbon in the atmosphere. The cows would actually need to die on the land to create the illusion of the human-guided process mimicking natural cycles of life. The dead bodies are necessary to feed the grasses, which is not the point of raising livestock. The point of raising livestock is to eat meat, not let the meat decompose to feed the grass and the soil. Plus, the animals suffered when subjected to continual moving from pastureland to pastureland. They were thin. Bad for them and bad for ranchers. They wouldn't get much price at a slaughterhouse. Also, there's a difference between overgrazed land and real desert. Real desert has cryptobiotic soil on the top. It holds down erosion. It keeps the desert soil alive. Cows break that up, making the soil more prone to erosion, letting whatever carbon is sunk in the soil to fly high into the sky. When I worked at ORLO—educating the public about the environment through the creative arts when I lived in Portland, we had bumper stickers that read "Cows Kill Salmon." Cows turn tiny salmon spawning streams into mud. Not even dam-catapulting salmon can swim through mud. It's hard to imagine so many hooves being good for the sand. But I admit, I tried to put this out of my mind. I will make room in my brain for science that lets me eat steak.

My parents didn't think about the garage again until they went to the Park City condo to clean it for imminently arriving renters. They thought they would just be washing windows and toilets. They didn't expect beer cans and ashtrays, empty bottles of Jaegermeister. For a minute they believed the previous overnight renters to be the culprits but then they noticed the door to the garage had been left unlocked. The only way to unlock the door from the garage to the house was the key on my mom's key ring. The key ring with the key to Mom's minivan. Only someone from our house would have access to that key. When they asked Paige if it was she who had had a party, she said no. When they asked about the key, Paige blamed Dad. Dad was tired of being blamed for stuff he didn't do. He had enough guilty baggage carrying the bad stuff he actually did do. When they said they didn't believe her, she said, "I can't believe you don't trust me." They grounded her for two weeks and did not let her get her driver's license for one full year after she turned sixteen. High rhetoric always gives you away.

Perhaps if Savory hadn't been so brash when he said that with these new grazing practices, we could return the amount of greenhouse gases in the atmosphere to preindustrial levels. Perhaps if it hadn't been so obvious that Savory clearly liked to eat meat. Perhaps if he'd made a distinction between plains that had been turned to deserts and happy deserts where the microclimates and the microorganisms in the soil are so intricately dependent and unique that it's pure hubris to think humans, with their big clumsy hands, can mimic them. Science sucks. As I was researching mycelium, these fungi and their hyphae, and how they work with trees to suck extra carbon out of the air and sink it into soil, researchers at my own university discovered that yeah, it's true. Microorganisms in the soil love carbon and they suck it up. But the more the sink, the more they emit. I keep looking and looking for the scientists to save us, but there is no easy way out. We want a deux ex machina. Or, better, a science ex machina. But we only have what's inside the machine. I still eat red meat sometimes. I love this idea of prairie lands restored, carbon sunk, the cows living full happy lives before they become hamburger but it's hard to trust someone who advocated the killing of 40,000 elephants, even if he later admitted he had been wrong. And now is probably wrong again.

My mom hated lying. She left my dad not because he was a drunk but because she found a receipt that showed a pair of boots bought in Houston, Texas, and he lied and tried to say he bought them for her.

"You would never buy me boots. You don't even know my shoe size."

"Nine," he tried to sound convincing.

"Seven and a half." She met with a lawyer the next day.

But the other day, we were talking about Paige, how she snuck out with the car. "I was so proud of her," my mom says now. I raised my eyebrows at her.

"No, really. She was so brave to drive at fourteen. Up the canyon. And to bring the car back, unscathed. If she had just cleaned up the condo, we never would have known."

"What about me? Were you proud I'd tried to find that cabin with Monty?"

"I would have been. Had you found it."

Paige and I both lied but my lie was all air. Paige's lie was air and accomplishment. Lies don't last very long. Neither does the truth. I would like to believe in this "Graze more! Sink carbon!" crusade but I already know I'm prone to believing in any God that lets me eat a hamburger. You may be able to only believe the dirt you hold in your hands. Maybe not even that. Can you tell dirt from carbon? Can you tell carbon from cryptobiotic soil? If you crush it in your hand, was it you who tipped us over from comfortable coldness to Jurassic-like heat? And you, you who advocated killing 40,000 elephants? Who can trust you? You are like the God who prohibits drinking and then tells us your wine is your blood. You always keep elephant blood separate from your own.

DNA

IT'S JUST DINNER. It's just the Lumberyard, a beer pub. It's just the last day of the semester. I want a glass of wine. Erik wants a beer. The kids want root beer. I pick the kids up from school. While we wait for Erik, we play tic-tac-toe. Already no one wins. When Erik gets there, the kids interrupt me telling him about my talk with the dean. Zoë interrupts Erik's story about how they broke into small groups for his supervisor training lesson with a story about math—if 84, 27, 9, 3 then what? Erik interrupts her to tell Max not to pick his nose. I tell Erik not to yell at Max. Erik says he isn't yelling. I mimic his yelling. No one says anything for the rest of the night.

Max crawls into our bed at night. Max tosses and turns and the bed is too small for three of us so I go upstairs to the master bedroom to sleep. Erik and I have slept together in the master bedroom maybe thirty times together since we took down Max's crib about a year ago. Erik and I usually sleep downstairs in Max's room but tonight while Max sleeps in Zoë's room, Max wants to sleep in his own room. Neither of us wants the kids to sleep alone on a separate floor and since Erik can sleep through tornadoes, which is the manner in which the kids sleep, I leave the tornado-sleepers to Erik.

We fight when we don't sleep together. We lose our way toward any notion of "one." When we sleep together, our bodies share blankets and sheet and pillows, our breath shares the same air. It's like the DNA of the fetus embedding itself into the cells of its host-mother. In the bed, our alleles, our sloughed skin, our dust mites, our microbes get mixed up and shared. When we don't sleep together, there is distance between us. We can't operate as one. We are not as one as we are when we sleep together every night. We don't blame Max for interrupting us. It's easier to be mad at someone who shares no DNA. Verbs of anger, like "mad at," require a direct object and Erik who I didn't sleep with last week is not in me.

December is full of birthday parties. My friend Beya has kids born on either side of Christmas, one Zoë's age and one Max's. Erik and I take both Max and Zoë even though I think this party is the one meant for Zoë's age group. I can't keep track and Max would be sad to miss his friend's birthday, even if it's not his friend's birthday. Erik and I stand around, look at our phones. I reorganize the carrots and the vegetable tray. Erik takes pictures. A mom of one of the kids, sensing our awkwardness, starts talking to me and Erik.

"Mine is just a blur. He runs from one room to the next like he's Superman. I can't keep track of him."

"That sounds fun. Max is a blur too. A blur of two different superheroes, asking if he can watch Batman, crying if the right Batman isn't on."

"And then mine, in the middle of building a Lego tower, wants to stop and build a real tower. With the kitchen chairs. And asks me to sit in the middle, holding up one of the chairs with my head."

"Max asks me for the one piece. You know the gray one? With the two parts. And I say, what parts. And he cries, the two parts. The TWO parts. An hour later, I find the gray piece with the THREE parts and he says, 'that's it.'"

Erik turned the heel of his cowboy boot against the carpet, grinding his thoughts into the ground.

Later, Erik says what he was thinking. "Why would you say Max was a terrible kid to those people we don't even know?" I cringe. I wasn't saying Max was terrible. He's just a regular kid, I thought I was saying. And I say Erik's being horrible to me and Erik says, "I just don't get you."

I was already ready to be hurt. Erik said the mean-in-my-mind thing to me after he asked, on January 4th, if Max would like a birthday party. Max's birthday is on January 6th. As if one can plan a birthday party in two days. I take this the wrong way too. Erik doesn't understand how he's telling me I've failed. That I'm a bad mother. I neglected to organize a birthday party and Erik as a last ditch is going to, two days before the event, going to save it by throwing one together. And now I feel he's seeing the truth. That he married wrong. That I will throw my son under the bus for a good story. But he doesn't hear it the way I hear it so he doesn't see why I hit myself on the head, on purpose, to make the pain stop or start somewhere sharper. He doesn't see why I slept in the other room. He doesn't see what I see which is the gap between the way he loved me before and the way he loves or doesn't love me now. And, when he raises his eyebrows, pulls his eyes thin, and tells me I've done wrong by our son, I see the gap between us. I do not want to see. I kick the bag with the portable DVD player because I cannot believe I used to be so loved and am now so not, and I used to be the best mother, and now I'm not, and the gap is not only between me and him but between me and time. At least my toe and the DVD player are as one.

The gap is still wide. It is too much to expect him to close it? He does, just a day later. While I'm chopping broccoli, I bend my head toward him. He takes my sunglasses off from the top of my head so they don't fall onto the cutting board. He smiles at me. Married again.

I'm getting to see it. Like a geologist checking his seismograph. Erik said something about never spending money again for ten years. I said, fine. I don't like to spend money either. We moved on. Got the kids dressed for dinner. One snarky comment by me about shoes all over the floor. Then, maybe he said something about, good for her, his mom not drinking and then he was telling Zoë about Les Paul and his broken arm and how Les had his broken arm set purposefully bent so he could play guitar and I said stop, and he said, don't tell me to stop and I said I'm sorry, I just need your sister's address really quick. It's all fine. But the seismograph went from 3.0 to 4.0 to 6.0. Earthquake? Imminent disaster? This world is hard to keep.

But there are whole days when I think we're going to make it. Not the one when we were driving to Napa, leaving San Francisco airport, and Siri freaked out and thought we were on surface streets so we bailed on the freeway and you were so mad you said, "If you don't know how to look up the maps, then you drive."

It sounded a lot meaner when he said it. We didn't talk the whole ride up to Napa but fortunately everyone on the trip got sick but us, which made it kind of romantic, in the end. It's easier to squish together in a twin bed that is far, far away from noises coming from the bathroom. Trying not to laugh at other peoples' misfortune is a kind of romance too.

It is sweet to ask me where I want to go to dinner for my birthday but even sweeter when you decide. I know I said even Denny's is fine but I like it better that you know it's not.

"Is your mom talking to me, Max?"

"Nope," says Max.

"Can I give her a kiss on her head?"

"I guess so."

Erik kisses me on my head and the world levels out. A kiss sustains.

Again, I like to divide the world into two kinds of people. Some people are believers in potential energy—these people are the believers in God, ghosts, fossil fuels, football, *Dancing with the Stars,* and the power of baking soda. They are against abortion. The idea of potential human weighs heavily in their calculations about what to do about women's bodies. Inside that woman-body, the fetus, smaller than a mouse, with less volition than a mouse, with less hunger than a mouse, with less movement than a mouse, has the potential to become a human. Humans trump everything, in this group's mind. Potential energy is gas in a lawn mower, a car on top of a hill, students waiting to go home from school. The future is bright in this potential world. Everything is coming. They follow the physics of potential energy. PE = mgh where m equals mass and g equals gravitational force of acceleration and h equals height. This is where one gets the idea that the bigger you get, the harder you fall. But believers in PE believe that on this planet, mass equals human and mouse equals zero.

The people who believe in kinetic energy believe in birds, fate, bucking up, the fantasy of solar power (it's kineticking right at you), *The Walking Dead,* and the sovereignity of toothpaste. KE-1/2mv. Where the m is mass and v equals velocity. The nice thing about velocity is you're already going somewhere. It's nice to be on the road or even on the train that lets you know where you're going because you've already seen the tracks. The kinetics are bound by their love of movement to believe in abortion. Not only because babies slow you down, which they do, but that babies-as-mice are not even quite mice. They don't breathe on their own. They're like those creatures in *The Matrix*. Pods in *Aliens*. Peas more than mice.

The kineticstician values this: an equality of cells. You cannot eat a chicken, a fish, a steak. You might not even be able to drink a milk or eat a cheese. The vegan may be the judge of what is valuable but to someone who eats veal and decries the removal of an accidental chemical reaction between an egg and a sperm, well, potentially, they're hypocrites, and, worse, heirarchists. The humans-are-best argument seems like a good belief until you start up that lawn mower, drive that car down the hill, let those children out of school. And then, by nature, everything turns kinetic. The mouse wins.

Of course, maybe dividing the world into two kinds of people is just another way of making sure there is a crack in everything. When can you smooth out this fault line?

Here is a story about potential energy.

Walnut Canyon is a big crack in the limestone where Sinagua Indians once lived in pueblos built into the bedrock. At another end-of-the-world, possibly what is now Sunset Crater erupted, the Sinagua Indians fled their homes. The climate changed. The river that ran through the canyon narrowed. They moved on. Possibly to Portland, Oregon, where we shall all be reunited in our post–global warming lives. Until then, I am determined to find a way through Walnut Canyon to Northern Arizona Campus by bike. I'm done with the car. Or, at least, I'm done driving the car while the sun is shining and I don't really need to be to campus at any specific time because it is suddenly summer break.

The paths in the forest are circuitous. I can see campus from the hill where I live. It seems like a straight shot. I pedal out from Lake Elaine. The trail is ATV-ridden. Erik has driven his Four-Runner out here. But I am righteous and biking and hoping my tires don't pop on the sharp rocks.

I wend down to a neighborhood I didn't know existed where people raise goats and chickens. The remnants of a US ARMY helicopter and a paddleboat decorate someone's front yard. There are many "no trespassing" signs and NRA signs and "this is a private road" signs but I ride on because I am on my bike and I'm a short, blond girl and I use that as my force field today.

I ride along a fence. I find the Walnut Canyon loop. I'm too far south. I ride north. I find a fellow bike rider. I ask him if I can make it to Lone Tree Road this way.

"Are you good?"

I think on it for a while. Good? Like, if I'm pure of heart, I'm on the right road? And then I realize what he means. Good at riding a bike.

"Good enough."

"Yes. Then keep going this way."

I follow him but the path seems wrong. South again. And downhill. I hate to go down hills. That means I'll have to come back up. I turn around again. And again. And I'm not lost but I'm certainly not going to make it. Apparently, I am not good enough. I walk my bike up the hill. Ride past the helicopter. Walk again up the hill, wondering if I have enough energy to get back home.

Here is a story about kinetic energy.

A cure. Later that week, Erik and I ride together. I look at the map. He looks at the map. We argue about which way feels south. We argue about whether to trespass or not. He bikes down a hill that I know we're just going to have to come back up. The hill has too many rocks for me. It's too steep. I walk my bike down. We look at the map together. I sense we are close to the never-had-a-drop-of-water-in-it-that-I've-seen Rio de Flag.

"Is that the river?" In the distance, we can both see water.

"I think it is the river."

"That's the path we need."

So along what is called the Sinclair Wash, we ride our bikes. There are sunflowers as tall as our heads. To our left, the same limestone the Sinagua dug their homes into. To our right, a golden eagle. We ride under I-40, around the water treatment plant. We ride toward Rio de Flag, full of water. We have to get off our bikes and carry them across. We find a paved trail. We pass the labyrinth NAU students have made with lava rocks and Mardi Gras beads.

We make it to Lone Tree Road. We have made it from our house to campus through the forest. Maybe that's how cracks in the façade are forded. By potential energy at the top of the hill and kinetic energy at the bottom. By a map and a dialectical argument—no this way. No this. By a bridge of bike and dried up river.

Erik offers me a sip of water from his camelback. I suck on the plastic tube even though it's warm and frothy. It's hard to know where the spit ends and the water begins. We share a lot of spit. We could make a bridge out of it.

Sustainable Dogs—
On Time and Timing

MY DOG IS very sick. Almost as sick as my cat was before he died. At least my dog is drinking water but when I lift her up to make her walk, her back legs collapse. Her front legs buckle too. She can pee but she falls down right where she peed. There is shit collecting on her tail.

The book I'm reading about a hospital's meltdown during Hurricane Katrina, *Five Days at Memorial,* turns out to be a political piece against euthanasia. Although objective in the beginning, the author clearly argues that had the doctors who ordered Versed and morphine for the patients been able to see the bigger picture, had they been able to realize this wasn't a real apocalypse, that it was just a short-term natural disaster, then they wouldn't have put the patients out of their misery. The author does a good job at making the patients seem miserable. Choking on their own secretions. Excrement stuck to their buttocks. Animals who had been brought to the hospital for safety were put to sleep. One doctor tossed a cat out the window. But the tone in the middle of the book shifts. Narrative turns to accusation. Miserable circumstances don't last forever. If the disaster had been forever, maybe euthanasia would be right. But disasters are never forever. These patients, as nearly dead as they almost were, were not necessarily doomed.

The back of my legs are clean. The fur isn't clumped. I don't feel the skin loosening from the muscle. But if there were shit stuck to me and I couldn't stand up to wipe it off, I think I would like to die. But what do I know what I would want or when I would want it? The narrowing of perspective. This moment that seems to last forever. What do I know about death? The eyes sink backward. They glaze, then they fix, sometimes right on the person who put them to sleep.

If I have time to think about it before I can no longer move, if I have time to say, not only Do Not Resuscitate but If I Get Gross, here are my veins. But the gross meter might shift far to the right, depending on how fearful I really am of dying. I might be able to stand to lie in my own pee. I just washed feces off my dog. Some got on my hands. Maybe I could stand my own feces for a few minutes. Maybe even a few days. What is this life worth? At least, if I were alive, I could ask this question over and over while the bedsores mount.

My sister Paige used to teach environmental science. Now, she rolls her eyes at me whenever I poke around her house, looking for potential recyclables she might toss into the garbage. When I told her I was writing about her boyfriend Garrett's suicide when he was a fourteen-year-old and she was thirteen while also writing about "sustainability," I asked her, why is she an environmentalist no more? She used to be a vegetarian. She used to grow her own food. She composted. Why'd she stop?

"I said to my eighth-graders, 'If we don't stop using fossil fuels, the planet will flood. Or it will turn to desert. You might die.' They shrugged. I said, 'Your parents might be too old to change, but you aren't,' they just looked at their iPhones. If eighth-graders can't rebel against their parents' carbon-loving ways, there is no hope."

I think of my rebellious sister, sneaking the car out of the house. Of her becoming a vegetarian at fourteen. Of the way she shaved her head before her wedding. She always rebelled against what "she was supposed to do." No wonder that she's disappointed in her students. As she throws away an empty can of Coke instead of recycling it, I wonder if she's rebelling against me.

"Our time is over. It is all over. Why fight it?" she tells me. It's not like I don't agree.

It's 67 degrees outside in Flagstaff in January. An image of a map of snow depth in Arizona recorded every January from 2010–2014 shows a beige state slashed with a swath of blue, indicating snowfall, across flat beige territory in 2010. In 2011, patches of blue. In 2012 smaller patches of blue. In 2013, still patches of blue. In 2014, hardly any patches of blue—indistinguishable beige from corner to corner.

The snow depth graphs of Salt Lake City, where Paige lives, where we were both born, looks much the same. I told her about the plan to shoot the sulfur into the sky. If individuals won't change their habits to save themselves then there's a last-ditch effort to save the whole species. One big hospital in the sky.

"Sulfur? How do they get it up there?"

"They shoot sulfur dioxide into the sky."

"Sulfur dioxide is toxic," she tells me.

It depends on the amounts. Like time, toxicity is relative.

My nephew is sitting at the table as we sort through recycling, Paige still noting that it costs more energy to recycle glass than to chuck it. He'll be going into eighth grade the next year. "You would love the TV show *Firefly.* It's about how the planet becomes too toxic to live on. So they live in space. And the space pirates attack each other. They have zippers for mouths," he tells me.

It's hard to take the real apocalypse seriously when you've seen it happen so often on TV.

My mom reminds me every time I see her that, when she is old and feeble, I will need to "do her in."

"I promise, Mom. I will. But you need to get the pills or whatever. I'm not a real doctor."

I wish I had been a real doctor. Or a psychologist. I like this idea of helping people. But my bedside manner is not so good. I'm too callous. I just hurt my mom's feelings by telling her she had to procure the drugs. If I loved her, I would figure out how to join the Hemlock Society or at least plant some fox glove in the backyard. It's one thing to be willing to do it. It's another to be matter-of-fact in tone when you agree to bump your mom off. But of course, I'm not serious. How could I kill my mother? I believe I believe I believe that she does not want to live with a weak body or mind but we've all been weak before. I pretend that I could do it. I can imagine myself sticking my fingers between her teeth, prying her mouth open. I could stick the pills down her throat, pour some water. Hold her nose closed. Keep my hand over her lips like I do when I have to give my dog Advil. I can imagine standing far above the scene, watching myself do it. But I am weak. Put me back in my real body. Put me back in my real time. Instead, I would stroke my mom's cheek saying, "I'm so sorry, Mom, I can't do it. If you meant it, you should have done it yourself." Because killing her would take more self-will than killing myself and I am not so willful. Dying is one thing but living is many. Living, like the weather, changes—all the time.

Our dog is so sick that Erik and I take the Cleo-carrying sheet out back where she lies in a pile of weeds and dirt to bring her inside. She is too big for either of us to carry alone. She smells bad and it hurts her to move but the temperature will get down to 15 degrees that night. We have to bring her inside. We pull her onto the sheet, bending her into a burrito. She makes weird gagging sounds that made us think we are choking her but we are probably just hurting her legs. She panics. Scrambles out of the sheet only to land on her back. She cringes. We try to help her walk into the house but she keeps collapsing. We end up half carrying her, half dragging her to her dog bed.

This will be the last time we will be able to carry her like this. We know that in the morning, she will likely be gone. Her eyes are sunken. Her fur has separated from her skin. She is a bag of bones, covered in a little bit of excrement. She can't hold her head up. I find her a pillow, lift her head, lay it down. I scratch her nose and tell her I am so sorry. That I will call the doctor after the long holiday weekend. That I am so sorry. That she could go, if she needs to. Zoë lies on the floor with me.

She says, "I love you, Cleo."

I say, "We love you, Cleo."

We lie by her for a long time. Cleo falls asleep. We can hear her breathe. The breaths are shallow and slow.

In the middle of the night, I hear something from behind my earplugs.

I ask Erik what it was.

"Cleo," he says.

I listen hard for the death rattle. I don't want to go watch but I don't want her to die alone. I force myself up, walk to the living room. I prepare myself for vomit and shit. For shallow breaths. For pleading eyes.

Instead I get a dog, wagging her tail, barking at the back door, scratching to go out. She has to pee. I let her go. Watch her walk around the house, a little wobbly, but walking nonetheless.

I eat butter. I eat cheese. I eat bacon. I would rather die of a heart attack than cancer even though it's possible butter and cheese and bacon will give me cancer too. But I remain hopeful for sudden. This slow dying. What is it good for? Thoughtfulness. Regret. Hope. And who knows? One nice thing about a slow death is maybe you're not dying at all. Every day, there's bad news: Your white cell count is low. The tumor's back. Your immune system eats the myelin sheathing your nerves. The Karposi's syndrome signals full-on AIDS. Lou Gehrig would have preferred to be remembered for something besides what killed him. The ocean's acid levels killed the oyster industry. Hurricane Sandy flooded your restaurant. The Cocos fire in San Diego burned down your house. The last known tiger was shot yesterday. The panda ate the remaining bamboo.

But you swallow your immune-supportive drug cocktail. You lie still for the chemo. You take your blood pressure medicine. You remove combustible materials from the edges of your yard. Hedge your bets.

You read about solar-shingles coming to your state anytime now. You hear on the radio that the Amazon rainforest isn't being deforested as quickly as it once was. The elephants might be coming back. There are otters in the river just down the hill from you.

You eat lentils for dinner and like them, even without bacon. You ride your bike to work. You have to share the road there are so many riders riding their bike to work. The oak trees, last to green, still green even though the snowpack was a third of what it was.

Hope and despair. A slow death gives life a slow chance.

Here's the solution and it has nothing to do with whether I can climb stairs or whether the otters, who I just found out existed less than forty miles from me, might be wiped out by the new water treatment plant in Prescott: Stop making lists of All The Bad Things. Make a list of a thing done well:

I danced to the "Sons and Daughters" song in the living room.

I picked the worm up from the garage floor and moved it to the dirt.

I sang, "Your dad has a funny beard. We think it's kind of weird. But at least it's less scratchy today." Max and Zoë like the lyrics. We sing it in the morning to Erik.

I serve as a trampoline for my children. Max's feet are small and Zoë's jumps are light.

I have recorded in words the stalks of Max and Zoë's spines. I have tried to triangulate their birth, their death, their long lives by remembering the way they said "jewelry." By the way they said "Ceelo" for Cleo, by the way they said "Mama" in the night. The way I say "goodnight, taco" and hear "goodnight, burrito" back.

I have thought of Erik's hair. How it is owl in the back and crow on the top. My head fits in his armpit. I could hibernate there. It is only funny the one time he crosses his arms imitating mine but it is funny, the one time. He would like to move to a smaller town, which means that we are enough nation for him. Erik picks up Zoë in his arms. Max climbs on his back. He is a mule and a donkey and a kangaroo to them both. I love animals. I wish I could cover myself with fur.

Erik says that he's calmest when he's playing the guitar. Just plucking at it. He doesn't need to be making a song or perfecting a riff. Just plucking. When I think about my calm place, I think about the time he said, "That wasn't so bad," after a dinner party he'd been dreading. I think about the time we came home from a restaurant and went through the Christmas cards to make sure we'd sent one to everyone who had sent one to us. I think about the time we were driving to go camping and I thought, this is the best life anyone could get. There was always a "we" in the car, a "we" in the mail, a "we" in the not so bad. He played guitar alone but I can hear him singing in the other room. I think he might have the "beard is weird" song stuck in his head. And me. Even this. I'm writing this song to someone. The maker of music is his own audience. The guitar surprises. The typewriter makes the same sound no matter how you strum the

"I." Wanting an audience is longing and longing is a wish for more time. To play music for yourself is to say, this is the time I have now.

Play the typewriter for someone later. Don't make them read, just ask them to listen. All those "I"-started sentences will make a music instead of an echo. The sound bouncing back to you off someone's ears. That's all you really need, at least this time, to get up from the backyard, shake the sticks off your fur, and walk back in the house.

A few months later, Cleo can't get up. She can walk but I have to lift her up, right underneath her belly. She's shedding, so I come away looking half malamute myself. She slips down again. She can barely take a few steps. Is this the time? I think so. I call the vet.

He comes, looks at her paws, saying, "They don't look too worn down. You know, you can get a sling to help you help her walk." I silently say, "Please take her out of her misery. Don't make me say it." Aloud I say, "Great. Let's try the pills."

"And, one more thing," he mentions. "Keep your eye out for maggots. Sometimes they don't get so clean back there and flies land. Breed."

You would think "maggots on the butt" was a clear sign that the time is now for euthanasia. But no. The doctor says to split these pills in half. He writes the name of the sling company on the bill. $80.50 for a still-living dog.

Later, I let her outside. She falls down a few feet from the back door. I leave her there. I don't know what she wants. That's the problem isn't it? She looks at me. She still likes biscuits. She just drank a bucket of water. Her ears point up. She's alive. Conscious. Fully present.

I go upstairs, take a shower. I will her to die. "C'mon, Cleo. Let go. Tell your heart to stop. Please don't make me do this."

If she were human, I wouldn't have to do this. It wouldn't be legal. And, even if I were willing to break the law, at least the human could tell me to do it. It's the worst-case scenario—something that seems like it's suffering beyond what's worth it but might not want to die. Who am I to say what worth is? When I go to her and put her head on my lap, she still looks up at me. Isn't every second of love I can give her worth it? Shouldn't she live her forever as long as she can? Who needs to walk? I can wash the shit off her one more day. I can wake up at 3:30 in the morning to let her out. To think about how cold she must be. To get back up and carry her back in.

But she cannot eat anything but biscuits. She cannot walk. The flies.

I make her stand up again. I lift her hips to stand her up. She can't step over the threshold. I lift her over the centimeters. I give her another biscuit. I'm the parent. I'm the human. I call the doctor. Friday? No. Thursday. It's time.

Does the *hu* in *hubris* come from *hu* in *human*? No, not according to the online etymology dictionary. *Hubris* is probably from the Greek *hybris,* "wanton violence, insolence, outrage," originally "presumption toward the gods"; and *human,* besides meaning "man," means, probably related to *homo* "man" (see *homunculus*) and to *humus* "earth," on notion of "earthly beings," as opposed to the gods.

Humans are defined as opposed to gods. And yet, here we are, with such hubris, acting like gods. Putting rivers over here. Moving mountains stuffed with coal over there. Mowing forests like ants at a picnic when the humans have gone off to play their picnic games. Opposing god's will? Will is temporal. I am holding out against time, like a one-woman rope pull. Rope burns and time always wins, but at least the full force of time is felt by willful hands.

When people say they "had" to put their cat or dog to sleep, I'm not sure I get the "had." Nobody made you do it. You chose to do it, and that's sometimes OK. I think of the five days in which the people were stuck in the hospital during Hurricane Katrina. If only the doctors and nurses had some perspective, the author insinuates, that this disaster wasn't going to last forever, they wouldn't have done what they did. But five days with shit floating in the toilets is forever. Cleo has shit stuck to her legs again. I look out the window to see flies circling. They are always circling.

The vet gives her a sedative. I give her one more biscuit. Erik gives her even one more. Cleo falls asleep. But ten minutes later, when Dr. Kurmes gives her the barbiturate, she wakes up, startles, looks me right in the eye.

Her eyes say, help me.

I say, I am sorry, so sorry, but you can't walk. I could have stayed with her another hundred years, giving her biscuit after biscuit but I can't pick you up any more and a dog has to be able to walk.

Today is less sad than yesterday but not by much. Max left his bowl of yogurt on the floor. I'm waiting for Cleo to come in the room to lick the bowl so I don't have to waste the water to rinse it out.

Sustainable Caulk

I GO WHOLE hours not liking Erik. I'm sure he goes whole hours not liking me but he just came home with a new tube of silicon to caulk the kitchen backsplash. If you don't like someone who is constantly armed with a caulking gun, who can you like? My house is impenetrable by any seal. Zombies could infiltrate neither through crack nor seam.

Judgey McJudgerson

FIRST OF ALL, he's driving a Cadillac Escalade. Estimated 16 miles per gallon city, 21 highway. Second of all, he's taking up two parking places. Third of all, he is sitting in the car, with the engine running. He has been since I pulled into the parking lot, completely turned my car off, walked down to the gym doors, waited my turn to call Zoë out from the line she sits in perfectly alphabetically, helped her carry her guitar, asked her how her day was while truly listening, walked back to my car, Honda CR-V, 21 city, 28 highway. (I wanted a Prius but with another baby on the way, it didn't seem practical for a family of four plus our dog and two cats, which is why having kids is bad environmental logic.) He was still there when I, perfect mother that I appear to be in the parking lot, hold the door open for my daughter and wait to start my car until the last possible minute, saving at least a cubic centimeter of oil. I glare at the Escalade driver who makes his kids open the huge doors to the SUV by themselves. Who have to haul themselves into the seats, using whatever handrails are made available to the first-grade set (seat belts will be used as climbing devices), who hoist their guitar cases and backpacks up the five feet into the cavern of the might-as-well-be-a-Humvee. Car idling all this time, the dad doesn't even drive off immediately. He waits in his car, staring out the window, ignoring my nasty look and my windshield-penetrating thoughts of thanks to you, this whole state is in a drought, this whole country's climate is wildly out of control, and this whole planet's glaciers are melting. I'm glaring at you on behalf of the polar bears.

Nature is rebellious and bad. In Woods Hole, Massachusetts, the Woods Hole Oceanic Institution trains a camera on an osprey nest. The scientists are not ornithologists at the Oceanic Institution. They study oceans and ocean-dwelling creatures. But outside the windows of the institution, where scientists work on their ocean work inside, is a nest of ospreys. The camera watched an empty nest for three years, after one of the ospreys, named after the founder of this osprey nest, who also died, died. Dead founder. Dead bird. Empty nest. Three years. Then one day, an egg appeared. Then another. Then another. Much rejoicing. The eggs hatched. Baby birds! But then, the mother bird started treating the babies not so well. She stopped feeding them. She pecked their heads. The babies turned on each other. "Tearing to shreds" comes to mind when you watch the mother interact with her babies. People-of-the-internet emailed the oceanographers. "Save the babies, please!" But the oceanographers, since they knew the ways of jellyfish dolphins and the rapidly disappearing starfish, but not so much the ways of birds, checked in with osprey experts who thought a) the mom was acting weird but b) in no way to intervene. The oceanographers didn't like looking at the mom harass the babies. No one wants to see babies die but the nature cam is recording nature, not human beings saving babies.

Car idler is not rebellious or bad. Cadillac driver has no idea why I am giving him the stink eye. He probably thinks I just have crusty-face, or I'm racist, or I'm jealous of his big car, or

I think he parked badly (which he did). He has no idea that the crusty face I'm wearing is the "you're just idling, wasting the planet, with your gigantic car idling machine." And what do I know about him? How is crusty-face helping anything? Perhaps my thoughts will penetrate the windshield, he'll turn off his car. Nay. He'll drive his car, one last time, to the Toyota dealership where he'll turn in the Escalade for a Prius, or, better yet, one of those new BMWs, the kind run entirely by wind power. Then, next time when I'm in the parking lot, still driving my 21 city, 28 highway Honda CRV, he can give me the stink eye.

The mother bird tears at the first baby's feather. She kicks at the second baby's chest with her talons. She puts food in the third baby's mouth and then takes it back out and swallows it herself. The babies are malnourished. The oceanographers wring their hands but they know that wringing their hands is all they can do. One baby bird gets a ribbon from a balloon tied around his claw. The website reads:

> On rare occasions, a bird may become entangled in items that they've brought into the nest, such as rope, balloon string, plastic bags, etc. Please know that in our area they usually free themselves with no harmful result but that it might take some time, and some behavior that may appear frantic and distressing could take place as they do so, so please be patient. Calls for immediate response are understandable, but please know it could cause the animal to fly off with the item, or struggle more, potentially putting it at greater risk of harm.
>
> In the extremely rare case of the animal being completely immobilized by human-introduced material, we will evaluate and consult with experts and proceed as they deem best.

Humans should get out of the way of humans eventually but possibly immediately out of the way of birds.

How do I know why the dad idles his car? Perhaps he's charging his cell phone to make a call to the dealership to buy his Prius. Perhaps he is recovering from hypothermia and needs the heater to heal his toes of frostbite. Perhaps he doesn't even have toes! Perhaps he is worried about the call he just got from his boss and the layoffs at Walgreens distribution center and the last thing on his mind was whether his car was on or off. Perhaps he didn't notice that it hadn't snowed this year. Perhaps he doesn't equate his idling his car with the lack of snow. Perhaps he knows that even if he drove a Prius, the snow will not come back. It's too late, even if we all drove Priuses. Perhaps the reason he didn't get out of the car to help his kids walk up from the gym to the parking lot is that he knows that what his kids will need to do is learn to climb and hoist and bear the brunt of heavy things.

No one knows why the mom osprey was acting weird. Maybe she knew in advance that the small territory, with the encroaching institutions and departments and malls and complexes, left to these osprey couldn't support three baby osprey. Maybe survival of the fittest begins in the nest. Maybe the sweet, tender preening of the ordinary osprey is a thing that doesn't happen on camera. Maybe the bird, watched by humans, knew these baby birds would be human-seen and therefore, disrupted. Maybe she was teaching humans pity—please, bring some food to my babies. Maybe she was teaching empathy—these babies, don't hurt them. Maybe she was teaching a lesson in how nature works—toughen up, children of the snow. It's going to be another sunny day.

•

The other day, my sister Valerie posted a picture of her lunch on Facebook. Frisée aux lardons, or, as we like to call it, salad with bacon, croutons, and poached eggs. Valerie noted in her post, made with cage-free eggs. I wrote back, "They still sell eggs from caged hens." She countered, "I only buy cage-free when they're on sale. I'm on a budget." I went to the internet to Google the cost difference. I had no idea. I don't even look at the price of the caged-hens eggs. I guess it is about $1 or $1.50 different. But I didn't want to be a jerk. Instead, I found a website that noted California has banned caged eggs. I wrote, "California, über alles" in a comment on her post. I didn't post that, after debeaking the hen, egg producers put eight to nine chickens in a small cage, allotting each bird sixty-seven inches of space—less than a sheet of paper. I don't say this but I'm still a jerk. I shouldn't say, I still love you. I should say, I love you. And maybe send her $20. Or a chicken. Notice that no one, pig lovers all, said anything about the bacon.

I was thinking today as I dropped my kids off and three of the five cars dropping off were Chevy Suburban-type gas guzzlers, and I thought about how hard it is to get people to change their beliefs, about, for instance, global warming. And then, I thought, Fox News makes people believe things all the time. And then I thought, it's easy to believe stories that don't make you change your mind about anything ever. The best propaganda makes us think about ourselves. The best stories make us think about other people.

Straw Men

THERE ARE TWO kinds of straws in the world, flexible and not. (There may be other kinds of straw, like cocktail, Slurpee, and hay but for the purposes of this argument, there are two. Picture white with red stripe. Accordion ribbing on the one. Flat plastic on the other.) Perhaps this is the end of that argument. But keep it in mind. Two straws.

Before we left for Phoenix to catch our plane to Salt Lake, Erik put on his trucker hat.

I shook my head. "Please, please don't wear that. You have nice hair. That hat is so ugly."

I have a lot of problems. Worrying about other people's appearance and that hat are two of them. The first I have tried to quit. I don't bug Erik anymore about wearing his stretchy pants to the store or the shirt with paint stains on it to dinner. But this hat. It sits on top of his head like an extra head—and Erik's head is already big. He doesn't need two. The brim goes out instead of down, making his brow look wide and square. There is mesh on the back of the hat for easy cooling. He could grab a can of chaw and look more the part. This hat strikes the fear of God, or perhaps, Burt Reynolds, into my heart.

I should shut up. It's just a hat. It's his life. He probably wears it extra just because I complain. But I don't shut up.

"Just please, don't bring the hat to Salt Lake." My eyes roll. Erik mocks my eye roll and adds a *tsk*.

"That's fine. I won't bring the hat. I won't bring anything. I'm not going."

It is rare that we get out of the house for a trip without one of us threatening to stay home. I'm usually mad because I'm the one cleaning out the sink before we leave. Erik's usually mad because we're going to be late and the sink is fine with coffee grounds—we won't be here for them to bother us.

We also both always finally get in the car, hat and coffee grounds and all.

On the drive, I kept telling the kids we'd stop in Prescott, but everyone knew I meant Camp Verde and Erik didn't bother correcting me which was when I knew he wasn't mad anymore and I knew I was being an idiot about the hat. He bought cracked pepper sunflower seeds. I bought beef jerky. On the way down the mountain, he shared his seeds. I handed him pieces of meat. The kids and I sang "Baby You Can't Love One" as Erik drove. Our skin puffed up from all the salt. Max's ears wouldn't pop. I told him to open his mouth wide and wiggle his jaw. "What is wiggle?"

"You know, like move it back and forth."

"Like my booty?"

"Like your booty."

I put my naked feet up on the dashboard like I did when I drove Erik home from the night we first hooked up. We'd gone camping in the San Raphael Swell with a bunch of friends. I drove down alone because I had to stay in Salt Lake. I'd signed up to volunteer for the Sierra Club. I didn't do much. Handed out bumper stickers? Asked people to sign a petition? I left early anyway. I wanted Erik to know I meant it when I said we could go camping together. That I meant the together part. And that's how we drove home. My feet on the dashboard, spitting the shells of sunflower seeds unsexily into old Diet Coke cans.

At the Chevron, I'd filled up my Nalgene. Erik forgot to get a drink. Sunflower seeds and beef jerky are really only salt. Erik asked for a sip. I offered him my water bottle—the kind with a straw. His hands were full, driving and sunflowering, so I reached over to bend the straw, which really isn't bendy, but will bend, if pressed, toward his mouth. He drank it. Max asked for some. Maybe it would help pop his ears. Zoë wanted some too. By the time we were in the real desert—the one with the saguaros, we were almost out of water but we were almost to the airport. One straw, four people. That must be some kind of conservation.

In this light, Erik looked kind of good in his hat.

Action

SOMETIMES YOU HAVE to go down to the bottom. Sometimes, you take the bad stuff with you and sink it. Sometimes you drown. Sometimes, you take the bad stuff with you, sink it, come back up, bringing gifts like sturgeon and carbon-sucking algae and delicious Dungeness crab from the ocean floor. Maybe a joke too.

To go into the darkness, the airy darkness as opposed to the watery darkness, means you might find bats. Your fear of bats is irrational you know. Where does it come from? Is your neck that precious? Your hair? You know it's thanks to them that you can walk outside without a country of Deep Woods Off applied to your delicate skin. It's thanks to them that there's not malaria around here. "Intricate balance" is the love-child phrase of the environmentalist. I don't have to see the bats to know they're there.

Jennifer Michael Hecht, an author and a suicide-prevention advocate, wrote an essay for VOX called "10 Things I Wish People Knew About Suicide." She begins by arguing, as I have argued in the past, since I was seventeen, applying to Reed College and citing St. Augustine, probably erroneously, that suicide is morally neutral. That it's a person's choice. That, perhaps, it is the only real act of free will one can exert.

But fuck free will. Free will suggests individualism. It suggests that the ego is supremely isolated. It suggests that the will of one person outweighs the will of us all. The all here, according to Hecht, is this: suicides sometimes spur other suicides, making your singular suicide a kind of murder. That suicide suggests for all of us that life is not worth the paper it's written on. That almost everyone has suicidal thoughts. If we knew each other's thoughts, we would not be so afraid of our own. And, in a parallel-universe-many-lives-in-one-body kind of way, Hecht argues that we owe it to future selves, and our future moods, to give those future selves a chance to live. If spatial dissociation—I can see myself walking toward the gun, I can see myself pull the trigger—sometimes makes it possible for us to kill ourselves, perhaps temporaral dissociation—I can see myself as an old woman in a rocking chair, I can see myself with grandkids—might prevent it. A community of selves. A community of suicidals, who do not, in the end, suicide. A community of saving the self so that others may live.

Fungi are morally inert. The mushrooms that tuck extra carbon into the ground seem good but they, in the end, might die and release that carbon back into the atmosphere. Points for trying, I suppose. Mushrooms can fell a tree and mushrooms can turn a tree into food for a sapling. Mushrooms can grow in your carpet and they can grow in your teeth but mushrooms can give rice a reason to live. Truffles and chanterelles can turn a carnivore vegetarian, or at least fungiterean. Mushrooms erupt like volcanos or horny penises. Mushrooms grow in centrifugal rings called fairies, because another word for magic is *ecology*.

The white-nose fungus that smothers bats, forces them to awaken from their hibernation and flail against wintery cave walls is obviously bad. But the fungus is happy, living life on the warm snout of a sleeping bat like an Arkansan on a Hawaiian beach. Life proliferates. There is grass everywhere. There are people everywhere. Every other centimeter of this planet boasts a fungus. A community of fungi. Perhaps what we fail to understand about white-nose syndrome is how the next-door-neighbor fungi could be of use. Perhaps another fungus could intricate-balance its way into the nose and figure out how to save the bat, not because it's the right thing to do but because that's what fungi do.

Drug and alcohol addiction might be morally neutral. Drugs certainly don't care if you take them or not. Your drug dealer might care if you take them, but only if you pay for them. When I worked at the Oregon Winegrowers' Association, we put a lot of time into publicizing studies that showed how good red wine was for your heart. Did we care about Chardonnay drinkers? No. Pinot noir is the wine of Oregon. We had nothing for beer or whiskey drinkers. Let their arteries clog! We were wrong to abandon our fellow drinkers, even if they drank white.

Johann Hari, author of *Chasing the Scream, The First and Last Days of the War on Drugs,* writes for the *Huffington Post* about a study done in the 1970s to show that jonesing for the chemical in cocaine or heroin isn't what leads to addiction—isolation is. He points to a study done by Bruce Alexander in the 1970s, showing that rats, alone in a cage, will certainly drink the cocaine-tainted water. But when he put rats in "rat park," a lovelier cage filled with colorful balls and delicious snacks and rat-friends, the rats shunned the drug-tainted water.

Hari cites studies where trauma patients are given morphine for months and yet, when they return to their normal lives, they generally stop hankering for morphine no problem, as long as their normal lives included the human equivalent of colorful balls, delicious snacks, and rat-friends.

Heroin-using soldiers returning from Vietnam, citing further research by Alexander, immediately upon return to their normal lives, stopped using heroin.

This normal life may be a little bit middle-class hegemony, a little reactionary in wanting to keep the prevailing social structure intact but perhaps if you think of normal as "intricate balance" instead of two-car garage, you won't accuse me of such things. Hari writes,

> Nearly fifteen years ago, Portugal had one of the worst drug problems in Europe, with 1% of the population addicted to heroin. They had tried a drug war, and the problem just kept getting worse. So they decided to do something radically different. They resolved to decriminalize all drugs, and transfer all the money they used to spend on arresting and jailing drug addicts, and spend it instead on reconnecting them—to their own feelings, and to the wider society. The most crucial step is to get them secure housing, and subsidized jobs so they have a purpose in life, and something to get out of bed for.

I think of my dad in his kitchen, the one without any brown sugar or flour. The house where only people who wanted money went to visit. I used to wonder how he got so sick so fast after my parents divorced—my mom was one of the only things connecting him to the larger world. He cut her out of his life by taking another woman to Club Med, buying her a pair of expensive cowboy boots, and leaving the receipt where my mom could find it. Then he lost his job, the last tenuous connection. No colorful balls. No delicious snacks. No rat-friends.

Sometimes it's safe to go into the darkness. Go into the suicidal thoughts? What's there? A picture of me and my thumbs typing. Then, the thumbs type. "A book is a suicide postponed," observed Emil Cioran, the Romanian philosopher.

> Globally, suicide is on the rise. According to a 2013 *Newsweek* cover story it took more lives worldwide than "war, murder and natural disasters combined." We're apparently killing ourselves at a greater rate now than we're killing each other. Whatever that high watermark for humanity implies of our times, authors are said to commit suicide, and suffer the mental illness that can lead to it, at twice the rate of the general population. E. L. Doctorow joked to *The Paris Review* "writing is a socially acceptable form of schizophrenia." Or was he joking? The long list of self-murdering writers includes Virginia Woolf, who suffered mentally while capturing those torments on the page, to Ernest Hemingway, whose family has had five suicides over four generations, to Auschwitz survivor Primo Levi, to Anne Sexton and Sylvia Plath, Richard Brautigan, Hunter S. Thompson, Spalding Gray, and David Foster Wallace.

And maybe it's because these authors went deep and could never resurface. That the fear of life was worse than the fear of death, as David Foster Wallace himself wrote in *Infinite Jest.*

> The so-called "psychotically depressed" person who tries to kill herself doesn't do so out of quote "hopelessness" or any abstract conviction that life's assets and debits do not square. And surely not because death seems suddenly appealing. The person in whom its invisible agony reaches a certain unendurable level will kill herself the same way a trapped person will eventually jump from the window of a burning high-rise. Make no mistake about people who leap from burning windows. Their terror of falling from a great height is still just as great as it would be for you or me standing speculatively at the same window just checking out the view; i.e., the fear of falling remains a constant. The variable here is the other terror, the fire's flames: when the flames get close enough, falling to death becomes the

> slightly less terrible of two terrors. It's not desiring the fall; it's terror of the flames. Yet nobody down on the sidewalk, looking up and yelling "Don't!" and "Hang on!," can understand the jump. Not really. You'd have to have personally been trapped and felt flames to really understand a terror way beyond falling.

You have two choices. Jump or flames. Or rather, "you only have two choices" is you're the fulcrum on the scale, if you're the linchpin, if you, individual, are the only one making life or death decisions around here. But perhaps you're holding up the ceiling with one arm, holding open the window with another. Perhaps your breath is simultaneously fanning the flames and putting them out. Perhaps if you jump, you'll land on someone else. Perhaps you'll land on your mother, which, for most people, is never the jumping intent. Fear of flames or fear of jumping are just fear. If you would just look at those wild, opposable thumbs holding up that ceiling, propping open that window, chimpanzees, gorillas, and humans would remind you, you're not alone. Look at the polydactyl cat, the East African maned rat (in fact, many of the genus *muridae* have thumbs—like most of the rats and mice). The bat—it too has thumbs. "Like humans, bats have 4 fingers and a thumb on each hand, but the fingers are very long—each about as long as the body—and very thin. The thumb is relatively small and has a claw that is used for gripping when the bat is at rest, whereas the fingers have lost their claws (except in many fruit bats of the Old World, which have a claw on their second finger).

You are not alone, human.

Writer, who is always already two, is like a pregnant woman. Only in the cruelest movies do they let the pregnant woman die. The writer, who goes down to the ocean floor to dig up the dark matter, the writer, who goes outside into the dark to triangulate the distance of alpha centari, the writer, who delves into their addictions and their suicides and finds a good joke.

The writer/artist/scientist/bat is everyone who gets something out of the dark. Perhaps anyone who does anything writes. And therefore lives. And anyone who has people, also lives. I realize that if Oregon calls, it doesn't matter. I will be with my people and the bats wherever we go, no matter how thirsty we or our forest gets.

There are only two things to fear: loneliness and thirst. So you go outside. You step out into the evening. The sun is going down. You know where the bats hang. You can stand beside them. Feel the spores of various fungi land on your eyelashes, on your fingernails. Invite that athlete's foot into your sock. You, humans, so numerous, should look to the largest organisms in the world. Two vie for first place. The honey mushroom and the aspen forest. Either way, they each win first place for the way they're tied together—underneath, using mycelia-type connectors to keep their fruiting bodies up through the surface where, in the aspen's case, the branches bend and wave and, in the honey mushroom's case, the caps themselves undulate. Hello, fellow fruiting bodies. Hello, they say. They wave. They, even rooted to the ground, act.

On Beauty

I WOKE UP this morning, having gone to sleep thinking about some lines Eric Lemay wrote in his book *In Praise of Nothing*. He is writing about returning to Ohio as a now-married man, having grown up in this town in Ohio (Athens?) but had moved to New York for a decade or so. The essay is about how he feels like two people at once, or, rather, feels as if his old self was never interrupted. That his old life and his current life are parallels, nearly one-in-the-same, but different because he observes both selves as if from outer space. He witnesses his past life and his current life from a dissociated distance. "Every time we went [to the lake] I wondered if I'd entered that pattern, if I was my younger self or the self in my swimsuit." But that sense of dislocation, of dissociation falls apart when a thunderstorm hits at the lake he visited in his past life, at the lake he is visiting in his current life.

> One afternoon while we were there at that lake a thunderstorm came up. It was like a message from a far-off country that I'd once lived in and left for good. The momentous

> feeling that arrives with an electrical disturbance over a lake in America hasn't changed in any important respect. This was the sublime, still the sublime. The whole thing was overwhelming, the overcast clouds that rolled in and the general worry on the beach about whether it'd rain. Then before long (there was no question now) a dark greening of the sky, and a lull in everything that has made life tick; and then the way the leaves suddenly turned up and showed their silver sides with the coming of a breeze across the water, and the premonitory rumble.

There is no more wondering who is who. The essay ends with LeMay saying, "Suddenly I felt the joy of my youth."

In the feeling, in the moment, in the beauty of those leaves-turned-silver, the fractured self comes together in one trembling, unified mass. It didn't matter if it was the LeMay or any other book or painting or actual silver shimmering. What mattered was the notice.

Having awakened thinking of this passage and thinking about how this sublime brings the selves, the writer self, the younger self, the swim-suited self, the married self, the young turked self, the observer self, and the observed self together, I wondered what did it? What allowed for the collapse into unity?

Sublime beauty. I think. It takes an overwhelming event to bring the senses to bear, to bring the selves together.

How does beauty work? Or sublime beauty. I would have to look it up. Perhaps Montaigne would have an idea. I wrote an essay for an anthology dedicated to Montaigne's work. Maybe Montaigne could help me with sublime beauty.

So I opened up the Google Docs collection of Montaigne's essays. I looked through the table of contents. No "On Beauty." I did a regular Command + F search. Nothing in the table of contents. However, the "Find" function took me to the word *beauty* on the first page. I hit the return key.

The "Find" function took me to page 66. Then 95 then 156, 205. Every thirty pages or so of the nearly 3,000-word document the word *beauty* appears. Although there is no single essay "On" beauty, beauty stitches the whole collection of essays together.

Maybe this is the point, maybe beauty is the stitch, I thought, although I did dread reading through *all* of the Montaigne essays. Montaigne is good on a subject or two but to read them all at once, to read them to distill his views on Beauty, to trouble anyone who might read this with a series of beauty quotations, is to akin to looking for Max's monkey that he may have left under his bed, in the car, on the back porch, in his closet, or, possibly, at the restaurant. It's very good to have read/looked, but the reading/looking is taxing. We will read all of the Montaigne. We will find the monkey. Just perhaps not today.

But the idea that the word *beauty* existing so often but not as its own thing made me think about the big bang, how elements from the big bang are in each of us—how we are physically connected through matter and the "we" is wide. Me, you, and the lilac bush, the tree with the widest trunk in Oaxaca, General Sherman, the tree with the biggest mass in California, the tiny stick and the microorganism, the largest spider and the titmouse, the Doberman and the orange tabby. Molecules all expanding, expanding. The big bang was a big break. Humans are good at tracing that break back together. As David Kirby has said,

> Everywhere the world is broken,
> and only the poets can make it one again.

In the Slide fire, a pair of nesting herons lost their chicks. A ranger found four heron babies lying on a picnic table under their nest. The mother heron flapped around the campsite all day, frantically looking for her children. I wondered how many animals had died in the fire. Emily, the one who packed up our things during the pre-evacuation order for the Little America fire, said, "As we breathe the smoke, we are breathing them." For a minute I thought she was being very woowoo Sedona, and then I knew what she meant. Animal particles going up our noses. It was horrible. It was kind of beautiful. Horrible beauty shocks.

The Navajo people have a ceremony to restore returning war veterans into the community. These ceremonies help the Navajo war veterans return to a state of balance, or beauty, within the universe. This state of balance is called "Hozho" in the Navajo language.

> Happily may their roads back home be on the trail
> of pollen.
> Happily may they all get back.
> In beauty I walk.
> With beauty before me, I walk.
> With beauty behind me, I walk.
> With beauty below me, I walk.
> With beauty above me, I walk.
> With beauty all around me, I walk.
> It is finished in beauty,
> It is finished in beauty,
> It is finished in beauty,
> It is finished in beauty.
> 'Sa'ah naaghéi, Bik'eh hózhó
> —a Navajo Ceremony Song

Beauty is such a spacey word. It doesn't hold much weight on its own. But Eric LeMay's silver leaves hold some weight. And the lilac bush holds some weight. The human-sized cracks in the bark in the tree called General Sherman, the snow on the eyelash, Max's chin, Max's monkey, Zoë's eyelashes, the snow on Zoë's eyelashes, Erik's cheekbone,

Erik's hand in my lap. Even the smoke holds a little weight when you inhale deeply every animal that it burns.

Last week, Safa Motesharrei published a report using data from NASA research, argues that civilization as we know it will last only a few more decades.

> Motesharrei's report says that all societal collapses over the past 5,000 years have involved both "the stretching of resources due to the strain placed on the ecological carrying capacity" and "the economic stratification of society into Elites [rich] and Masses (or "Commoners") [poor]." This "Elite" population restricts the flow of resources accessible to the "Masses," accumulating a surplus for themselves that is high enough to strain natural resources. Eventually this situation will inevitably result in the destruction of society.

I feel bad for my kids. Forcing them to live in a world full of big brown bats with rabies was bad enough. I did not intend to saddle them with a big brown planet. When I imagine the worst of my fears coming true—no food, no electricity, no water, no trees—I have the capacity to delude myself: Max and Zoë will find a nice spot in the Northwest to hole up while the worst of the violence and depredation rages. They will live among the bears, learn to pick salmonberries, learn to catch salmon. When it's over, they'll return to a smaller, more egalitarian world where everyone is happy just to eat the fruit of shrubberies, just to watch the bears. Less happy visions include Zoë and Max, living underground, siphoning water from Malcolm McDowell's water monopoly like Lori Petty and her band of mutant kangaroos as in the movie *Tank Girl,* or fighting over canned beans with other desperate end-of-the-worlders like in *The Walking Dead*. There is good news. Motesharrei reports no zombies.

It's my ability to imagine this prelapsarian Eden for my kids that I deny the images of the misery they most certainly will inherit.

Later in the day, NASA distanced itself from the report, saying that although Motesharrei used their data, they in no way support his findings. "As is the case with all independent research, the views and conclusions in the paper are those of the authors alone. NASA does not endorse the paper or its conclusions." I breathe a sigh of relief. If only NASA could alleviate all anxieties through a statement or two about its endorsements and conclusions.

The poet Marie Howe, in an interview with Terry Gross on NPR's *Fresh Air,* remembered her brother saying, as he was dying of AIDS, "Everyone feels pain. You can choose whether or not to suffer." Terry balked. "I don't think I choose. I suffer." And Marie Howe said, "Well, I guess suffering does tie us all together." Later, Howe said, "Poetry holds the knowledge that we are alive and that we know we're going to die," Another kind of negative capability, another kind of intelligence—being able to be so happy we are alive even though we are so sad we are going to die. There's something beautiful about the idea we are all dying together.

That Philip Larkin "This Be the Verse" poem ends like this:

> Get out as early as you can,
> And don't have any kids yourself.

That misery. It keeps us together. That coastal shelf is growing and it is beautiful. Look, kids. The tide is coming in. It is beautiful.

Images will sustain us. Bad images. Good images. The image of a broken-necked dove. The image of a bald eagle as tall as you are. I can see the lilac bush, tilted half way in the wind. The last petals hang on. The bush bends so hard, the petals touch the ground. The petals sweep the ground. The ground is clean and purple now. I put my nose to the dirt and smell the spring.

Real images. Imaginary images. Our own brains looking infiltrated by images. How are we one with the world? Because the images reverberate in our heads. The images go to the paper. The paper goes to the eyes. The eyes see the paper. They send a message to the hands. The hands plant a lilac bush because they want the dirt to smell of lilac.

Even the sky breaking blue holds a little weight. Everyone finds something beautiful. The ATV rider finds the stream just as beautiful as the hiker finds the stream. The hunter finds the grizzly bear just as beautiful as the photographer finds the bear. The gun lover loves his metal as much as the car owner loves her metal as much as the solar panel loves its metal. Erik sands and polishes the baseboards. He plays the guitar. Karen learns time-lapse photography. Rebecca paints a painting of her mother in a posters bed, draperies frame her mother's body as if she's in a painting.

The most beautiful thing is rain because it rains a little bit everywhere even if it's raining upward as the clouds pull water from the pines.

You Can Choose What You Remember

YOU CAN CHOOSE what you remember. You can even choose what you think about. When you think of love, you want it to flow like water. You want to go in it like you go into a stream, naked-toed and body-hot, like you want to lay your body against the warm waves of Bermuda, like you want to jump from the edge of granite into the murky brown lake water and come up swimming. You want love to swirl around you like it swirls through your hair. The currents of water you want to be the same as love: constant. Always in motion. And completely beyond your control. But love doesn't work like that—it's not all floaty and swirly. You can't always feel the water move. Sometimes the current stops. To make motion requires the work of the swimming. It is up to you to make your brain swim in a loving direction.

We had only been dating three weeks when Erik woke up at six-thirty, whispered in my mostly sleeping ear that he would be right back. Two hours later, he returned. He dug through all his drawers and boxes. He upended his mattress. He lifted nightstands and checked in Levi pockets until he found the ring that his dad had given his mom. The metal was hammered. The stone was as dark, uneven, mottled with what might have once been lichen. His parents had been divorced forever. The ring didn't mean perfection. It didn't mean forever. It meant, *I only have one of these. I'll give it to you.*

He asked me to marry him again on the deck of a cabin in Torrey, Utah, and he asked me again by the Provo River in Sundance. He asked me to marry him all over Utah. I said yes every time.

I remember how I insisted you listen to me tell you who I'd slept with before to make sure you knew that I had a history, that I was a bit of a Superfund site, not pure Evian—that I wasn't fresh, unsullied but complex, murky. I poison quickly. I could, if I wanted to, remember how we argued over the word *collateral*. You insisted it came from the idea to collect. That collateral couldn't be avoided. I argued that no, collateral is what you owe me. If I don't take out any loans, no one will be hurt accidentally. You didn't understand. You brought up Iraq. I brought up gambling in Wendover, Nevada. That poor dog we tried to rescue. That dog that we waited with at a Humane Society that never opened. That's collateral. Wendover owes me. You said, "only if the dog lived," which led me to cry in the bathroom and to you driving off in the car with our dog named Cleo who we got at a Humane Society that was not in Nevada. I could remember this but instead I remember the way I went out to the car before you drove away and handed you part of a toenail that I had torn on the bottom of the bathroom door. I handed it to you and you shook your head but ate it anyway.

How else will I dive into him?

It is only through water that memories are made. Like oysters, nothing changes us too much, until it does. Erik read me a story from the *Salt Lake Tribune* even though we lived far away from Salt Lake and oil drilling at the time. He was bothered by the way the water turned oily in Liberty Park. A man-made lake that when he was young he rode paddleboats on and where when I was young I threw bread to the ducks and where when we were both young and both there at separate times and spaces, we threw sticks under the bridge to see the water usher them under but then later when we were old and almost stick-less, an oil pipe broke nearby flooding the lake and the ducks and the bread and the sticks. He took his metaphorical stick and raised it high. He said, they are ruining that lake. They must be stopped. And although neither oil nor spilling stopped at his very insistence, the stick he holds reminds me that memories float.

One day, we were talking, fighting really, about pi. When our daughter asked how to define pi, I said that pi helps describe a circle. Erik said no. He laughed at me! He said, pi is used to define circumference. The area of a circle is pi times *r* squared. I know that. I hate it when people think I can't do math. I took my wine and marched upstairs to watch TV without him. A divorce of staircases.

He did not apologize. Nor did I when I said maybe it's not a math problem but an English problem since you don't seem to understand the word *describe*. *Scribe* means "to write." I'll draw a circle for you. But he has a system. A three-touches-to-the-shoulder system. And then he says something stupid to me, instead of "I'm sorry," he says, "You can never have too much cheese. Especially if it's in a circle." And I have no idea what he's talking about but I laugh and I'm lost and the staircase carries me back to the ground floor where we avoid talking about cheese or circles ever again or at least for an hour.

It was Erik who told me the oysters were dying as the oceans turned acidic from global warming but it was also he who strapped on his camera and said let's make a movie about people who are not fucking up. About how people are unfucking if not whole oceans than at least whole puddles of nitrate-ridden water, about how people understand how microclimates pinch their Grenache grapes cold but ripen their Chardonnay grapes sweet and how, if we begin to follow microclimates that maybe we can be like the grape and reorganize the way we bend into the flow of canyon air streaming down to us in Sedona from Flagstaff on high, that if we massage micropreemie babies they will go home sooner and sooner and he brought the information to me in the way the internet brings information, in a flow, similar to water when I'm sunk in sadness at the memory of water broken by oil spills, broken by stupid fights, broken by nitrates, broken by pi, broken by global warming, broken by choose, he stands in front of me and agitates. Like a washing machine.

We used to spend a lot of time in that cabin in Torrey, Utah. Right outside of Capital Reef National Park. Sandstone is dry and sculpted and you are in no need of clothes. I wore Levis without a shirt. Erik played guitar on the deck. We took hot walks to hot rocks and had hot sex on them. Once, we were walking up the river bed (this is later, after we had kids), and I suggested that maybe the hot sand in the dry riverbank would be a good place for hot sex but he said no, this is a thoroughfare. He was right. Five minutes later, a man came from behind us carrying the morning paper and coffee in the middle of the desert in the middle of a dry riverbank and Erik knows more than most about the ways of rivers and dry people in dry lands.

Sometimes we did not live together and so coming back together was like bringing the water to a dry land. Erik had been in the Northwest for school. He drove his truck there and he drove his truck back carrying this time thirty-six oysters for him and me to share in the desert city of Salt Lake, where I grew up loving oysters even if growing up there was the wrong place and time (desert, the eighties) and he brought three dozen to my doorstep. We had lemon and an oyster knife but no real shucking skills. We're from Utah. We know bees. But he found a notch. He knew where to place the knife and I watched to try to figure it out. I held the oyster in my hand. I pressed the knife against the lip although I couldn't tell if I was springing the back hatch and prying upon the front hood. I pushed with the knife. The shell flaked. The lip closed tighter. The one time I managed to slip the knife wholly through, the oyster clenched his hinge so tight, I lost the blade to the creature. Well-armed oyster militia. Erik took the oyster and the knife and twisted like he whistles—so softly you can barely hear him. The oyster opened. The muscle revealed. I slid the knife under the oyster to cut foot from food. Erik had really done the work but he let me take credit. "A perfect one. Good job."

There are water problems like flammable water. There are water problems like water full of dry cleaning chemicals, of rocket fuel, of nitrates, of pesticides, of birth control pills and Prozac, of coffee and of urine. There is dirty water. There are these awesome things though called water treatment brains and while there is a lot of water that can't be helped there is a lot of water that can be helped. In the cerebellum, you expose the water to air. This deletes almost 50% of the bad memories. Then, you anaerobically contain the water. Putting a lid on it. This deletes almost 45% of the other bad memories. The last 5% of bad memories can have their pollutants dissolved by acts of kindness by microorganisms that turn the bad memories good. It's like *A Clockwork Orange* for water although the water does not need to have his eyes peeled back. The microorganisms are more on the positive reinforcement side. They take a nitrate and say, hey you, let us mingle. I'll toss off one of your oxygens and you will turn into sweet, sweet, nitrogen. Nitrogen is safe for all. Perfect nitrogen. Good job.

Of course there was the bad time when we were walking on campus and two women were walking toward us and he nudged me off the path to give them more room. And there was the time when he bought himself a new toothbrush but not one for me. He leaves beer bottles and towels everywhere. He does not cook or really clean. One time, he claimed we went out to eat more than anyone he knew, which would be a fine thing to say, if he ever cooked. Of course, when he tries to cook, I try to oversee, checking on the temperature of the onions (should be on low), of the seasoning (more than you would think), on the adding of cold oil to a cold pan (you can't do that) so perhaps the cooking is less a *won't* than *a won't be let to* but sometimes he emails me to see which kid to pick up first and I say Max but then calls me when he can't find Zoë's dance room and I say *ask Max who is three but good with directions* and he says *I came to get Zoë first* and I say *I said to get Max first so he could show you where Zoë's dance room is. Why did you email me twenty minutes of typing* and I say *the dance room is at the very end of the elementary school* and I hang up all mad but I text and ask *where is the bad husband room* and he texts and says but *my heart is pure* and still we go to dinner and we take both kids, one who lies down on the bench-seat, the other who still eats at age seven with her hands and we sit and we talk all at once to each other and everyone is eating oysters and eating lots of cheese. We can talk about circles again. We have already forgotten what describes a circle. Nothing describes or defines a circle. Like love, like water, circles just are.

The oysters are not doing well but this is no time to waver in our love for them or for each other. We have a secret. One day, we are going to move north to where the oysters are. Erik is going to build a yurt. We are going to learn about harvesting biofuel from algae. We are going to have solar panels for the seven days that there is sun. We are going to live close enough to the water that we will insert, as into a womb an IUD, wires that will roll with the incoming and the outgoing of the waves, making turbines, filling batteries, making sure that the internet is off the grid but still turned to "on" because otherwise how would we know what kinds of oysters we should grow in these beds of ours down by the sea. Do we need a wooden box or some chicken wire? Do we need to feed the oysters or just sway the plankton over them with tree boughs from our nearby Douglas fir?

Speaking of Douglas fir. Perhaps I am wrong about love and water. Perhaps it is not the swirling of hair-in-water that is love. Perhaps it is in the choosing and felling of a tree. Perhaps it is in the sewing and hewing. The measure. The determination of tools. It should not take more than one or two trees to make a large yurt. Perhaps this yurt is not sustainable exactly although once felled you do plant two new trees and these two-long-lived, long-limbed trees can serve to build your off-the-grid home. Erik, although he knows many things about water and oysters, is, almost preternaturally, a carpenter. He leaves more saws around the house than beer caps. He makes perfect circles with his planer and his awl. I could describe them with pi but he will define them with sandpaper and oil. He will rub into them linseed and polyurethane. He will join and shim these circles. The circles will stack and the rooms will grow like hives. He will set windows through which sun will flow like honey and we will warm ourselves sustainably with the sun honey and the love that we chose to remember. Like misshapen rings inside this perfectly shaped circle on top of the impossibly polluted world, we will sit by the ocean, hoping our oysters learn to like a lower pH in their water as we will have learned to stop talking circles about the exact definition of words and instead circle our meaning in metaphor. Sometimes, when you've been hanging out in water for so long, you don't even notice that water doesn't need to move to be and that *to be* is still a verb.

Further Reading

How the earth is emotionally detached from human behavior:
https://theamericanscholar.org/what-the-earth-knows/#.VMkjg17F8YI

How without mushrooms there would be no forests:
https://treesforlife.org.uk/forest/forest-ecology/mycorrhizas/

How to calculate your carbon footprint:
http://www.carbonfund.org/how-we-calculate#Transportation

Some really cool statistics about McDonald's:
http://www.usatoday.com/story/money/markets/2013/11/19/five-things-about-mcdonalds/3643557/

What do Americans really eat?
http://www.npr.org/blogs/thesalt/2011/12/31/144478009/the-average-american-ate-literally-a-ton-this-year

Is being suicidal in any way related to creativity?
http://lareviewofbooks.org/essay/suicidal-thoughts-creative-lives-tragic-deaths-prince-pauper

Which is better, the live tree or the dead?
http://www.friendsoftheclearwater.org/praise-the-dead-the-ecological-values-of-dead-trees-by-george-wuerthner/

About Osprey Reality TV—except some viewers were too aggressive (on the site or to the birds is unclear)—so no osprey this season:
http://www.whoi.edu/ospreycam/page.do?pid=41055

Is suicide morally neutral?
http://www.vox.com/2015/1/23/7868621/suicide-help

On a place to live and how choice might be the help people really need:
http://www.huffingtonpost.com/johann-hari/the-real-cause-of-addicti_b_6506936.html

How much willfulness does suicide require? Are creative people incredibly stubborn?
http://lareviewofbooks.org/essay/suicidal-thoughts-creative-lives-tragic-deaths-prince-pauper

How societies destroy themselves—second verse, same as the first:
http://www.policymic.com/articles/85541/nasa-study-concludes-when-civilization-will-end-and-it-s-not-looking-good-for-us

21ST CENTURY ESSAYS

David Lazar and Patrick Madden, Series Editors

This series from Mad Creek Books is a vehicle to discover, publish, and promote some of the most daring, ingenious, and artistic nonfiction. This is the first and only major series that announces its focus on the essay—a genre whose plasticity, timelessness, popularity, and centrality to nonfiction writing make it especially important in the field of nonfiction literature. In addition to publishing the most interesting and innovative books of essays by American writers, the series publishes extraordinary international essayists and reprint works by neglected or forgotten essayists, voices that deserve to be heard, revived, and reprised. The series is a major addition to the possibilities of contemporary literary nonfiction, focusing on that central, frequently chimerical, and invariably supple form: The Essay.

Sustainability: A Love Story
NICOLE WALKER

Hummingbirds Between the Pages
CHRIS ARTHUR

Love's Long Line
SOPHFRONIA SCOTT

The Real Life of the Parthenon
PATRICIA VIGDERMAN

You, Me, and the Violence
CATHERINE TAYLOR

Curiouser and Curiouser: Essays
NICHOLAS DELBANCO

Don't Come Back
LINA MARÍA FERREIRA CABEZA-VANEGAS

A Mother's Tale
PHILLIP LOPATE

SCOTCH PLAINS PUBLIC LIBRARY
DISCARD
3 9523 00220 7930